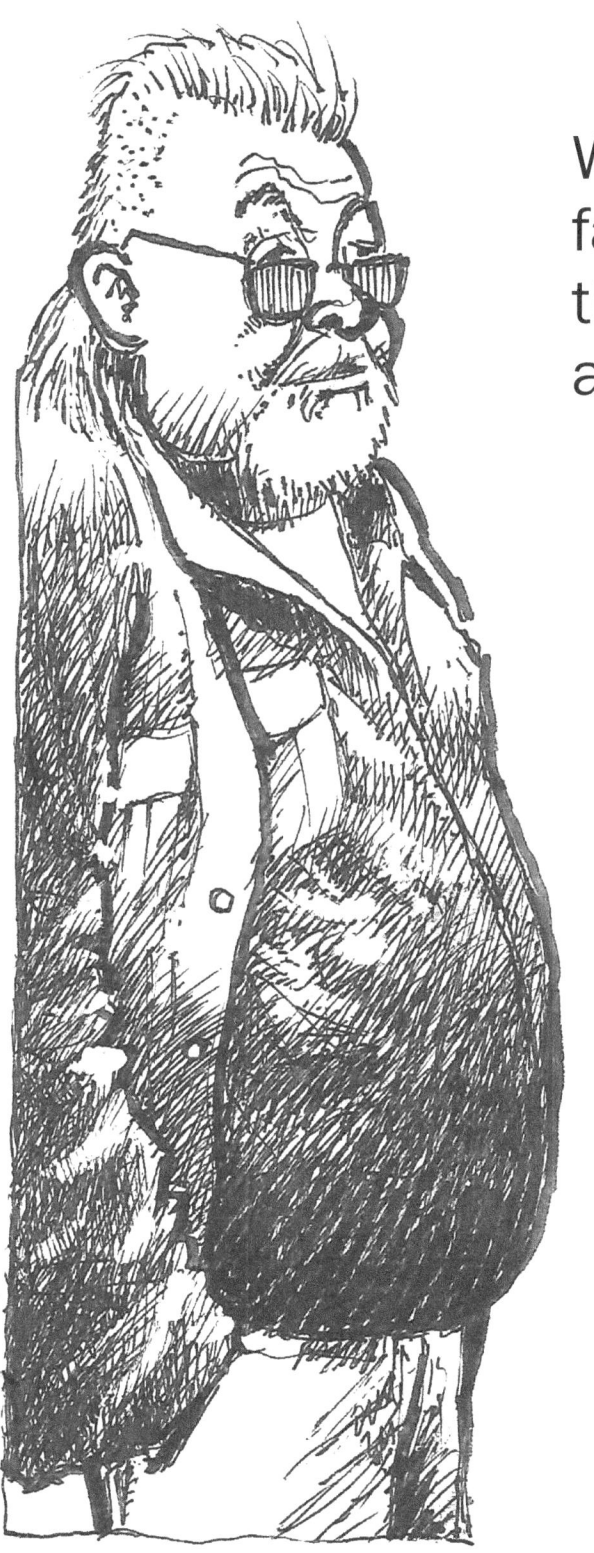

We interrupt this fanzine to bring you the following special announcement.

Portrait of Steve Stiles by Grant Canfield

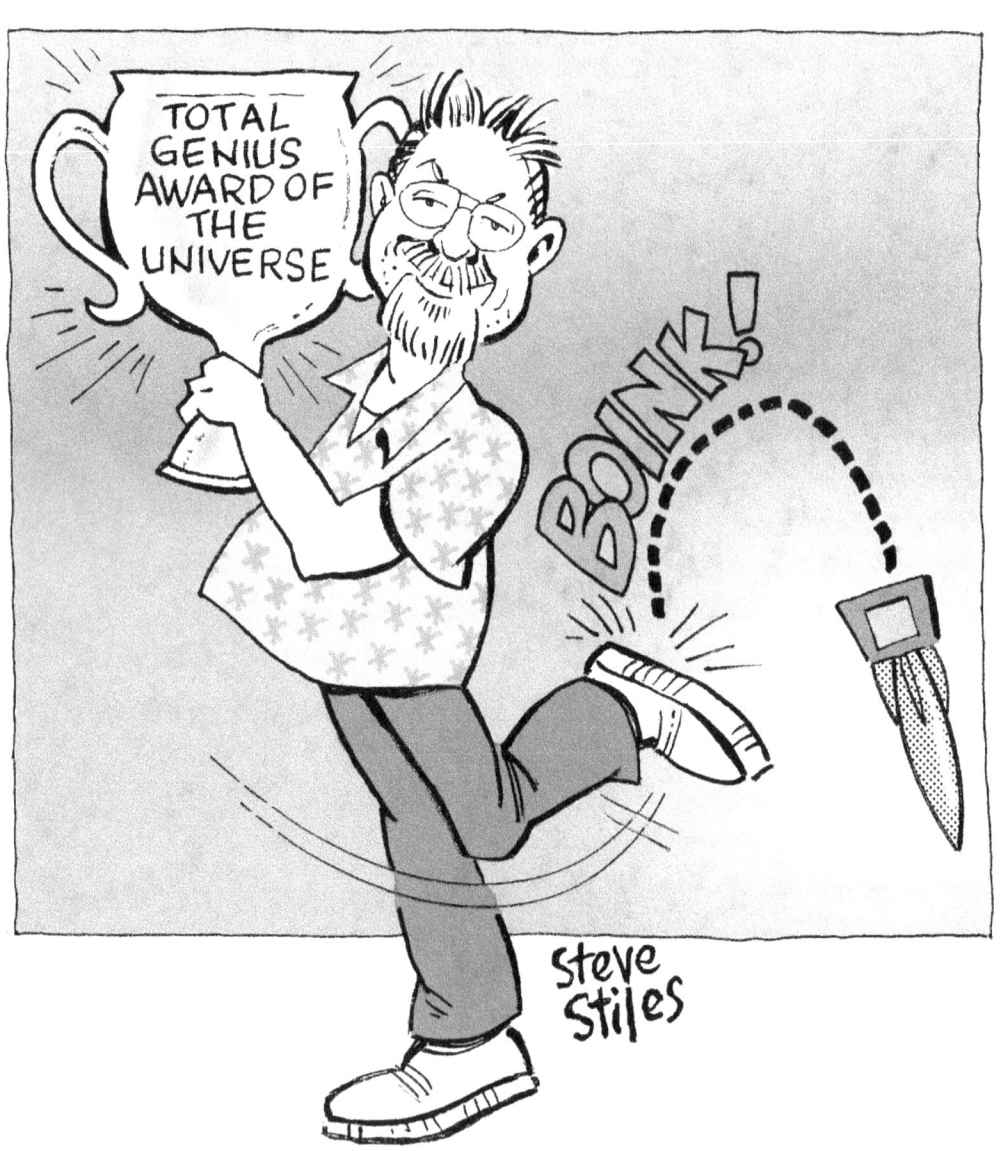

My Corflu Guest of Honor Speech
by Steve Stiles

Like many of us, Steve always brought a guest of honor speech to Corflu just in case. Because he couldn't deliver it in person, he wanted to share it here.

Every time I'm at a Corflu there's one major concern that bothers me and that's the awful possibility of being chosen randomly as GoH; there's no advance warning, no harbinger of things to come and that means the overriding opportunity of blowing it big time in front of an audience: I'm a second and third draft kind of fan and there's always the possibility of delivering *bla, bla, bla*, random boring nonsense. You know what I'm saying? I mean here's a good example of that right now!

For a while I thought that if it became my turn in this particular barrel I'd cop out by singing the Mighty Mouse theme song:

Mister Trouble never hangs around
When he hears this Mighty sound:
"Here I come to save the day"
That means that Mighty Mouse
Is on his way.

Yes sir, when there is a wrong to right
Mighty Mouse will join the fight.
On the sea or on the land,
He gets the situation well in hand.

I mean, you can't go wrong by dodging issues with the Andy Kaufman solution; he's one of my personnel heroes: I told him so just last week (although he got so flustered he messed up on my Burger King order).

There's also the possibility that Mighty Mouse, like Ben Grimm, the Thing, is Jewish, which I think would be neat. He's pretty much the opposite of Mickey, who is about the most Protestant rodent I can think of —like, there's that pitiable relationship with Minnie, which only seems to consist of going on long drives in the countryside, or taking her on picnics. I can't picture him giving her fellatio what with that weird little laugh of his; *"Ah shucks, Minnie!"*

Of course, Mickey and Mighty both have the same surname but that might not mean anything: Mighty's folks might've arrived at Ellis Island from the Old Country and their processor was too lazy to spell out Mouseberg or Mousekowitz. That happened all the time back then.

But I digress.

To change the subject, how many of you still read science fiction? (

(Two or three hands hesitatingly go up.)

Yeah, me too. I think what doused the old science fiction flame was the realization that faster than light space travel was flat out impossible and that we'll never ever find out if there's other intelligent life in the universe other than dolphins, even if we pedal as hard and as fast as we can. Myself, I'd hardly manage a light year. What a bitch! (And if there is intelligent life, are they Democratic Socialists?)

(I would really love to read a space opera where one starship crewmember says to another *"Isn't it amazing that that 20th century Albert Einstein guy turned out to be a total flaming asshole?"*)

So it seems to me that today's science fiction sadly has only one way to go and that's down. Now I love a good dystopia as much as the next fan, but there's so much of it that's been done already. I exclude alien invasion dystopias because of the FTL issue. Liu Cixin covered that in *The Three-Body Problem*: By the time they get here, many generations later, the aliens just might not give a shit. And if they did give a shit, assuming they had anuses, the plumbing might not be still working after four hundred years; we've had our place for merely over thirty years and it's gotten to the point where we send our plumber annual birthday and Christmas cards. We're putting his kid through college!

Aside from alien invasions in science fiction, we've had dictatorship dystopias, after the bomb dystopias, brainwashed with drugs dystopias, sexual repression dystopias, sexual enslavement dystopias, corporate despotism dystopias, Christian dystopias, Islamic dystopias, Israel-wiped-off-the-face- of-the-earth dystopias, and faith-based dystopias.

s

There've been mass-migration dystopias, unstoppable plagues, dystopias, famine dystopias, flooding dystopias, mass extinction dystopias, and global warming dystopias.

The only difference between old-time classic science fiction dystopias, like those by Aldous Huxley, Sinclair Lewis, Walter Miller and the like, and modern day science fiction dystopias is that the former usually take place a few hundred years in the future while with the latter it's more like a mere thirty or forty years.

Now why is that, I wonder?

*Mister Trouble never hangs around
When he hears this Mighty sound:
"Here I come to save the day"*

Et cetera.

— Steve Stiles

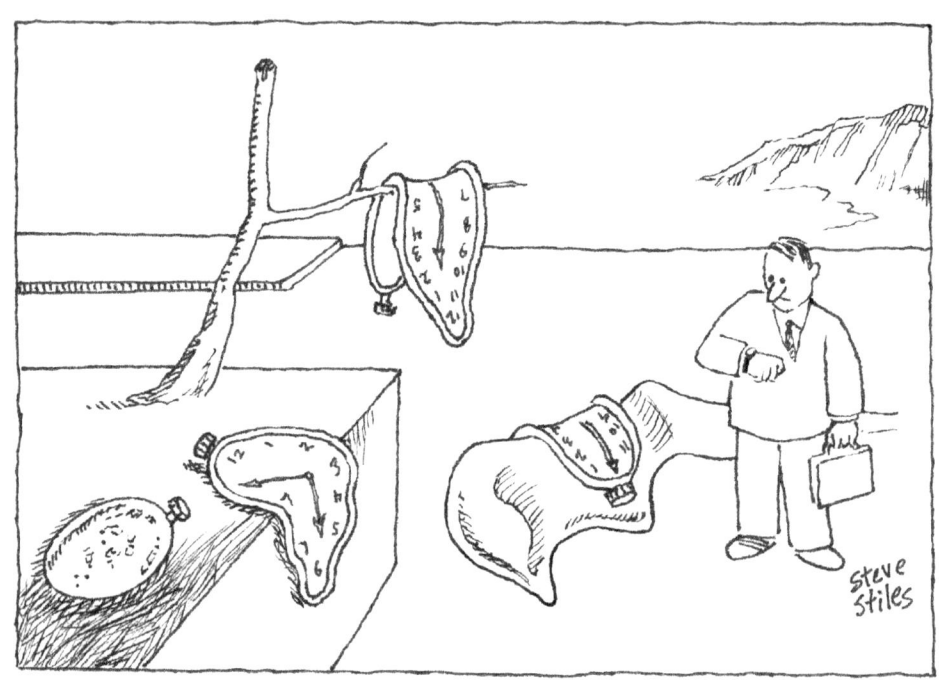

Corflu 36 FIAWOL
is dedicated to the memory of legendary
cartoonist and our very dear friend

STEVE STILES

1943 – 2020

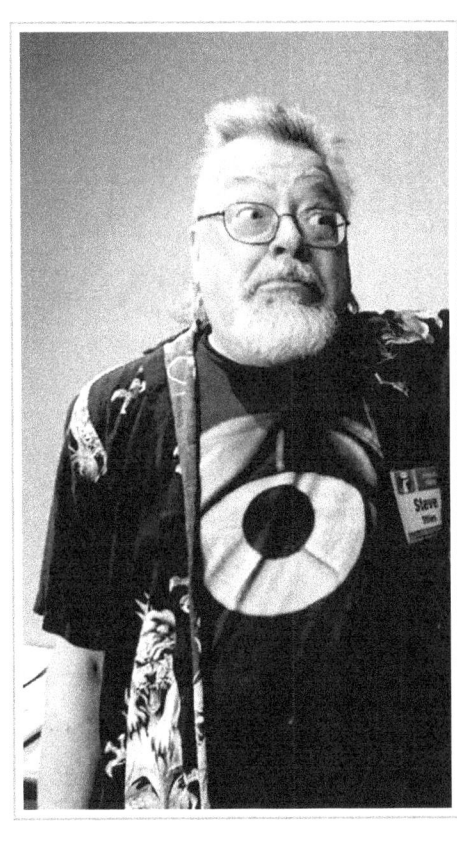
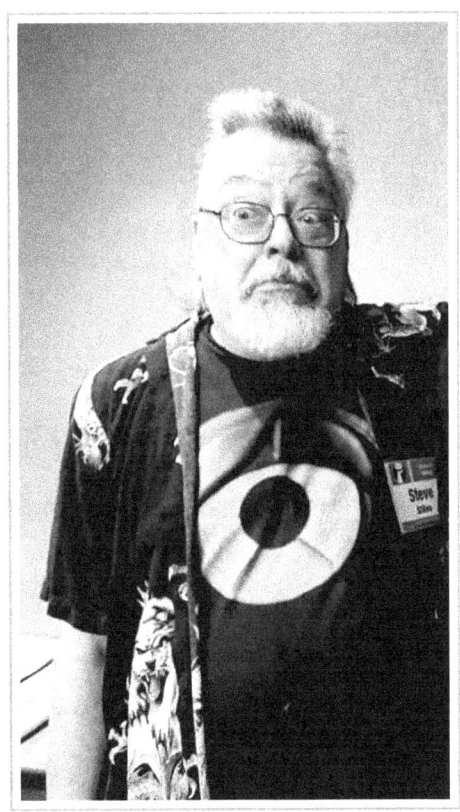

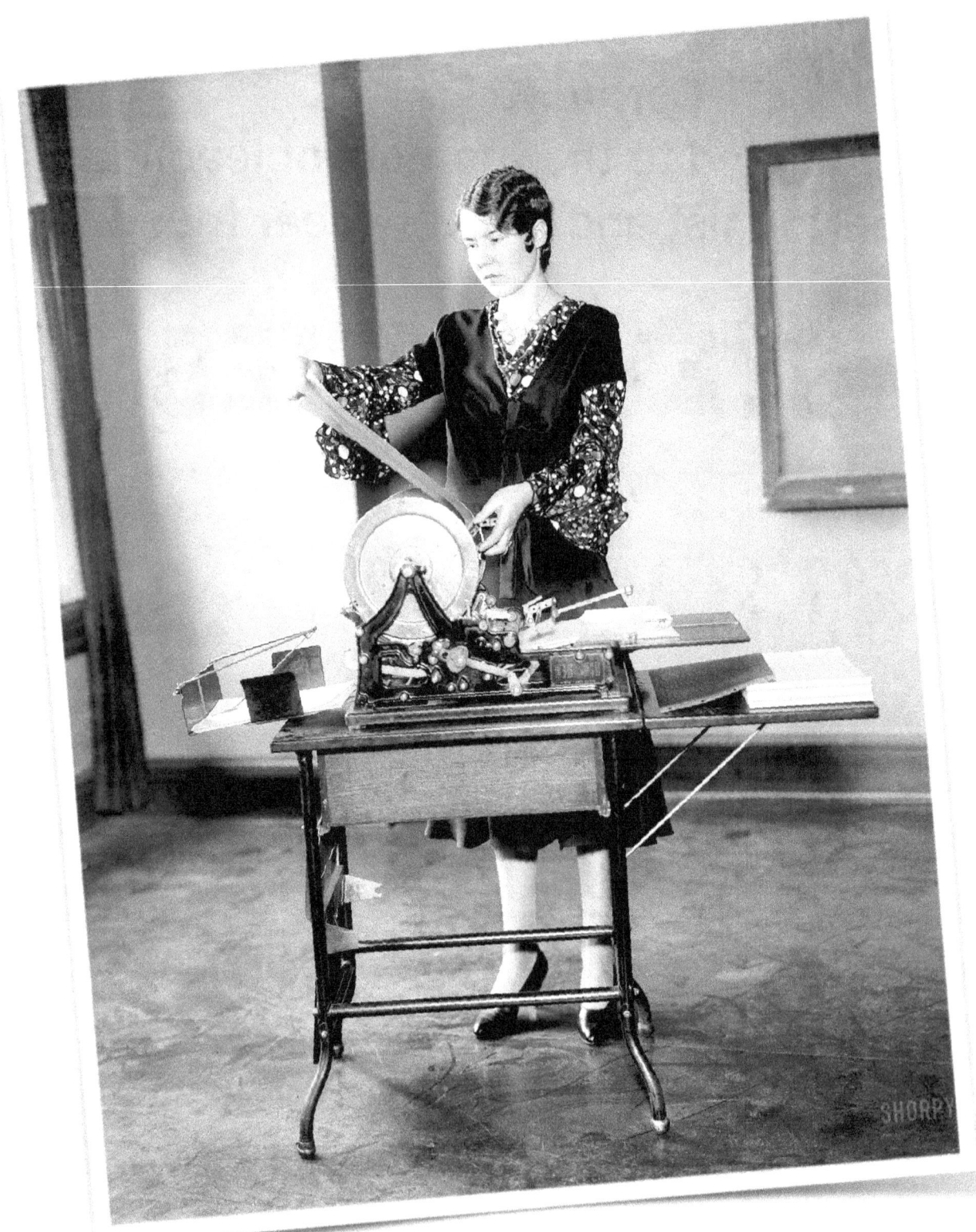

THE CORFLU 36 FIAWOL PROCEEDINGS

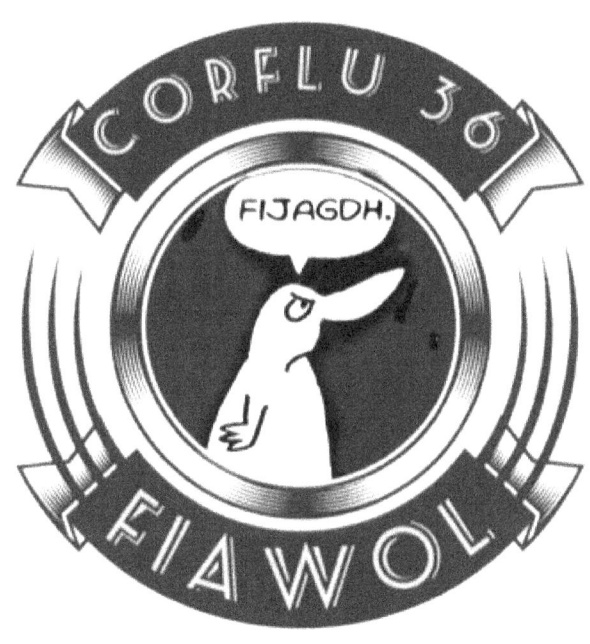

Random Jottings 20
The Corflu 36 FIAWOL Proceedings

TABLE OF CONTENTS

My Corflu Guest of Honor Speech (Steve Stiles)..................3
Editorial (Michael Dobson) 9
A Cast of Thousands (Committee and Membership).........11
    Corflu 36 FIAWOL Committee...13
    2019 Senior Class Yearbook...15
The Pre-Convention 23
    Welcome to Bawlmer, Hun 26
    Night of the Living Collators 30
    Arrivals and Excursions..33
    Museums off the Mall..34
Opening Day..37
    Official Corflu Begins 38
    Opening Ceremonies 40
    Bheer Tasting 45
    What Fans Do at Corflu 47
The Program 55
    Corflu Panels Sunt Omnis Divisa in Partes Tres 56
    A Bheer Can Tower to the Moon (Panel)......................57
    Facilitating Fan History Research (Susan Graham).....59
    The Void Boys Speak and (unfortunately) Sing (Panel)..62
    Doing *Void* (Greg Benford) 64
    Rotsler Award Winners (Panel)..68
    The Auction 72
Corflu After Dark 75
    Just a Minac (Game Show) 76
    Time Chunnel, a play by Andy Hooper 78
    Saturday Night's Alright (for Fanac) 89
    ~~Whining~~ Wining in the Consuite 92
    Plus de vin? (Spike) 92
The Banquet..95
    Corflu FIAWOL Banquet Programme..............................96
    Award Winners 98
    Ad Astra via Fandom (GoH Speech by Jim Benford...103
    Sunday Corflu Comments by Various 106
The Aftermath 109
    A Perfect Day in the Bloody Lane (Andy Hooper).......110

CREDITS

Cover: Leonard Stockmann (LS)
Cartoons: Grant Canfield, Steve Jeffery, and Steve Stiles
Photographers:
- Bill Burns (BB)
- Grant Canfield (GC)
- Andy Hooper (AH)
- Rob Jackson (RJ)
- Steve Jeffery (SJ)
- Curt Phillips (CP)
- Carrie Root (CR)
- Nigel Rowe (NR)
- Ian Sorensen (IS)
- Leonard Stockmann (LS)
- Geri Sullivan (GS)
- Michael Ward (MW)

Random Jottings 20: The Corflu 36 FIAWOL Proceedings, is edited by Michael Dobson (editor@timespinnerpress.com) and published by The Canal Press (thecanalpress.com). Members of Corflu 36 FIAWOL, both attending and supporting, will receive paper copies as part of their membership. Both grayscale and color versions of the printed edition are available for purchase on Amazon, along with previous issues of *Random Jottings*. A color PDF is available at efanzines.com/RandomJottings. Thanx and a tip o'the Hatlo Hat to British agent Rob Jackson and Corflu webmaster Bill Burns. Copyright © 2020 The Canal Press on behalf of the creators; editor-written material is CC BY-SA 4.0.

EDITORIAL / Michael Dobson

About This Issue

The 20th issue of *Random Jottings* is the third print volume dedicated to Corflu 36 FIAWOL, the 36th annual assembly of the increasingly small number of fanzine fans, held in Rockville, Maryland (a suburb of Washington, DC), from May 2-5, 2019. (Some events happened before and after the official convention.)

Random Jottings 17: the Corflu 36 Fanthology, with over 160 pages of classic fanwriting, appeared at the convention itself.

Issues 13, 14, 15, 16, and 18 of *Random Jottings* were only published as PDFs (although physical copies of *Random Jottings* 13 were distributed at the Toronto Corflu as the bid package).

Issues 14, 15, and 16 were progress reports, and *Random Jottings* 18 served as the post-Corfu report and assessment. All those issues, as well as some other Corflu 36-related material, are being published as *Random Jottings 19: The Corfu FLAWOL Papers,* released at pretty much the same time as this issue.

Because it's of such specialized interest, there will be few print copies, but as is the case with all my CreateSpace/KDP fanzines, it's available on Amazon if you just have to have a copy.

This issue is *The Corflu 36 FLAWOL Proceedings,* chronicling the convention itself. Next issue, as usual, will be Something Completely Different.

Previously in RJ

Each issue of *Random Jottings* has had its own theme. Here's what's happened so far:

- #1 The Genzine Issue (1970)
- #2 The Name-Dropping Issue (2003)
- #3 The Not-So-Good Samaritan Issue (2008)
- #4 The Alternate History Issue (2009)
- #5 The Odell F. Dobson Memorial Issue (2010)
- #6 The Cognitive Biases Issue (2011)
- #7 The Sidewise Issue (2012)
- #8 The Watergate Issue (2013) *First CreateSpace/KDP issue; published in print and ebook form.*
- #9 My Brilliant Fannish Career (2014)
- #10 The Improbable History Issue (2015) *Published separately in book form.*
- #11 Not the Fanzine You're Looking For (2016)
- #12 The Wheaton Murders (2017)

Credits and Acknowledgements

Thanks to all of you who provided memories and photographs, and to those who have allowed me to reprint convention materials from elsewhere.

- **Inca 16, Rob Jackson**

  Rob kindly granted me permission to use his "Notes for a Corflu Conrunner" in *Random Jottings* 19, and "The Rockville Diaries," his con report, in this issue. I've edited out some secondary material and added in new material from several people.

- **File 770, Martin Morse Wooster + Mike Glyer**

  I used several paragraphs of Martin's Corflu con report with his permission.

- **Beam 15, Nic Farey, Ulrika O'Brien + Steve Jeffery**

  With Steve and Nic's consent, I've used a few paragraphs of Steve's Corflu report, plus some additional material written for me by Steve.

- **Captain Flashback 7, Andy Hooper**

  Andy Hooper has allowed me to use his report on the post-Corflu Antietam/Harry Warner trip. It's been edited for length.

  Thanks also to Andy for permission to publish his play "Time Chunnel," which premiered at Corflu 36.

Several people shared original material.

- **Facilitating Fan History Research, Susan Graham**

  An article by the UMBC special collections librarian who oversees the Coslet-

Sapienza Science Fiction Fanzine collection.

- **Doing Void, Greg Benford**

  To accompany our *Void* panel, Greg Benford shared some reminiscences.

- **Plus de Vin?, Spike**

  To accompany the wine tasting, Spike is stuck in Lodi again.

- **Ad Astra via Fandom, Jim Benford**

  Jim wrote up a less technical version of his well-received Guest of Honor speech.

John D. Berry, Grant Canfield, Elaine Stiles, and others sent in various con-related notes, mostly combined into the chronological report. A lot of this was scattered through various emails, so I apologize if your own brilliant *bon mots* are not included.

There are more than 200 photographs here, and in looking through the pages I know you'll all agree that we've only gotten better looking with age. Thank our skilled photographers, listed on the first page and (by initials) on the photos.

Cartoons are by Steve Stiles and Steve Jeffery. Technical drawings are courtesy Jim Benford. Mimeograph ads and other visual trivia are all in the public domain because they were first published in the US prior to 1963, and either were published without notice or with notice and the copyright was not renewed. There's a credit line on the Antietam map, which came from Wikimedia Commons.

While I've done my best to identify people correctly and provide proper credit, the chances I've made some errors approaches certainty. I've also probably missed some wonderful comments and photos that have slipped into the morass I laughingly call a desk. While I can't change already-mailed print copies, I can fix the online version, so let me know.

If you came to Corflu FIAWOL, thanks. I hope you had a great time, and that this volume brings back some pleasant memories. If you didn't, here's a taste of what you missed. Either way, enjoy this album of memories.

— Michael Dobson

Corflu 36 Videos

Thanks to Rob Jackson, you can watch much of Corflu 36 online. Here's a list with links. I've provided shortened versions for those typing from the print edition.

Opening Ceremony (Friday evening)

https://youtu.be/GgfW7UcLx0A
https://tinyurl.com/C36Friday

Saturday daytime panels

https://youtu.be/RUstxv0rmRk
https://tinyurl.com/C36Saturday

Saturday afternoon auction

https://youtu.be/zLYKzOXk2_k
https://tinyurl.com/C36Auction

Saturday evening entertainment

https://youtu.be/lMr806_kzMg
https://tinyurl.com/C36SaturdayEve

Sunday Banquet and Awards Ceremony

https://youtu.be/l0yHFIh6sFg
https://tinyurl.com/C36Sunday

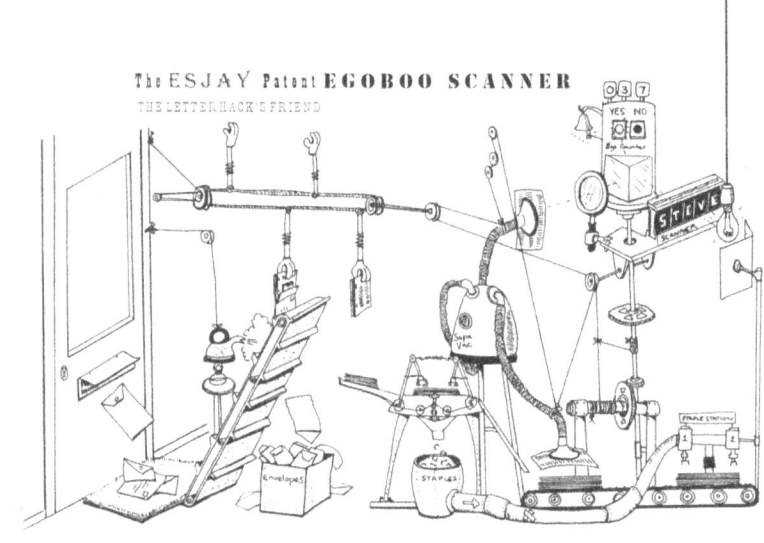

Steve Jeffery

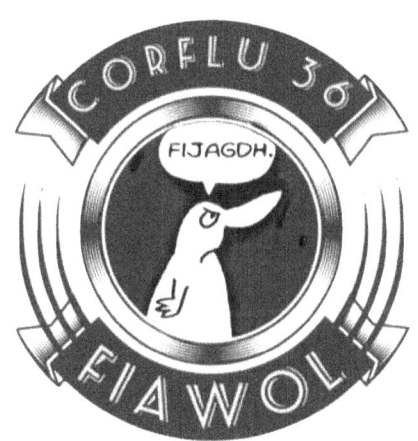

A Cast of Thousands

The Committee and the Membership

SNIFFIN' CORFLU AND OTHER SNFAL HABITS

FOR... ~~YOU~~ WHO CARES! ②½

THIS ISSUE IS RARE....RIP IT UP AND IT'LL BE RARER. OR AUCTION IT FOR TAFF

SCIENCE ← THIS IS A WORD

FICTION ← THIS IS ANOTHER

THIS IS A THIRD → FANDOM

<u>NOW PUB YOUR ISH</u>

Steve Jeffery

The Corflu 36 FIAWOL Committee

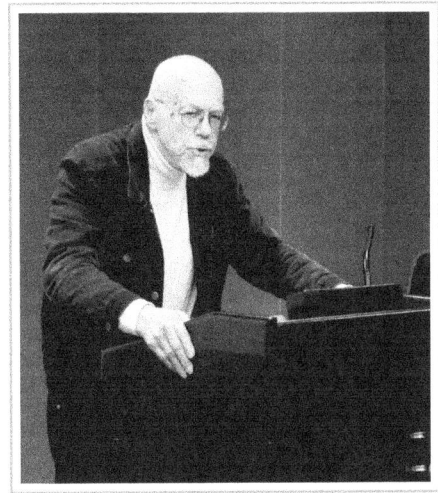

Chair, Michael Dobson (NR)

Programming, Ted White (LS)

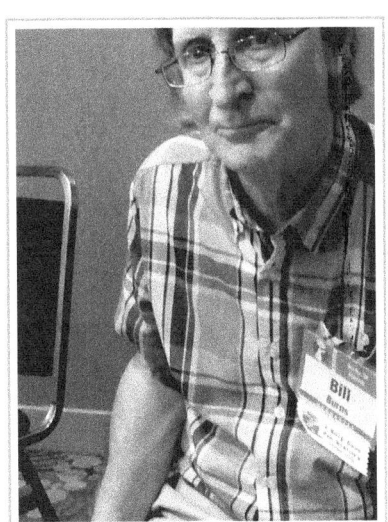
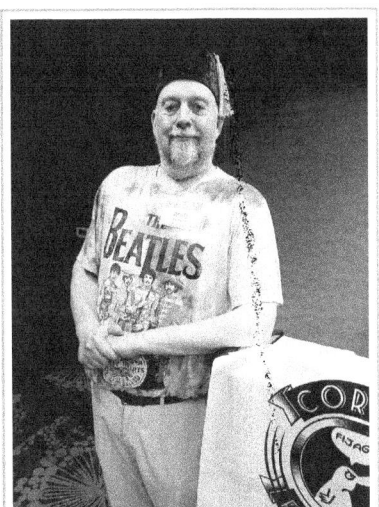
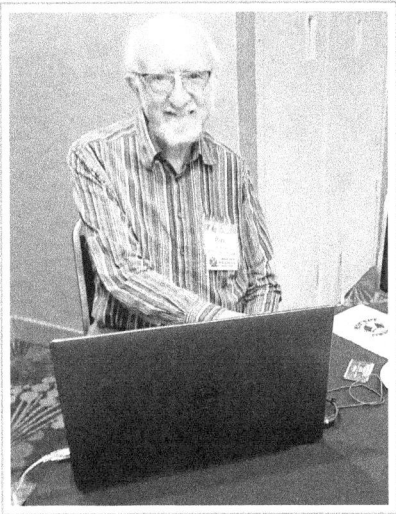

Webmaster, Bill Burns (SS)   Auction, Andy Hooper (NR)   Online Corflu, Rob Jackson (NR)

WITH

- Patti Ross, Treasurer
- Pat Virzi, Logo
- Doc Morgan, 3-D Trophy Designer
- Alison Scott, Clothing
- Steve Stiles, Logo/Tour Leader
- Colleen Brown Stockmann, Tour Leader
- Dan Steffan, Art Print
- Geri Sullivan, Bheer Tasting
- Spike, Wine Tasting

Featuring the Masterful Hospitality of
Curt Phillips
International Man of Mystery

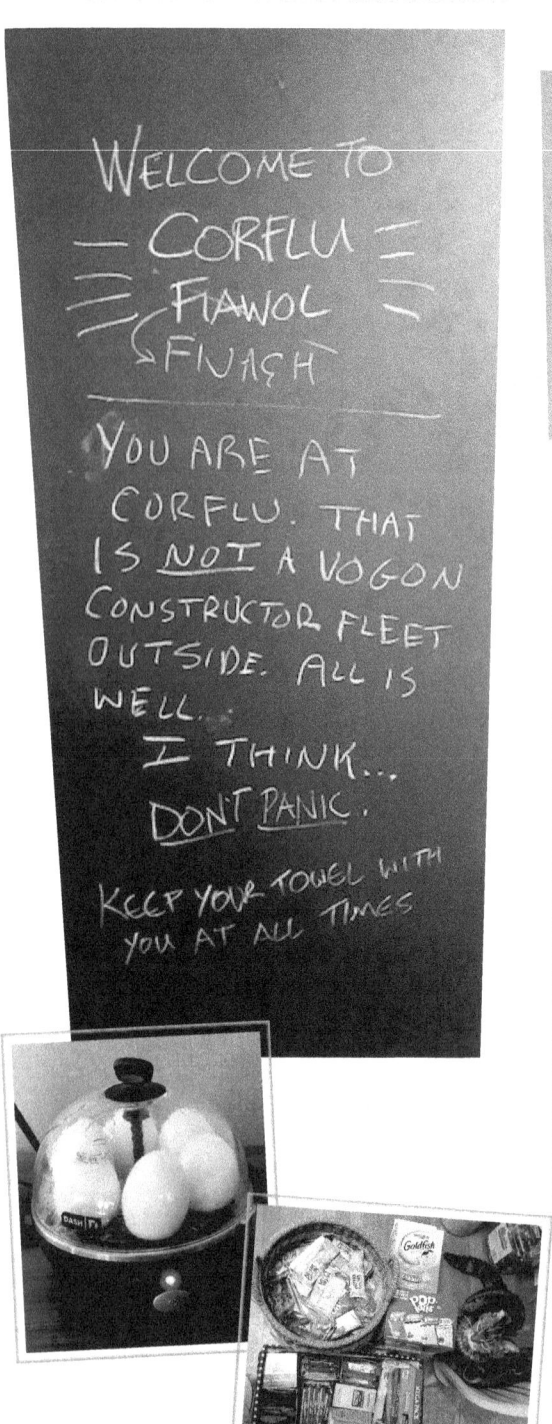
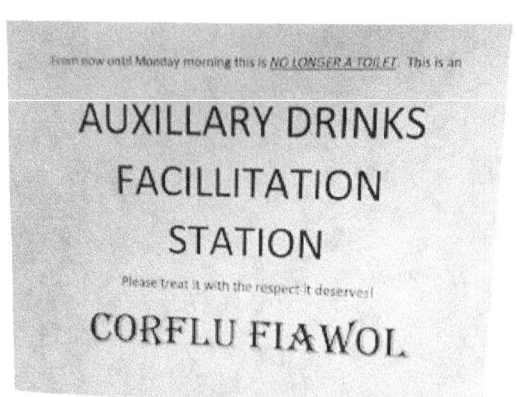
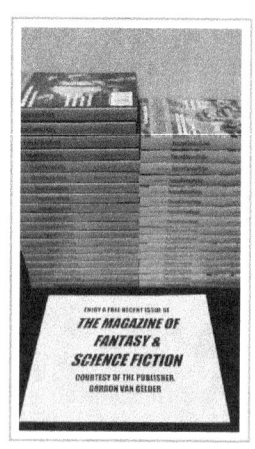
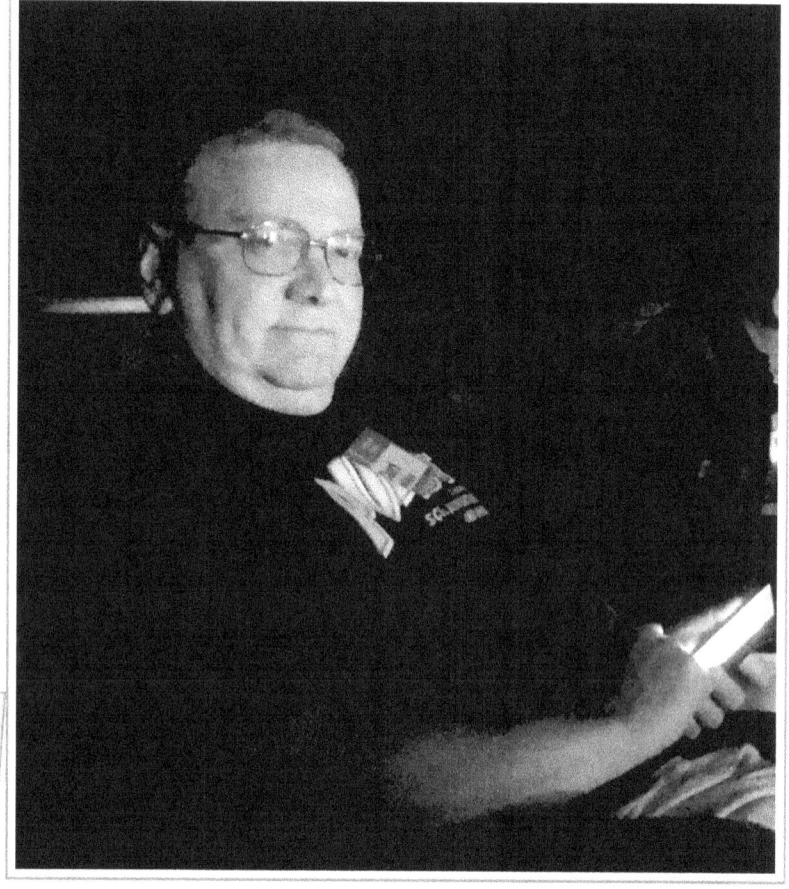

all CP except eggs (BB) and portrait (RJ)

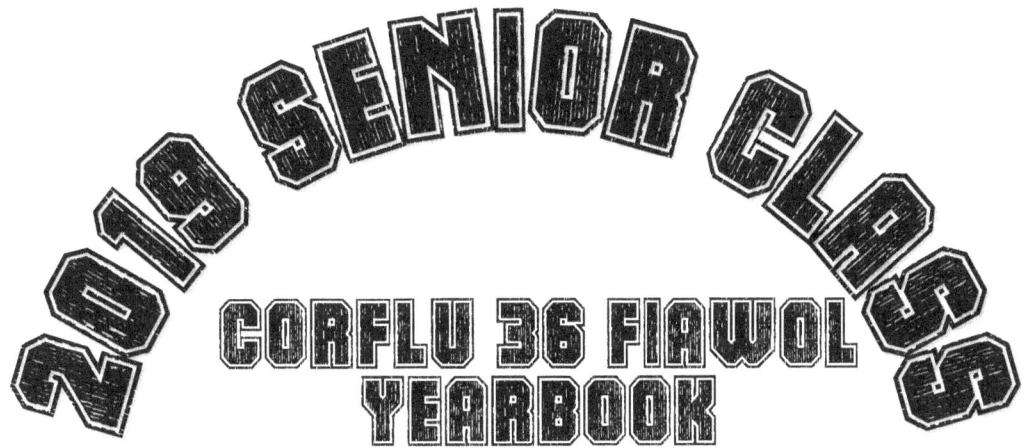

2019 SENIOR CLASS
CORFLU 36 FIAWOL YEARBOOK

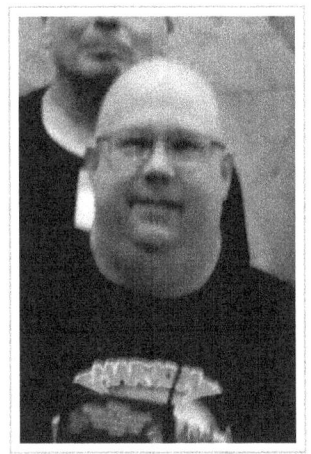   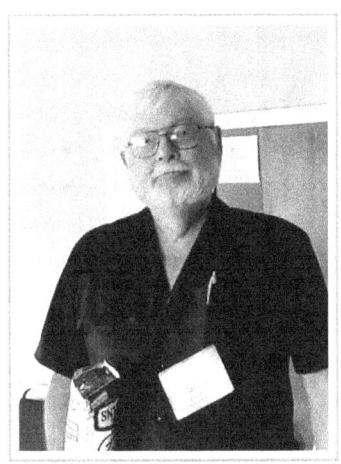   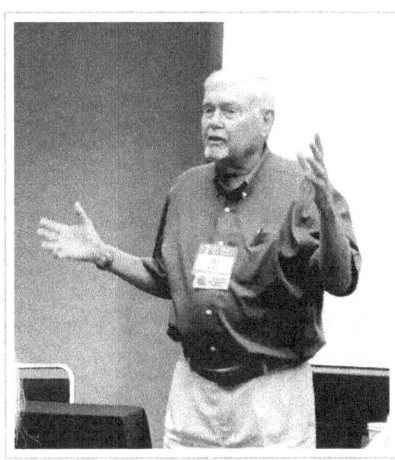

Mowgli Assor   Greg Benford   Jim Benford

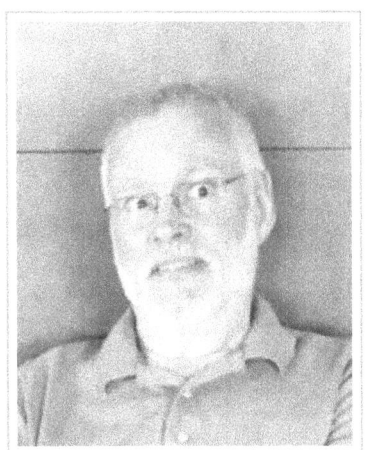   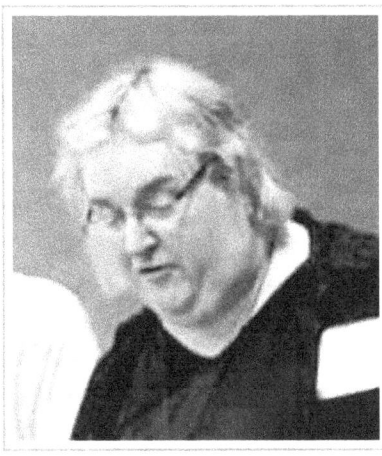   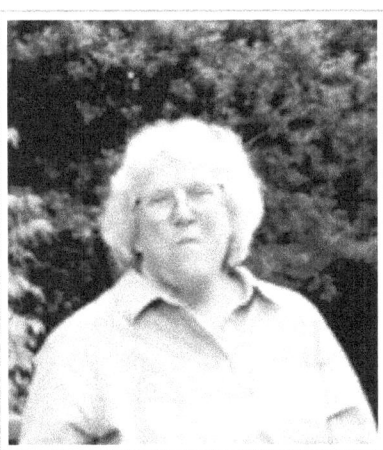

John D. Berry   Sandra Bond   Jeanne Bowman

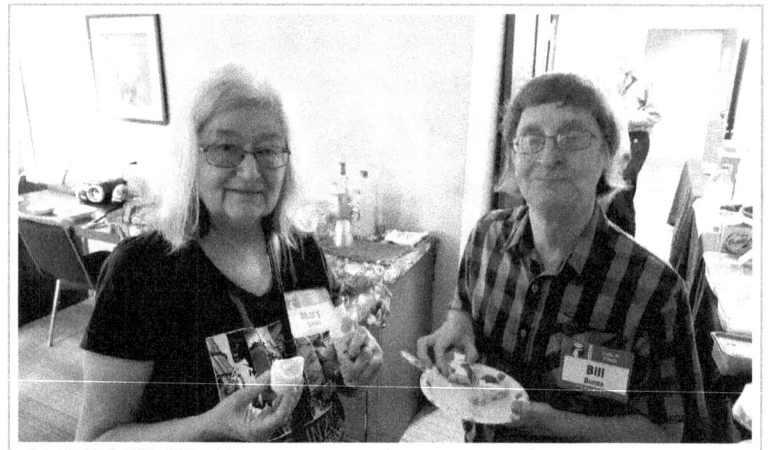
Mary and Bill Burns

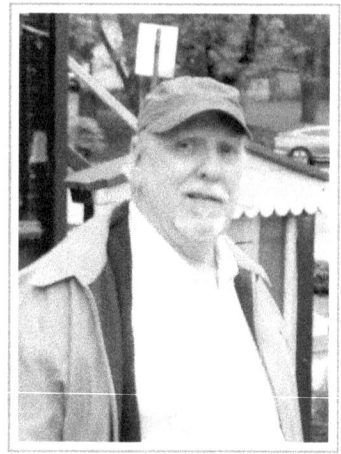
Grant Canfield

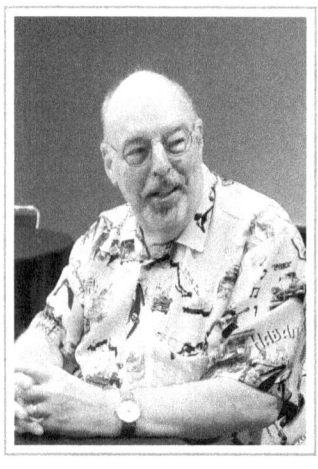
Rich Coad

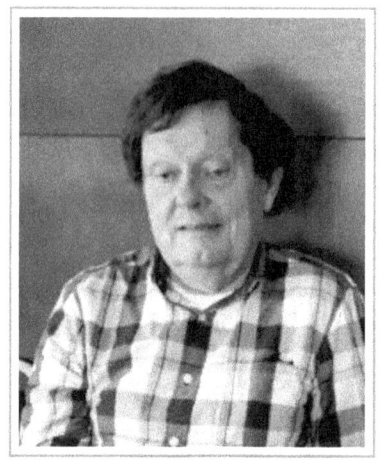
Chris Couch

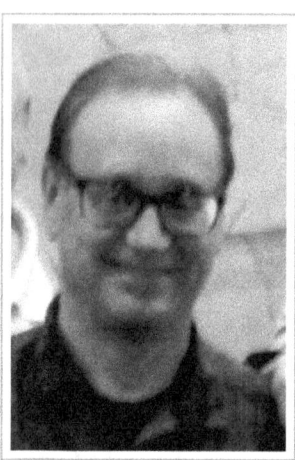
Bob Crain

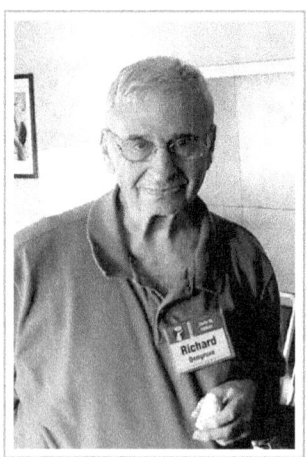
Richard Dengrove

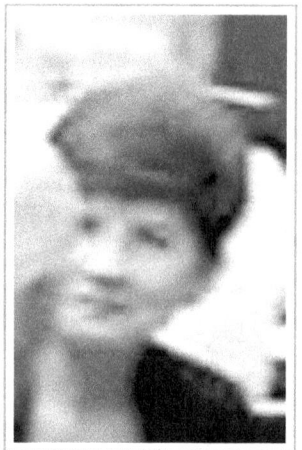
Deborah Dobson

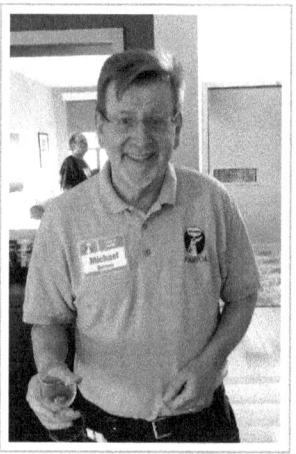
Michael Dobson

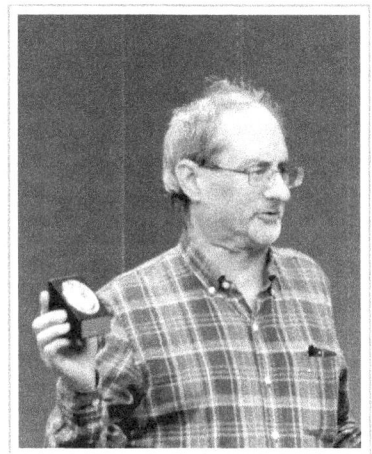
Victor Gonzales

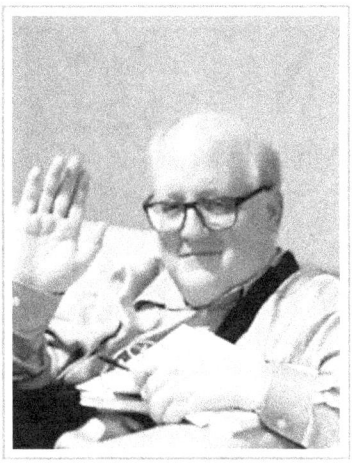
Frederic Gooding III

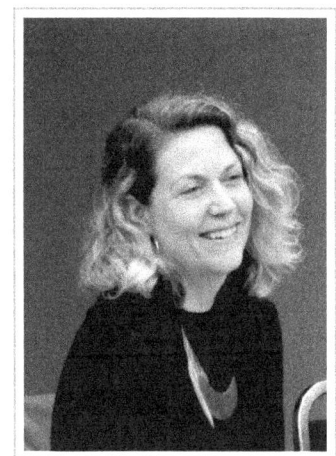
Susan Graham

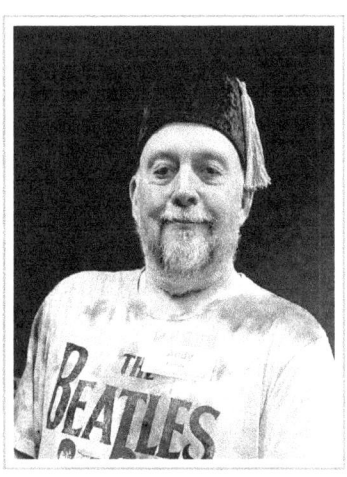
Andy Hooper

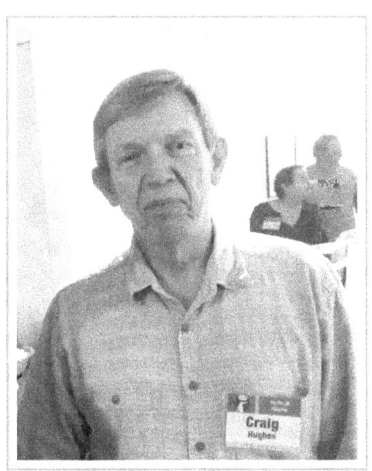
Craig Hughes

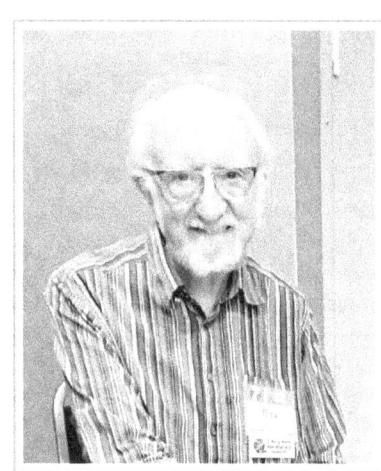
Rob Jackson

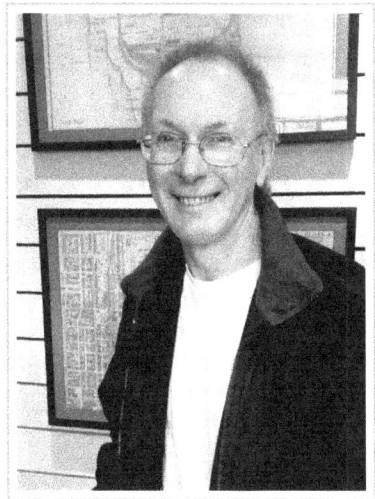
Steve Jeffery

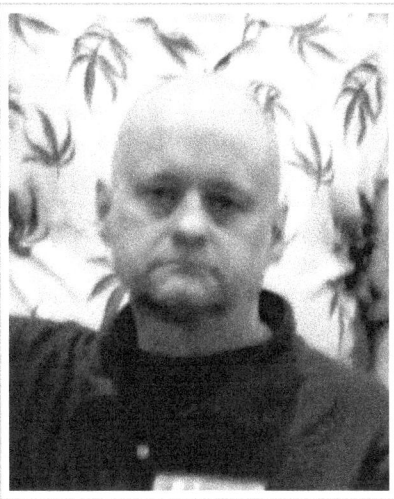
Dan Joy

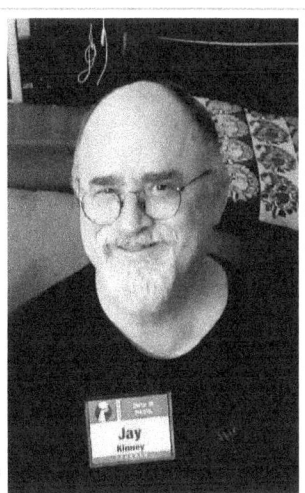
Jay Kinney

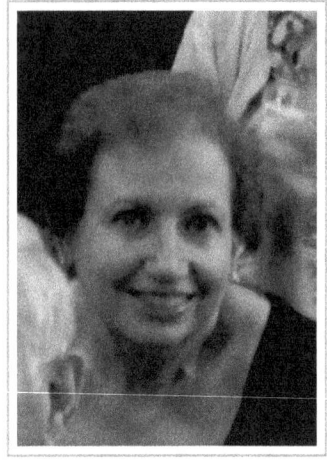
Lynn Koehler

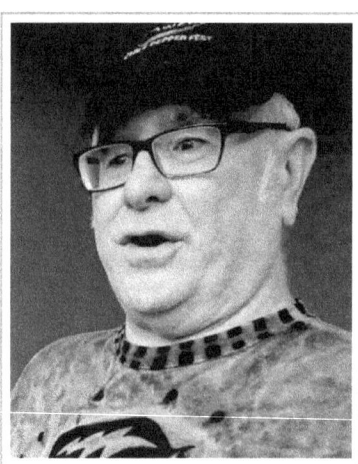
Frank Lunney

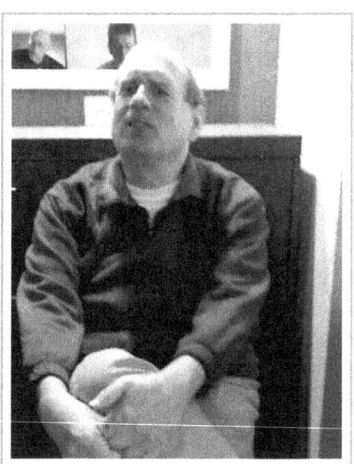
Keith Lynch

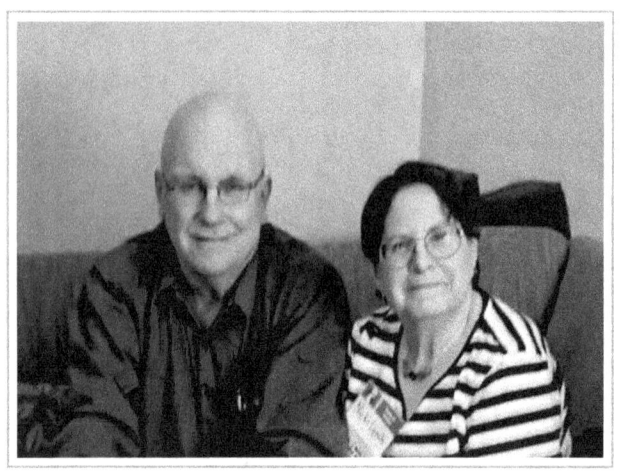
Rich and Nikki Lynch

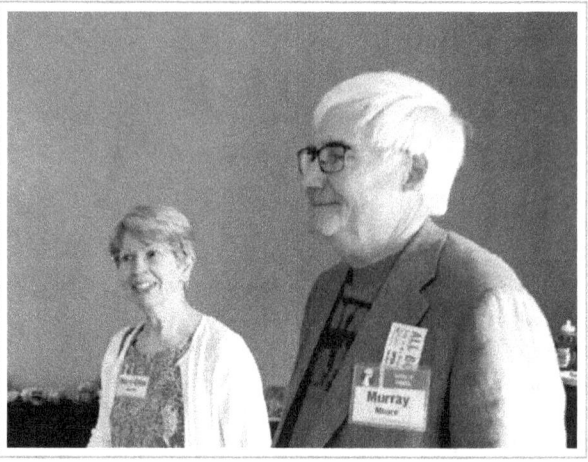
Mary-Ellen Moore and Murray Moore

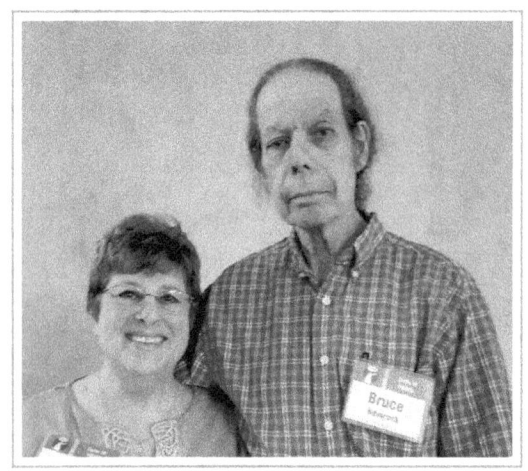
Flo and Bruce Newrock

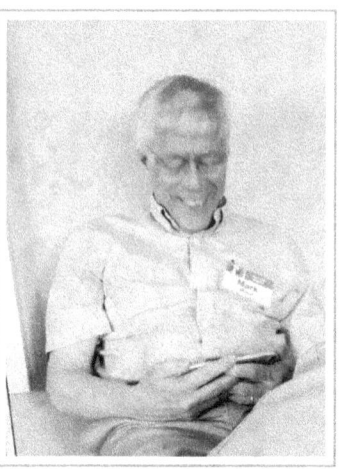
Mark Olson

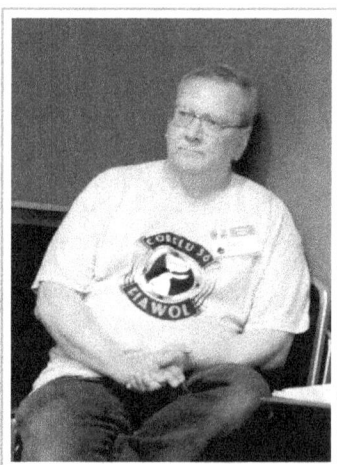
Curt Phillips

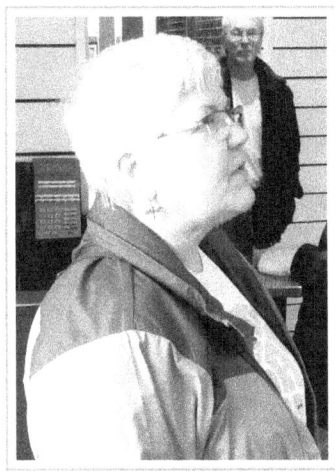 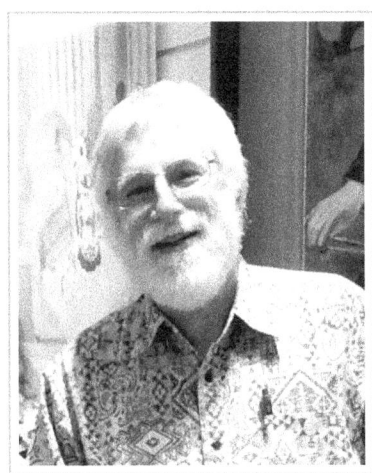 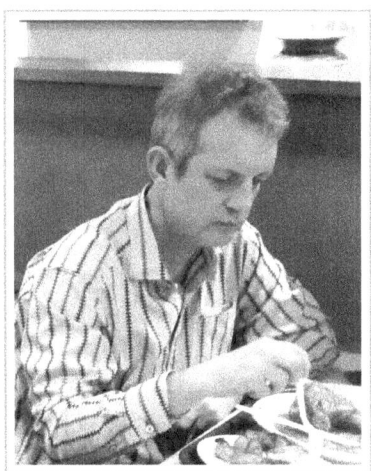

Carrie Root   Alan Rosenthal   Nigel Rowe

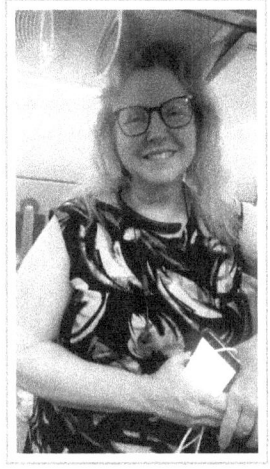 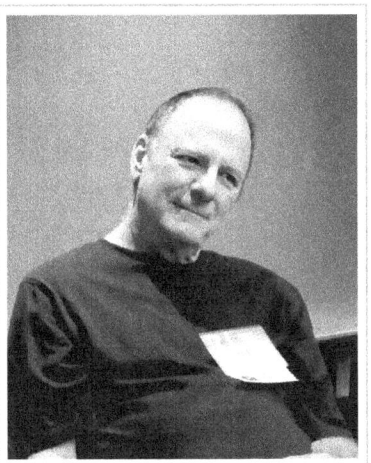 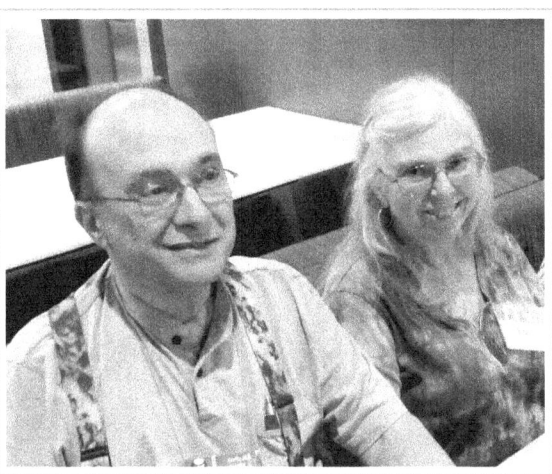

Karen Schaffer   Jeff Schalles   Joe Siclari and Edie Stern

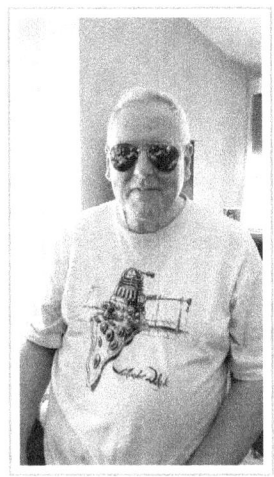 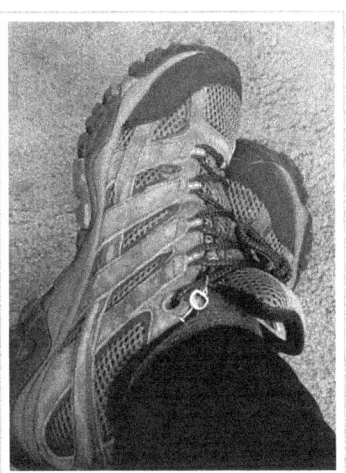 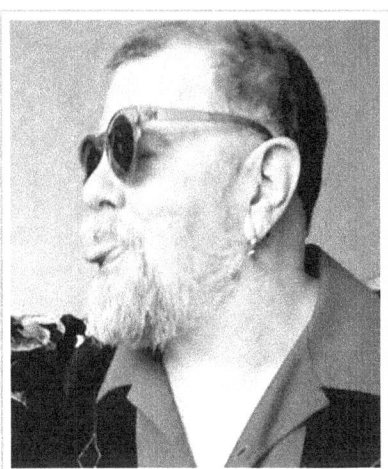

Ian Sorensen   Spike   Dan Steffan

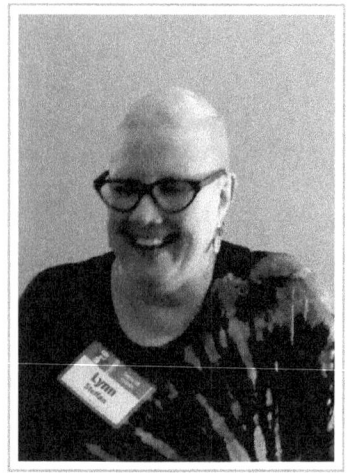
Lynn Steffan

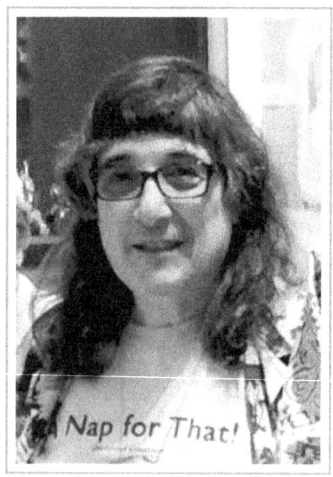
Elaine Stiles

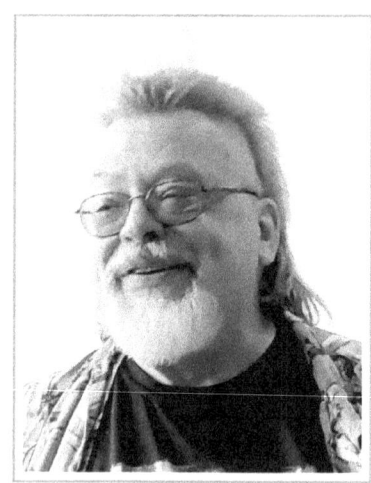
Steve Stiles

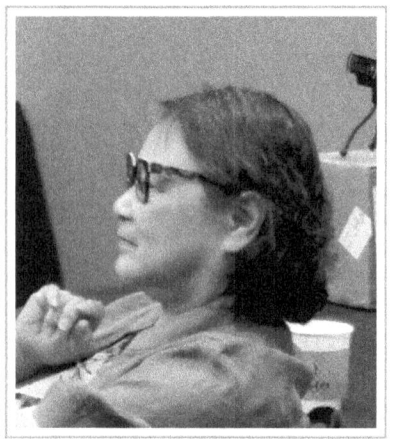
Colleen Brown Stockmann

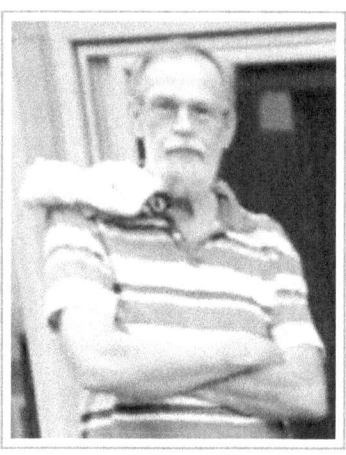
Leonard Stockmann

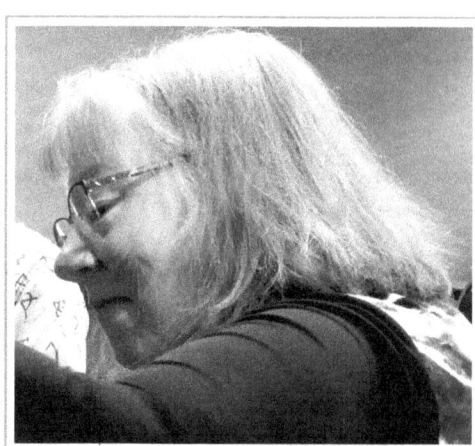
Geri Sullivan

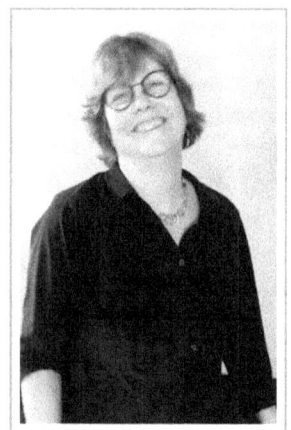
Pat Virzi

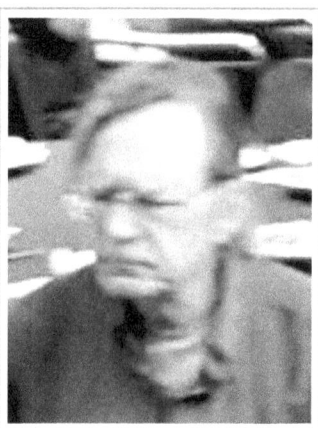
Michael Ward

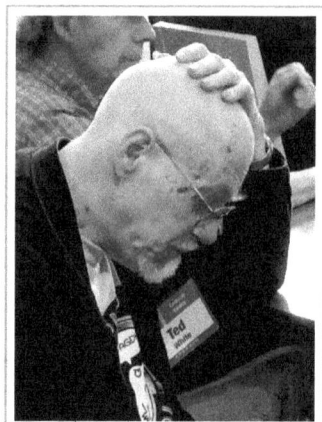
Ted White

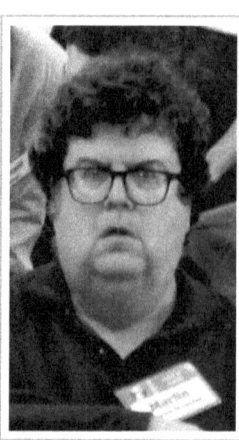
Martin Morse Wooster

Attending but Not Shown

Matthew Moore
Priscilla Olson
Dan O'Neill
Marla O'Neill

Supporting and Non-Attending Members

Alta Sligh Ayers	Jerry Kaufman
Stephen Beale	Dixie Kinney
Tom Becker	Robert Lichtman
Claire Brialey	Bob Madle
Pat Charnock	Matthew Moore
Catherine Crockett	Doc Morgan
Gordon Eklund	Ulrika O'Brien
Nic Farey	Lloyd Penney
Illi Ferriera	Mark Plummer
Ken Forman	John Purcell
Motya Gershunkskiy	Patti Ross
John Hertz	Susanne Tompkins
Colin Hinz	R-Laurraine Tutihasi

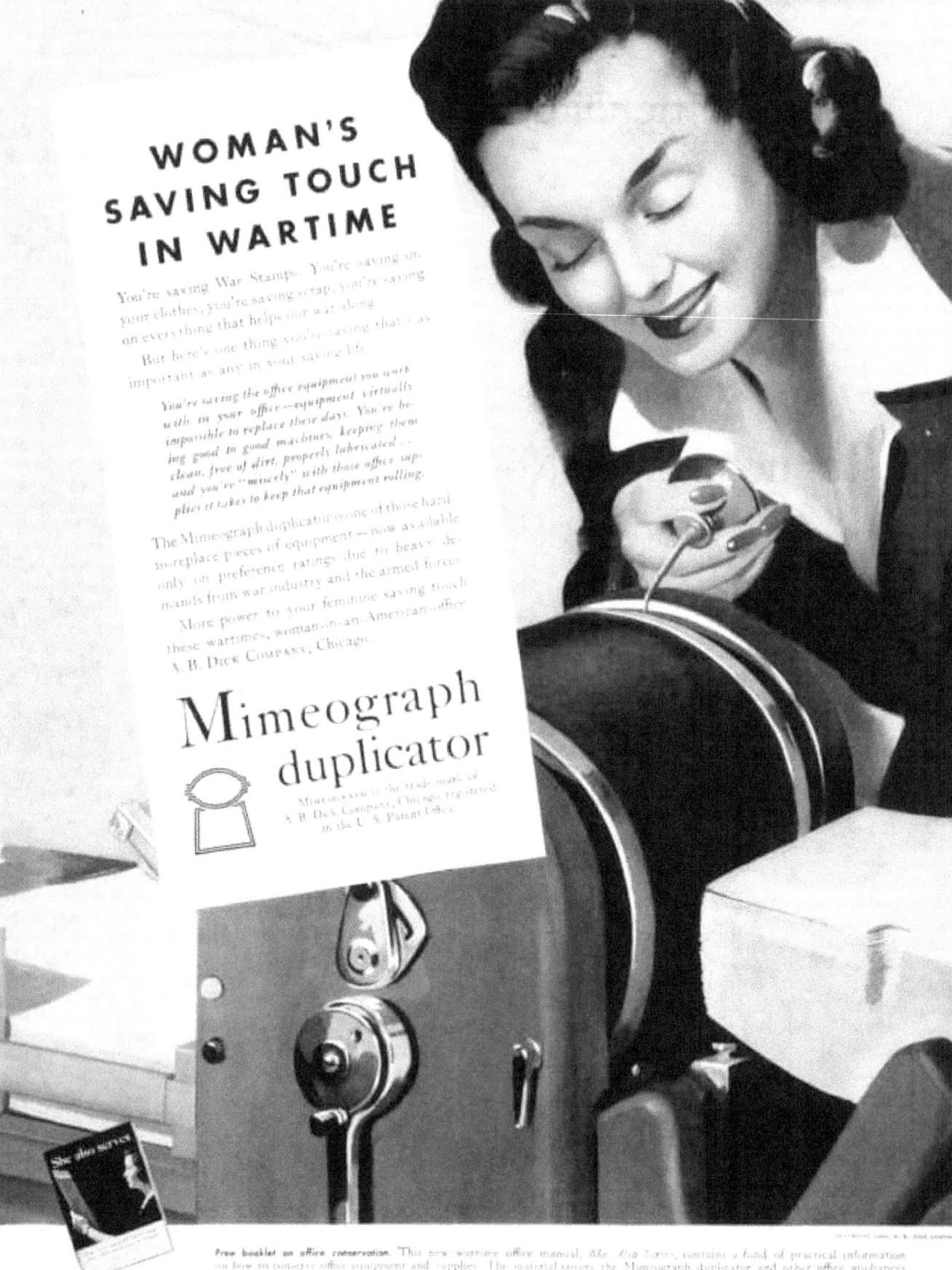

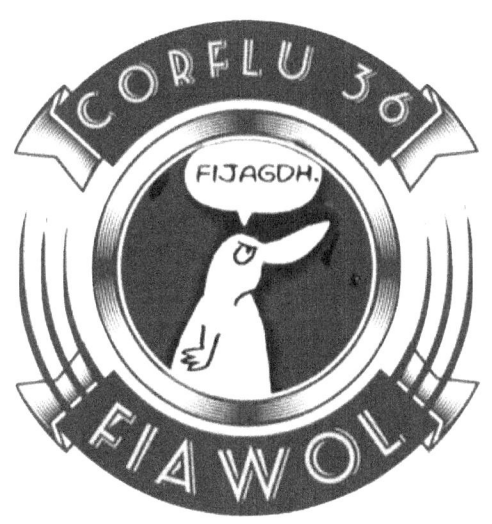

THE PRE-CONVENTION

Sunday 28 April to Thursday 2 May

THE PRE-CONVENTION
SUNDAY 28 APRIL — WEDNESDAY 1 MAY

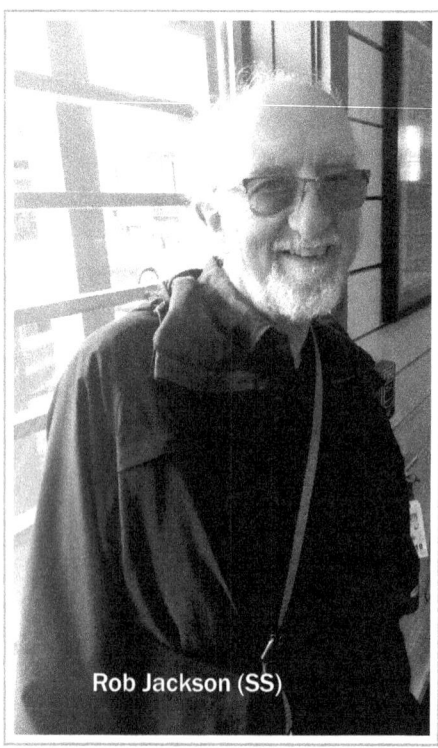
Rob Jackson (SS)

SUNDAY 28 APRIL 2019

Rob Jackson

I am on my travels again, staying at the Premier Inn at Terminal 4 tonight before getting the Underground to T3 tomorrow then flying into Dulles at 3 pm EDT tomorrow afternoon. As well as the usual large case with Incas and old Corflu Cobalt T-shirts to get rid of, I also have a small but deceptively heavy case with fanzines kindly donated by Skel, for the attention of Andy Hooper either at the Corflu auction or eBay. Some of these are seriously antique. They are also likely to get Joe Siclari and Mark Olson seriously interested, and be scanned for Fanac.org. Having looked through them in more detail, I realise how much they will benefit in the long run from being re-stapled anyway.

Back to the con and the fun.... almost exactly 24 hours after flying in, I return to Dulles to pick up Steve Jeffery, and call at Michael D's on our way back to the hotel. Then Wednesday is round Baltimore with Steve and Elaine followed by an early-bird welcome and collating party at Michael's (gussets may be involved), and Thursday round lesser-known DC-area museums with Colleen Stockmann.
I may return early from that to help Curt set up the con suite and Spike buy the wine for the wine tasting.

MONDAY 29 APRIL 2019

Rob Jackson

Email from Murray last night which I have seen this morning in the departure lounge — plan now for Tuesday is I pick up Steve at the airport, go on to Michael's, then early evening meet Murray and Mary-Ellen for dinner. Hope that doesn't strain Steve's jet-lag too much!

Reporting in from the hotel now. We've already had that confusion once or twice.

That plan may have to change, as I had a 50 minute delay getting out of Passport Control. My flight was the last of 5 that arrived all together, and Steve's tomorrow is a quarter of an hour later still.

So by the time I had sorted my hire car out, I was into the notorious I-495 northbound rush hour, or should I say crawl hour, and didn't get to the hotel till 6.15 – without even a call at Michael's on the way.

But a nice surprise was – who should be at Reception trying to sort out a problem with his phone accessing the hotel's wifi but – Grant Canfield! I didn't know he was coming! I now have another passenger for the trip to Steve's, Elaine's and Baltimore on Wednesday.

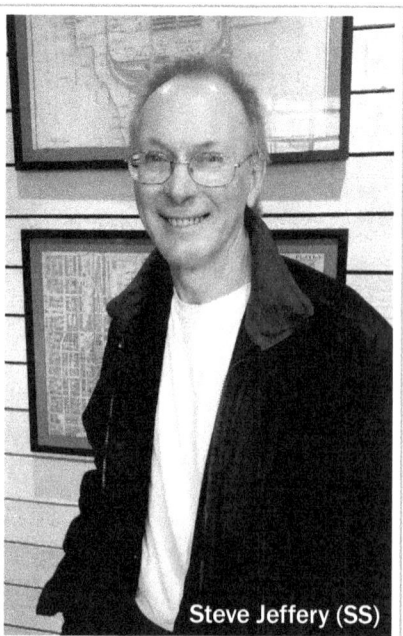
Steve Jeffery (SS)

The hotel staff are really helpful - but more of that some other time, as it's 1 am in my head and I got up at 6 am UK time this morning so I'm knackered. Early bed for me; but Grant was thinking of an early bed too as he got up at 4.30 California time to get here!

Tuesday 30 April 2019

Steve Jeffery

Hell is [queueing with] other people.

To say I hate queuing is something of a mild understatement.

I can be filled with the urge to kill at a supermarket checkout when the person in front of me, having put a pint of milk and a newspaper on the counter, then dithers before making up their mind about which combination of the many dozens of lottery tickets, scratch cards and lucky dips they also want that week and then have to turn out all their bags to find their purse and count out the money in small change.

Or when I'm waiting to board the bus and a couple who appear never to have seen or used a bus before have to have an interminable discussion with the driver about which combination of single, return, multipass or zone tickets will work out cheapest for their next three trip trips into town and back. So for me, air travel is a very special form of hell.

It doesn't help that I am inveterate early starter. Tell me that I need to arrive somewhere at 9 am and I will plan the journey so that I arrive an hour before, and then add another hour for starting out in case there are any delays on the journey. When my sister tells everyone to be at her house at exactly 4.30 for my dad's

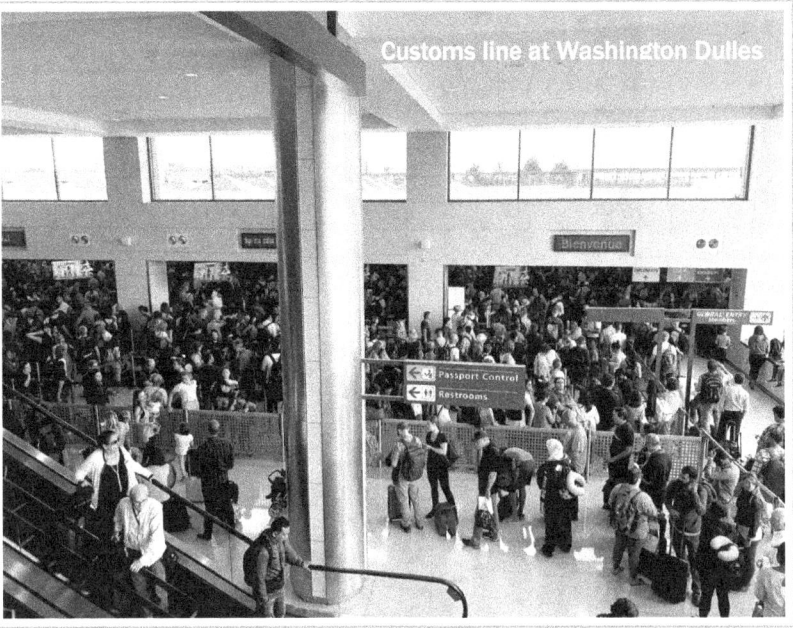
Customs line at Washington Dulles

special 80th birthday party I am standing in Thame High Street, about five minutes away from her house, at 3pm, wondering what to do for the next hour and a bit. So of course I go and find a bookshop.

I do rather bring it on myself.

Of course I arrived at Heathrow mere hours before my flight was even announced, let alone departed. I had anticipated endless queues at security and check in, questions about why I had suddenly decided to go to the States after a gap of 20 years, even bag or body searches to prove I wasn't trying to smuggle anything dangerous into the US, like Marmite.
(Flying back out of Copenhagen in the 80s on business, a suspicious security officer opened a box containing samples of white powders I was taking back home for laboratory testing. It took a fair bit of explaining and a sheaf of customs paperwork to persuade him not to dip his finger in and taste what was in fact a sample of flash dried lead acetate. Not a wise idea unless you fancy a week of stomach cramps and not being

more than thirty seconds from a convenient toilet.)

There was just one person in front of me at check in and I was through in 5 minutes with another two hours to kill before departure. Fannish wisdom saws never travel without at least one book. I had three and a half a dozen fanzines. I still only managed ten pages between compulsively checking the departures board every few minutes.

As it turned out all my queueing credits had been amassed and sent through to the other end.

Like hotels, all airports are constructed from endless identical corridors and passageways that are probably connected in hyperspace if only you could find the right door to go between one and the other. How else to explain why the security person interrogating you on arrival looks identical to the one at departure.

Arriving at Dulles International Arrivals, an endless queue of people stretched into the far

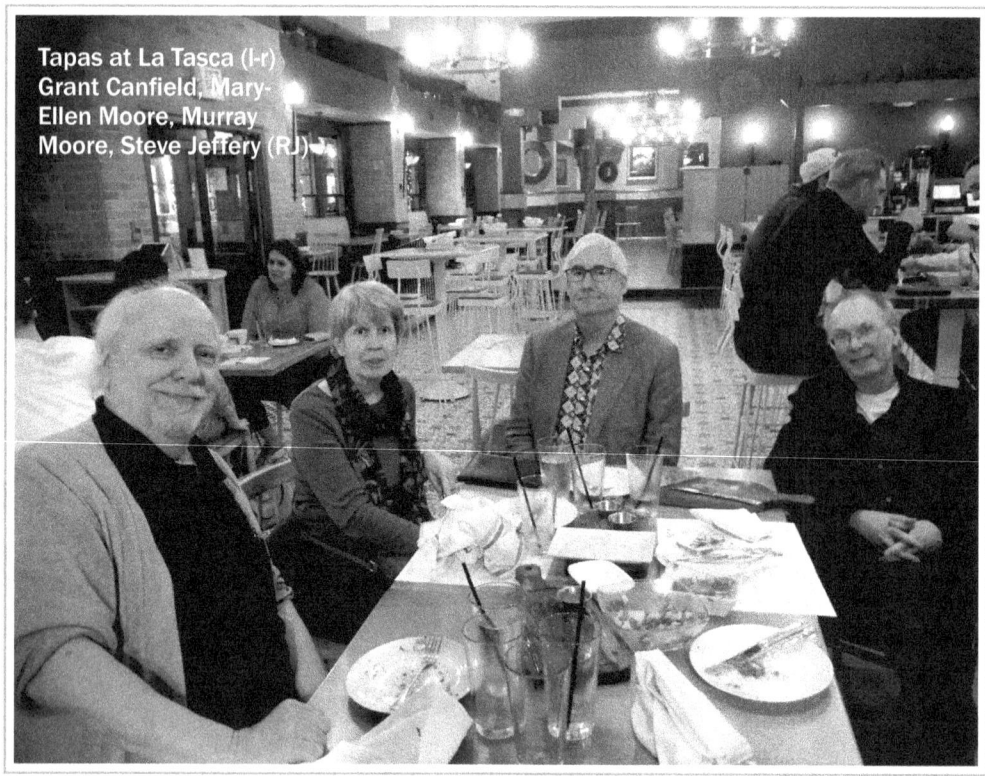

Tapas at La Tasca (l-r) Grant Canfield, Mary-Ellen Moore, Murray Moore, Steve Jeffery (RJ)

horizon, zigzagging around ten cordoned lanes, to be slowly released one every five minutes from one or other of just two security booths that were open in the middle distance. I did a mental count of how fast we were moving and how many lanes were still left to traverse and came up with an estimate of two hours. I wasn't far off. I managed to listen to two podcast short stories from Clarkesworld and Starship Sofa and the latest BBC 'Introducing in Oxford' line up of new bands on my mp3 player (all the while being kicked by a fractious child behind me who I increasingly wanted to kill) before finally finding myself at the front of the queue where I was photographed (twice), fingerprinted (several times), scanned, quizzed and finally welcomed to the USA.

Luckily this time I wasn't taken aside and detained in a side room for several hours while officials queried the status of my immigration visa. One up for the electronic ESTA system at least.

I had emailed Rob that my flight would arrive at 3.25PM. In the end it was almost 5.30 by the time I hit arrivals, having been told to look for someone with a trim white beard holding a placard stating 'Corflu 36 welcomes Steve Jeffery', although the first two people I saw fitting this description (although without placards) seemed remarkably uninterested.

We eventually found each other (Rob was older than I was expecting, but then again, we all are), retrieved Rob's car, and bundled out the airport just in time to hit the evening queue on the interstate out of Washington.

Murray Moore

Today shortly after 2 p.m. Rob drove to Dulles to collect Steve Jeffery. Steve's flight landed at 3:15 p.m. Steve rendezvoused with Rob at 5:15 p.m. Now I expect they are travelling slowly in rush hour traffic.

Rob Jackson

I was just about to report that myself! While waiting I tried to amuse myself looking at the varying degrees of shell-shock on the hugely delayed passengers' faces as they emerged from the utter tedium that is Dulles(t) Passport Control. Steve calculated it was about 2 hours by the fact that he listened to a short story that lasted about 20 minutes during just over one of the 8 lines of zig-zag queuing passengers. At one point they only had 2 booths open, but then some more officials grudgingly turned up. The arrivals hall was about 5 or 6 deep with waiting friends, colleagues, chauffeurs and relations around the area where passengers emerge from the customs hall.

We still had the I-495 crawl-hour traffic, but easier because (a) we were chatting and (b) I realised in a D'Oh moment that as I had Steve with me I counted as a High Occupancy Vehicle so could use the faster lane.

Then Steve, Murray, Mary-Ellen, Grant and I gathered downstairs to decide what kind of food we wanted to hunt for. Time to start the traditional con game of finding what sort of food is acceptable to everybody…. We eventually decided by the time-honoured method of going to the square where all the restaurants were, umming and ahh'ing with lots of "I don't mind – whatever you want!", till eventually I said: "That tapas place [La Tasca] looks OK…." It was. What they said was a meal for three was in fact plenty for five of us.

We had the strange experience of being partly indoors and partly out of doors, with Steve and Murray at an outdoor table which was right alongside the four-person indoor table which would have been next to the totally opened window. It was a warm and muggy night, but with no threat of rain till suddenly a medium-sized cloudburst emerged from nowhere. Though Murray and Steve only had the very edge of their table drenched, they were able to move to the inner end of the indoor table.

Wednesday 1 May 2019

Sandra Bond

The flight was lousy and I'm not impressed with JFK but what care I? Rockville looms large tomorrow. Sad I can't be there for the pre party tonight, but hope you are all having desperate fun as I sit waiting for my lonesome pizza here in Brooklyn.

WELCOME TO BAWLMER, HUN!

Our first official Corflu FIAWOL activity was a full-day tour of Bawlmer, Murland (Baltimore, Maryland to outsiders), where everyone is greeted with "Hun." (Honey, not Attilla). Hosts Steve and Elaine Stiles covered locations ranging from their house to Harborplace to the Visionary Art Museum. "Desperate fun" was had by Rob Jackson, Grant Canfield, Steve Jeffery, Andy Hooper, and Carrie Root, while Sandra Bond awaited her pizza. (It was evidently a long time coming.)

Rob Jackson

Not much lonesomeness if you had been in Rockville (or Randallstown/Baltimore, or Bethesda). Grant, Steve J and I got to Steve and Elaine Stiles's house soon after 10 am, but not till we had solved the Strange Case of the Disappearing Road. They are at 8631 Lucerne Road, OK? Yes, but my satnav turned us into Lucerne Road and at 8400-odd there were trees and a notice saying "Road Ends."

We retraced our steps and at the corner of the road were a couple of workmen doing something with a sign or some drains or something. We asked if there was anywhere that higher numbers of Lucerne Road could be found. One of them was a bloody hero and produced a street atlas of Baltimore including the other bit of Lucerne Road, involving turning left three times then third right. Turns out that years ago a recalcitrant landowning old woman had refused to sell her house to the people who wanted to build the road.

We were shown round Steve and Elaine's house with artwork

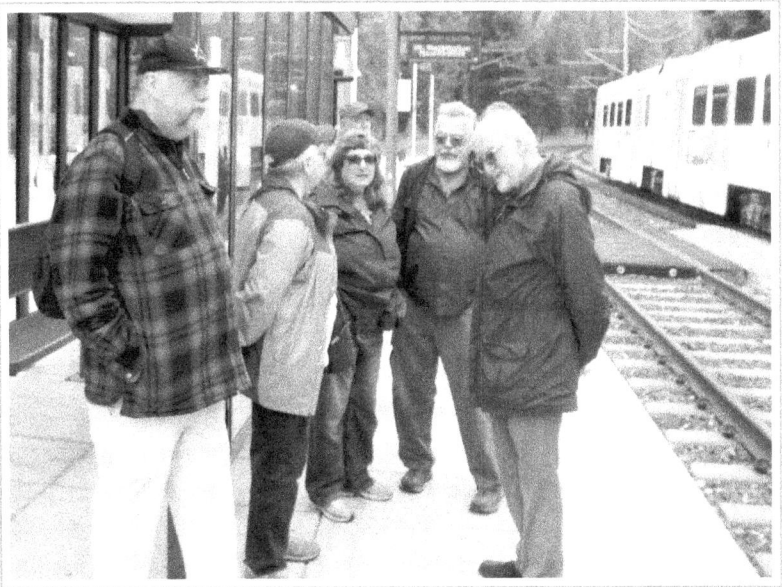

Waiting for the Baltimore Light Rail. (l-r) Andy Hooper, Carrie Root, Elaine Stiles, Grant Canfield, Steve Stiles, Rob Jackson. (SS)

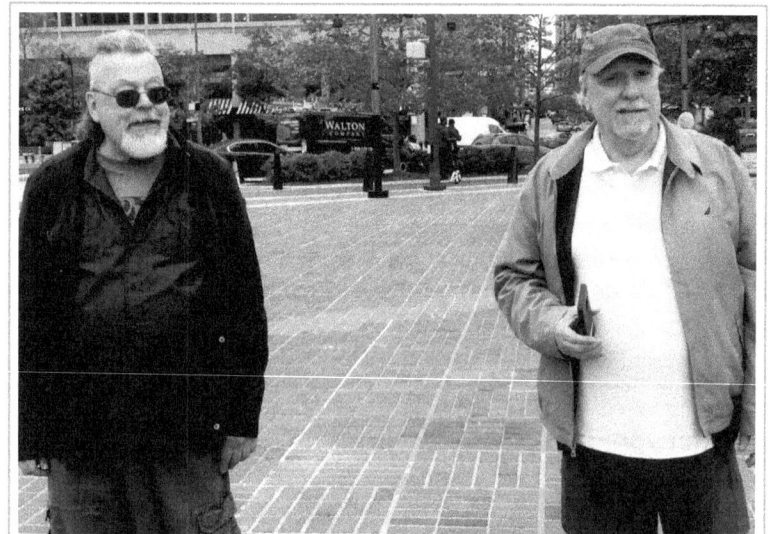

Left Top: Steve Stiles, Grant Canfield (RJ)

Left Middle: Grant Canfield, Rob Jackson, Elaine Stiles (SS)

Left Bottom: Grant Canfield, Andy Hooper, a small bit of Steve Jeffery's head, Elaine Stiles (SS)

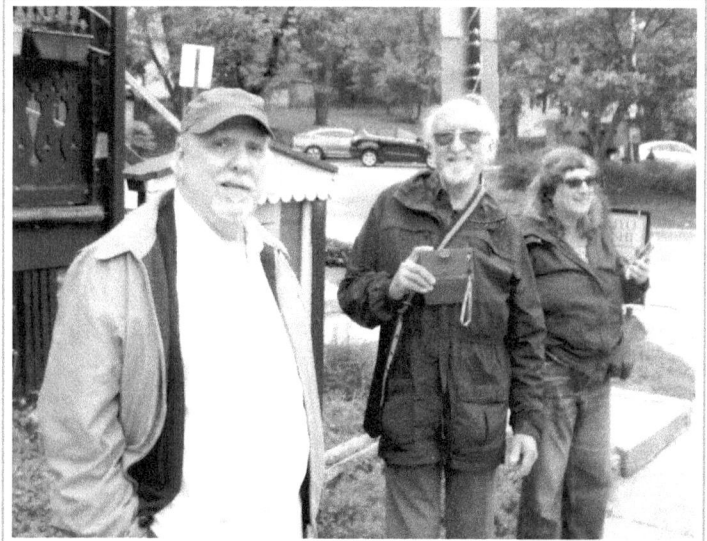

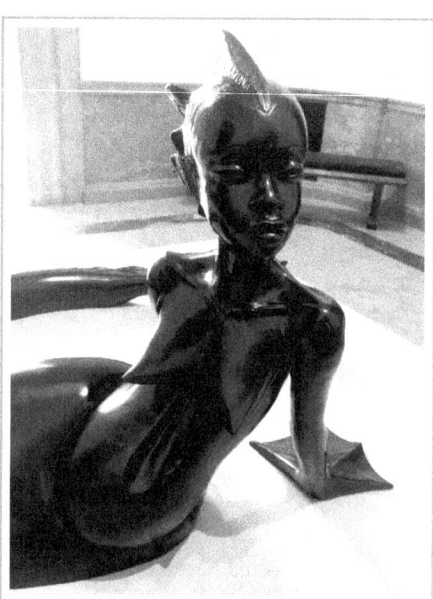

Visionary Art Museum (not a Corflu member) (SS)

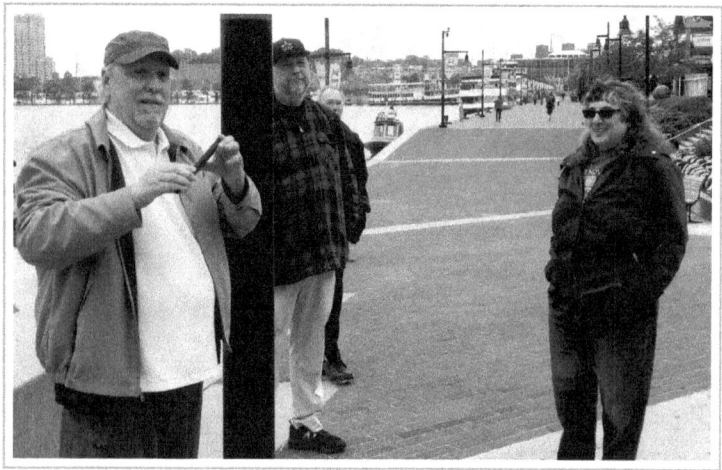

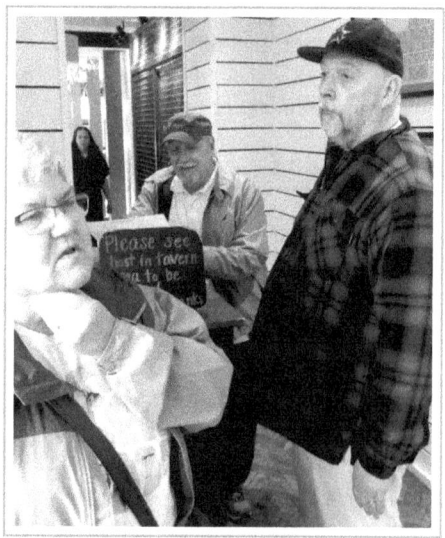

Carrie Root, Grant Canfield, Andy Hooper

everywhere except where there are untold thousands of CDs, cassettes or books, then Andy and Carrie arrived. We didn't leave till around 11.20, so the plan was to drive to Mount Washington where there is a cluster of fine restaurants in a mini bohemian quarter next to the light rail station. You can buy hippie dresses, have your dog groomed, or your Tarot cards read.

We ate an early lunch in the Mount Washington Tavern then it was onto the light rail to the Convention Center near Baltimore Harbour. Baltimore has an early but still very fine example of the gentrified, tourist attraction type of inner harbour, full of rich people's plaything yachts and lined by museums, restaurants and Ripley's Believe It Or Not. It was a bit of a hike to the American Museum of Visionary Art but totally worth it. Not only fascinating primitivist and other art, but a powerful message about the importance of decent parenting and of being kind to each other. (Hugely oversimplified here, of course.) Major feature: the brilliant Pratchett quote: "Evil begins when you begin to treat people as things."

Halfway to the museum I had a panic on realising I hadn't got my Corflu bag, which had a battery pack to allow me to take as many photos as I liked without running my iPhone down. The really irreplaceable thing is the Corflu bag! I remembered I had hung it on my chair on going into the pub/restaurant, and it was probably still there. Rang them: "Oh we found it. It's with the hostess at front of house." Phew. All that was lost was the chance to take as many photos as I would have liked.

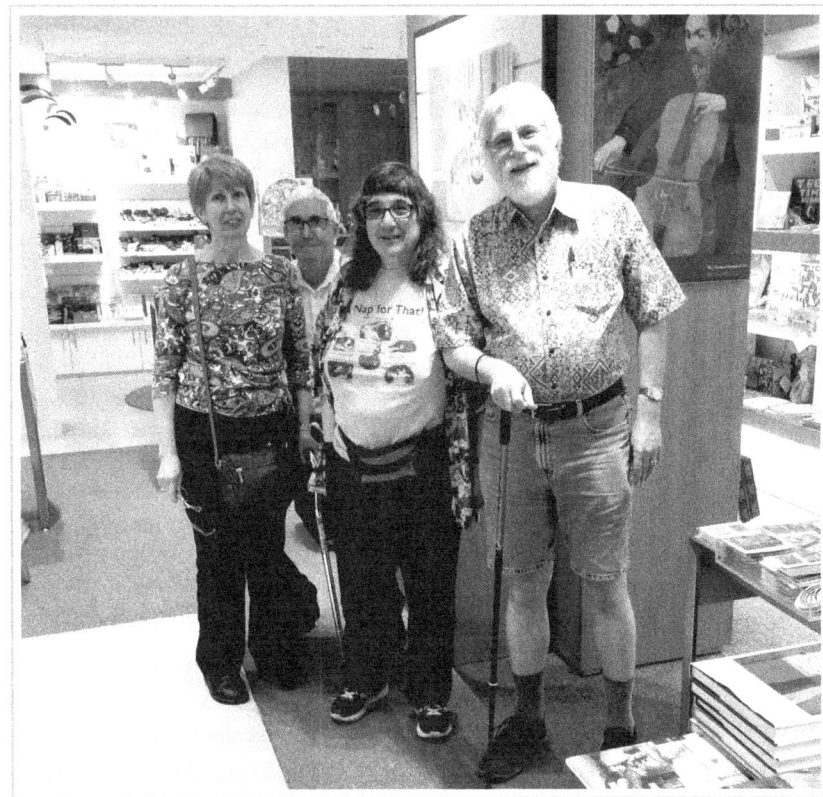

Mary-Ellen Moore, Murray Moore, Elaine Stiles, Alan Rosenthal (all SS)

NIGHT OF THE LIVING COLLATORS

Wednesday evening was a party at Michael Dobson's house in Bethesda, Maryland, about 20 minutes from the Cambria. Chicken tikka masala was used to bribe attendees into assembling the member packets.

Michael Dobson's house in Bethesda (RJ)

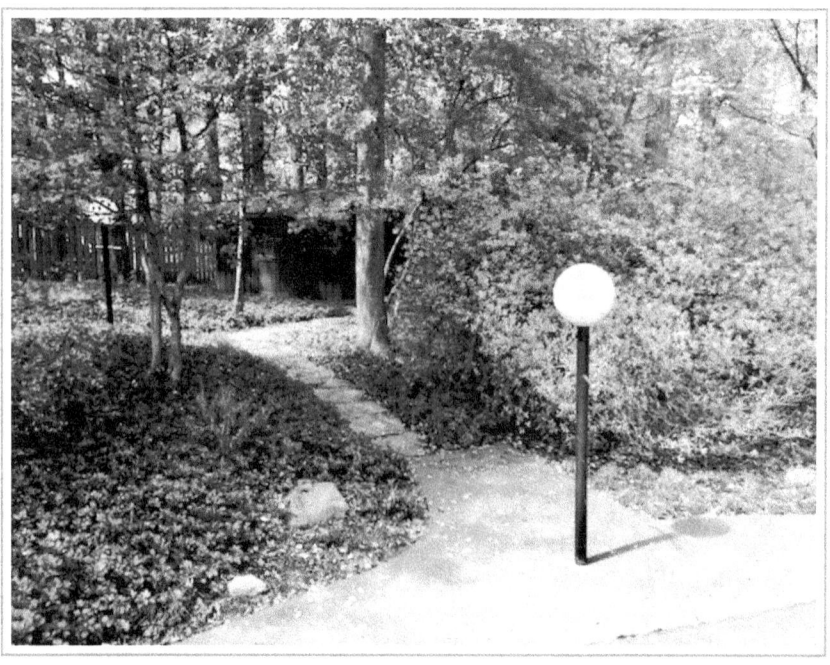

Rob Jackson

It was after 4 pm by the time we left Baltmore; our steps needed retracing to – in order – the city centre; the tram; the pub for my bag; the car; Elaine and Steve's house; the hotel (an hour's drive) and finally to Michael Dobson's place out on the rural outskirts of Bethesda by 7.30. There are still as many twists and turns as ever to get there, but the satnav coped OK. (I had previously been there in 2014 for breakfast with Michael as an advance thank-you for me giving him a lift to Richmond for that year's Corflu.)

Present, roughly in order of appearance in my memory, were: Greg & Jim Benford; Curt Phillipa; Jay Kinney; Jeanne Bowman & Alan Rosenthal; Murray & Mary-Ellen; Colleen & Leonard Stockmann; Steve J, Grant and myself; Spike (who came back to the hotel with us for a late check-in, making it a four-person carful); Andy & Carrie; Martin Morse Wooster; Frederic Gooding III (who had to ask who Ratfandom were), and others possibly not registering in my head.

A fine event, with much chat partly on the raised decking of Michael's upper-level patio on a balmy evening only slightly spoilt by regular planes descending into Dulles, and also indoors. Later on we all stuffed envelopes. Despite the massive wodge of publications and a surprise package of a

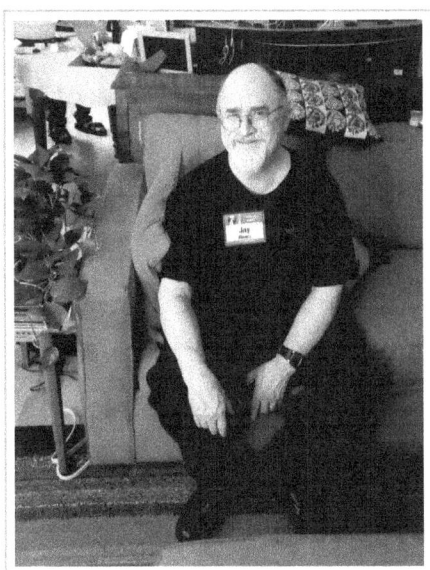

Jay Kinney (GC)

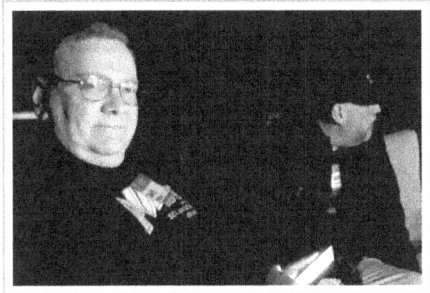

Curt Phillips, Andy Hooper (RJ)

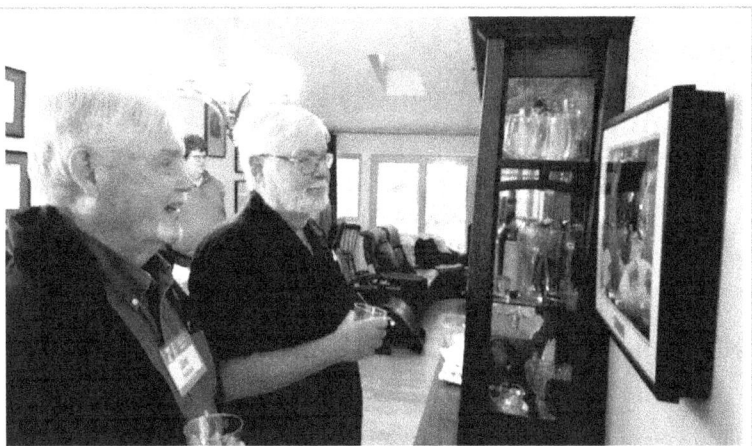

Jim and Greg Benford, with Martin Morse Wooster in the background

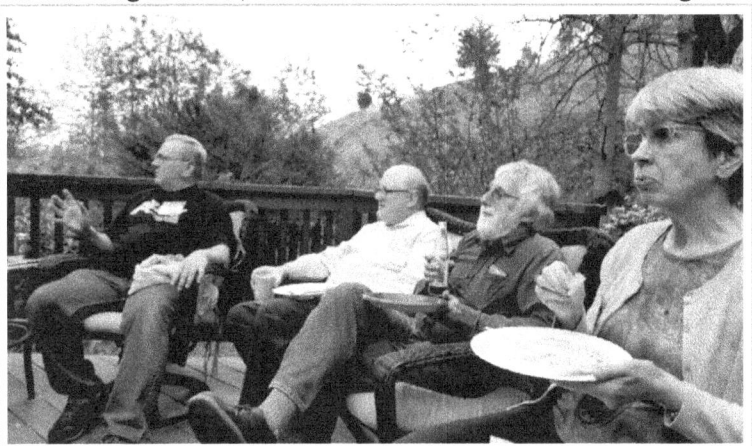

Curt Phillips, Frederic Gooding III, Alan Rosenthal, Mary-Ellen Moore

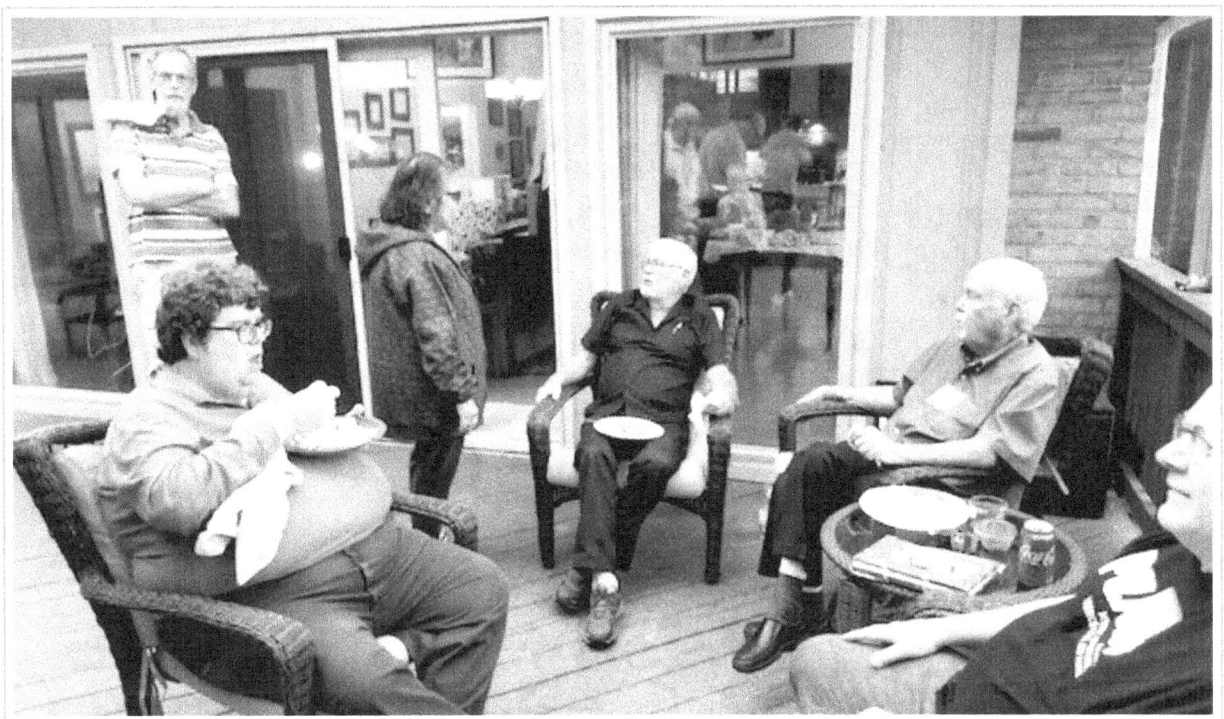

Leonard Stockmann, Martin Morse Wooster, Colleen Brown Stockmann, Greg Benford, Jim Benford, Curt Phillips

beautiful little illustration by Dan Steffan which Michael had framed for all attendees, many hands did indeed make light work.

Soon to be much welcomed, as well as those already known IntheBar such as Ted White, Rich Coad, Nigel Rowe, John D. Berry and others, were Dan & Lynn Steffan, and Craig Hughes.

Steve Jeffery

At the collating party, between frequent trips to a table overflowing with a very palatable tikka masala and some equally palatable wines, plus enough fruit, crisps, snacks and cheeses to feed a small army (or several dozen fans), Michael co-opted a small assembly line to unpick some 90 picture frames, insert signed and numbered pieces of artwork from Dan Steffan and reassemble and bag them for the convention packages. It all went surprisingly smoothly, showing that sometimes you can organise fans, as long as you keep them well fed and watered.

Michael's split level house is envious, from the spacesuit in its glass case in the den to the decking out back looking down on the garden and wooded hill behind the house.

I was presented with my official Corflu FIAWOL t-shirt and convention pack, which contained, along with Dan's picture (now sitting atop of my router) and the convention program book, *Random Jottings 17: A Corflu Fanthology* and an elegant spiral bound copy of *Thy Life's a Miracle*, a collection of selected writing by the late and hugely missed Randy Byers, graced with a beautiful cover by Ulrika O'Brien and Jae Leslie and carl juarez. In fact I think I paid for this last one as a Corflu fundraiser. I had downloaded the pdf before coming out, but the real thing is so much nicer and simply invites you to drop in and start reading, even if I didn't get a chance to do so myself before I got home.

I had almost forgotten what a good writer Randy was. I wished we'd met to discover, now it's far too

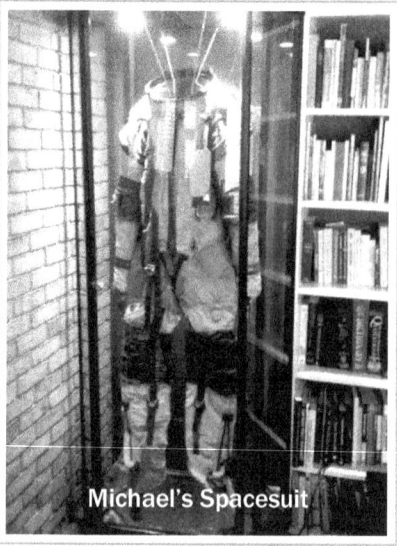

Michael's Spacesuit

late, how many things we had in common, from still liking and reading sf (I still haven't worked out whether that makes me a fringefan or real fan) and the writings of John Crowley (one of my favourite authors, and I'm hugely jealous that Randy knew him), to Chip Delany or the films of Pedro Almodovar. In a better world, he would still be here and we could have sat in the con suite into the early hours talking about the stuff we love.

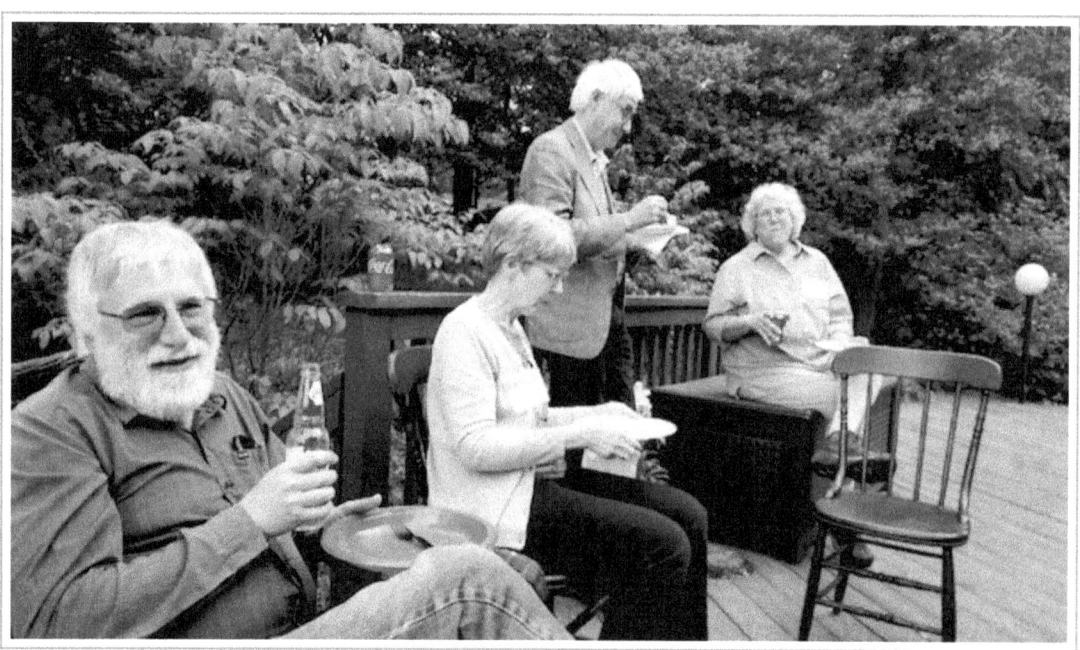

Alan Rosenthal, Mary-Ellen Moore, Murray Moore, Jeanne Bowman (CP)

ARRIVALS AND EXCURSIONS
THURSDAY 2 MAY 2019

Murray Moore

Our sat nav did not recognize the hotel address, 1 Helen Heneghan Way, because it has been in existence only a year.

We navigated to Rockville Town Centre and found the hotel after going into the Cambria Hotels building, which is not the hotel but Cambria Hotels headquarters.

Rob Jackson

I think the road was renamed recently – I am sure I saw a sign or map somewhere nearby with the old name. The hotel itself has a very new feel, and straight over the road they are starting to demolish an old street-level car park and build a new apartment block. With luck the construction noise (which isn't really all that bad) will stop over the weekend.

Curt Phillips (via Facebook)

The GPS address for the Corflu hotel is 196 East Montgomery Ave., Rockville, MD. I just found this out myself. Heading to hotel soon to set up the consuite.

Rob Jackson

I assume you are out buying further supplies? Or perhaps just now, sheltering from the massive thunderstorm. Which has only set in since 3.15 – weirdly, there was an utter cloudburst and flood first, and only now are we getting the thunder.

We were really lucky this morning, then. I was the only one on the planned tour of the Washington Gallery area with Colleen Brown and Leonard Stockmann, and the weather was gloriously sunny and

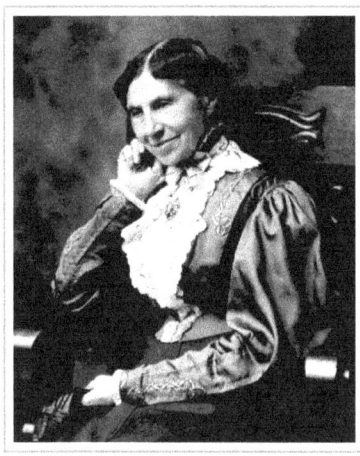

Clara Barton (did not attend Corflu)

warm. As there were just the three of us, Leonard drove into Washington DC as this was more convenient.

He dropped Colleen and me off at the Clara Barton House, which was fascinating and relevant to my Veterans Outreach work, as she not

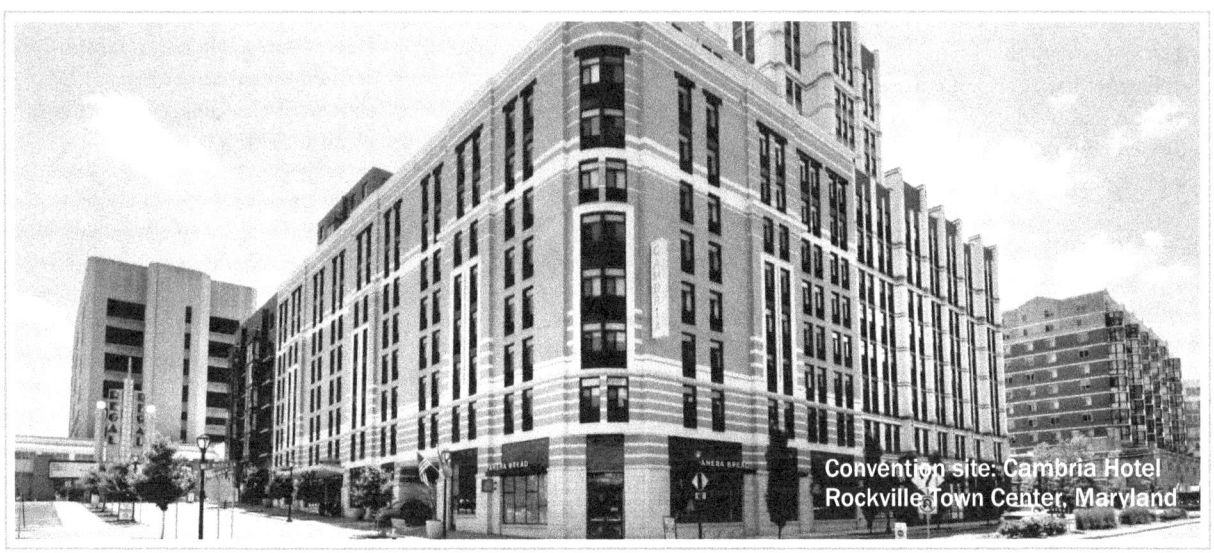

Convention site: Cambria Hotel Rockville Town Center, Maryland

Museums off the Mall

On Thursday, Colleen Brown Stockmann and Leonard Stockmann provided a tour of the Gallery Place/Chinatown area of DC to a packed audience consisting of Rob Jackson.

only pioneered humanitarian (and nursing) work with Civil War soldiers during the war but after it set up a hugely important and pioneering missing soldiers service, to try and find missing (often presumed dead) soldiers. 600,000 dead in that war; 62,000 letters of enquiry received, and 22,000 located one way or the other. Later she went to Europe, and her international humanitarian work included setting up the US arm of the International Red Cross.

Then to the American Portrait Gallery just up the street, where Colleen worked for 40 years till her very recent retirement. Saw the portraits of both Michelle and Barack Obama, then went to a pizzeria cafe called Ella's for lunch and by chance sat next to an old colleague of Colleen's who was showing a brand-new colleague round! Plenty to talk about – even old fanzines came into it, as we compared the states of preservation of their paper with that of the Clara Barton documents. Leonard got the car and we drove back. Just vaguely clouding over as we got back to Rockville....

Nigel Rowe

My flight was canceled so I have to wait another five hours. Who knew the DC area has weather in April that cancels flights.

I probably won't be at the hotel until midnight, although I now land at 10. Will be desperate for fun and

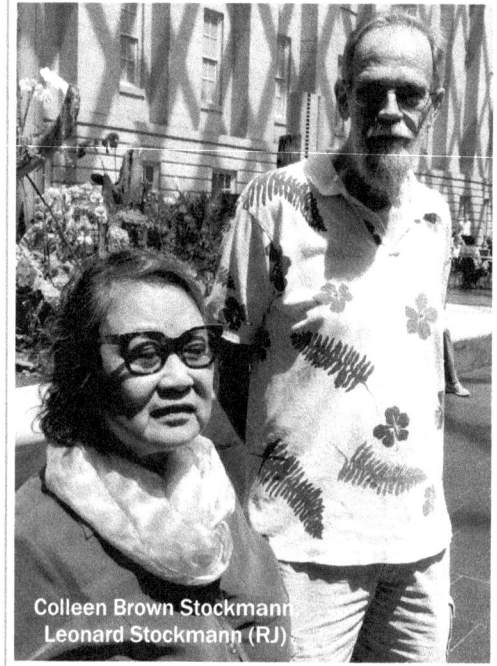

Colleen Brown Stockmann, Leonard Stockmann (RJ)

alcohol. Bummed that I'm missing Corflu dinner tonight. See everyone soon (hopefully).

Rich Coad

My flight to DCA was supposed to arrive at 4:30. Instead it's now 6:15 and I am stuck on the plane at Dulles. They are supposed to refuel and fly us to DCA sometime.

John D. Berry

The storm gods were against us.

Anyone coming in by air for Corflu on Thursday got diverted, redirected, delayed, and discombobulated by the intense thunderstorms that moved into the DC area that afternoon. Well, almost everyone: Dan and Lynn apparently lucked out, arriving on the first non-delayed flight into National, where they found no lines, got through Arrivals in mere moments, and caught the very first taxi outside the door. I think it spoke well of our fannish community that no one killed them upon hearing about this miraculously trouble-free arrival.

Since I couldn't get a nonstop flight into conveniently located National, I booked my flight into BWI (Baltimore-Washington International), figuring that it would be easier to get from there to suburban Maryland than from Dulles, way out in the Virginia suburbs on the opposite side of DC (especially since I was scheduled to arrive at 3:30, just in time to enjoy the start of the evening rush hour). All this good planning was tossed out the window when my flight got diverted to Harrisburg, Pennsylvania, where it refueled and awaited the go-ahead for another shot at BWI. I finally got off the plane at 6:30.

Then I made my mistake. I had been planning to take an inter-county Maryland bus that would have gotten me from BWI directly to the end of the DC Metro's Red Line, just one stop from Rockville, where Corflu was being held. But the bus only ran once an hour, and by the time I got in I figured it might be quicker just to catch the suburban MARC train into Union

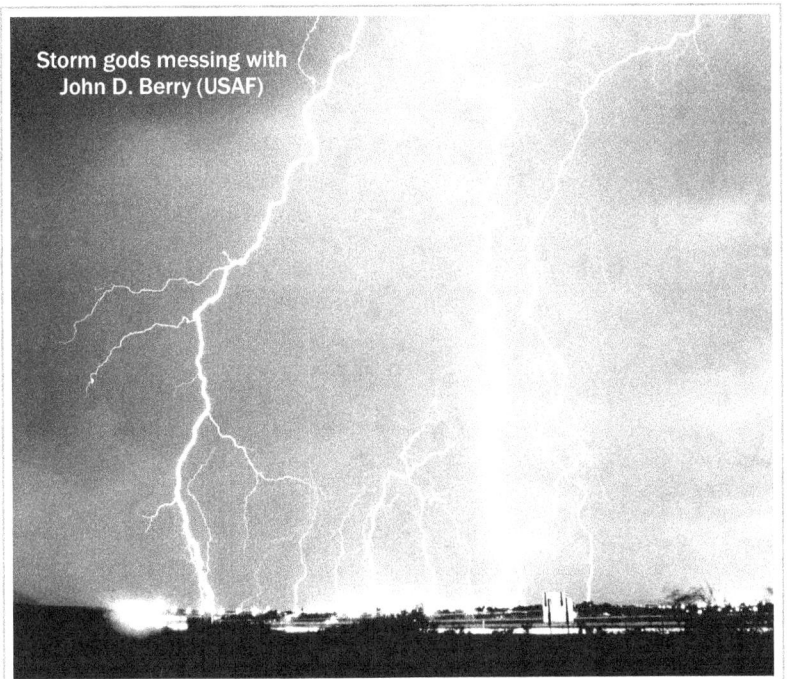

Storm gods messing with John D. Berry (USAF)

Station in DC, where I could hop on the Red Line and ride it out to Rockville. What I wasn't counting on was that the suburban trains don't run that often once rush hour is over. At the airport train station, I was helping a nice blind guy who had also just arrived use the ticket-vending machine; neither of us had any sense of urgency, but by the time we got over the tracks to the DC-bound side (which involved some slow elevators), we discovered that we had just missed the train we had seen, and that the next one wouldn't be coming for more than three-quarters of a hour.

Luckily, we were both in good humor, resigned to yet another delay (he had been through five airports already that day), and we sat on the platform chatting amiably while we waited. He was a programmer, and a parent with two kids and a husband. Also a good sense of humor. He was curious about Corflu, and impressed that such a large crowd was expected. He was just coming home from a family funeral in Tennessee, with family many of whom he hadn't seen in years and didn't normally interact with. We had such a good time talking that I gave him my card and encouraged him to send me email so we could keep in touch. (I haven't heard from him, though, at least not yet.)

Rich Coad

Latest word is we should move to a gate here at IAD. Hopefully I can then leave and get a taxi or Lyft or Uber to Rockville.

Pat Charnock

Am I the only one who always makes sure I've got a paper map when I make a journey? Everyone seems to be dependent on devices.

Rob Jackson

I used to want to have a paper back-up, but I usually look through a route on Google Street View so the route is in my head anyway, which is where the back-up always was in the first place.

I've now driven back to the hotel in Rockville from I-270 three times, so when Leonard Stockmann was driving us back this afternoon I was able to give him directions as to which lane to get into and so on. He & Colleen normally live further south and are not that familiar with Rockville.

Pat Charnock

Knowing you, that doesn't surprise me at all!

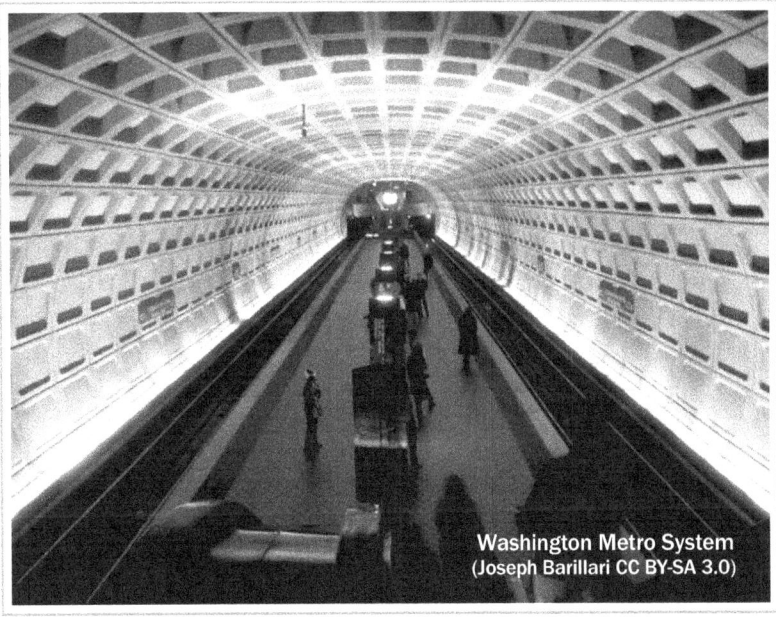

Washington Metro System (Joseph Barillari CC BY-SA 3.0)

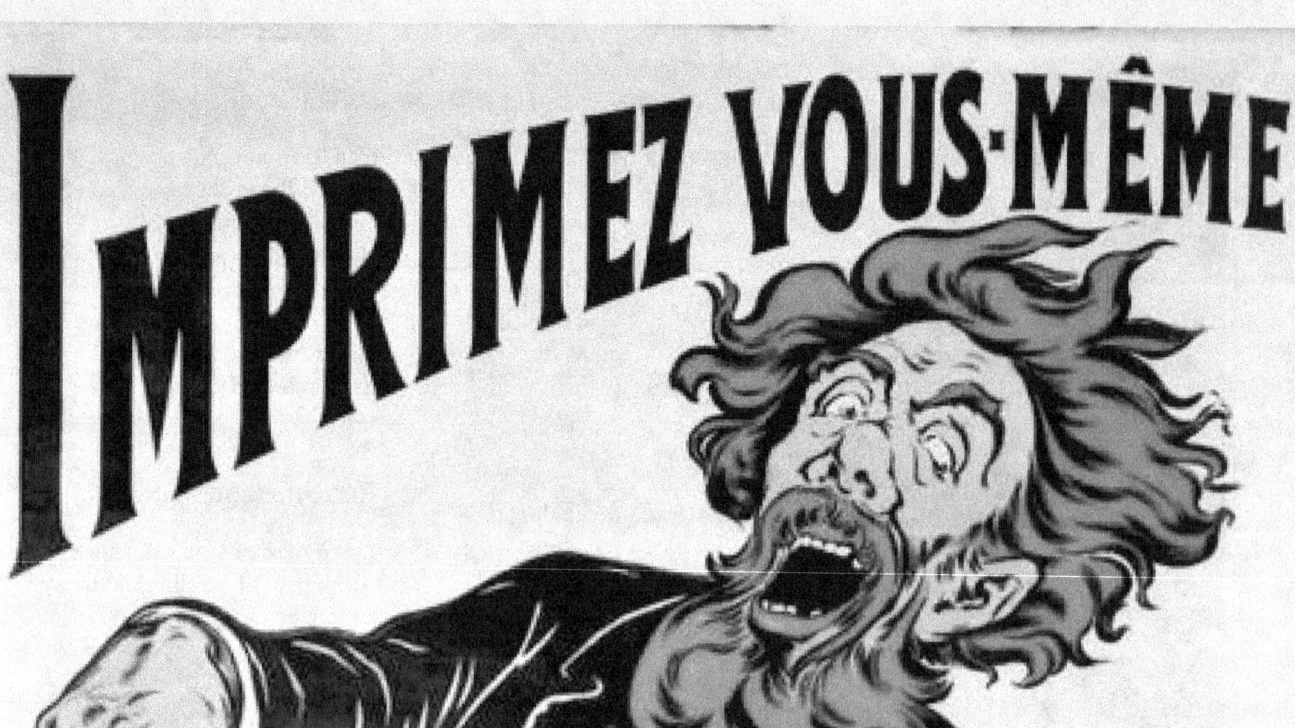

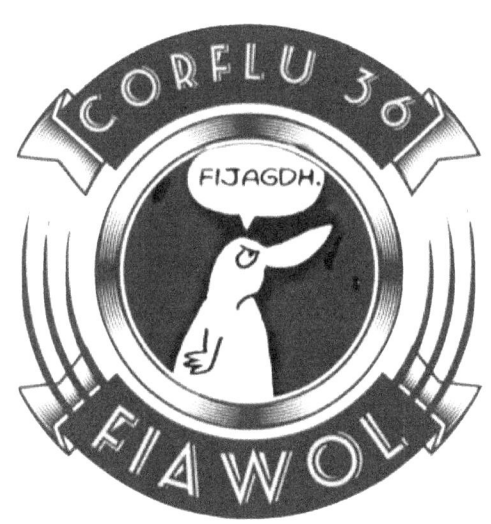

OPENING DAY

Friday 3 May 2019

OFFICIAL CORFLU BEGINS
FRIDAY 3 MAY 2019

Rob Jackson

The various wanderers with rebooked/diverted flights eventually arrived safely, though I hadn't yet seen Nigel by the time I went to bed (about 12.30 am). Rich's plane eventually got taxied to a gate at Dulles and they let people disembark, so he must have shot out of there like a bat out of hell and got a Lyft cab here. And JDB all present, correct and on good form.

Spike, Ian Sorensen and I went to the wine store round the corner for their tasting and came back with a dozen assorted bottles. There are still about half a dozen left but we are off out again at around noon to a different wine store, with Karen Schaffer also on the scouting party. But this evening it is Geri's beer tasting, so most of the wine will be kept for the wine tasting tomorrow (Saturday).

In between, Spike, Pat Virzi, Ian and I went to Gordon Biersch for dinner. This was good fun, especially when the waiter knocked over a nearly full glass of iced water. Most of it went onto the seat between Pat V and myself, but we both got slightly damp, and after a while I wondered why parts of my bum were cold – I was sitting on two ice cubes! As Ian said, definitely not a hot bot.

Steve Jeffery

The con suite, IMHO, was an ideal place to hang out, and so well stocked that there was far more food and drink than even 50 or so fans could get through in a long weekend. Huge thanks have to go for Curt for organising everything, and to whoever brought scones (complete with cream and jam) which proved to be a huge hit. There was some debate as to whether it should be cream first then jam or jam then cream, depending on whether you come from Cornwall or Devon (or possibly the other way around), and Murray and Mary Ellen Moore and I tried to resolve this by trying both options, although I can't recall if we came to any firm conclusion on the matter.

I wish I had more time to talk with Joe Siclari and Edie Stern about their fanac.org project, who set up shop on a couple of comfy sofas outside the main con-suite with a scanner and a growing pile of rare or historic fanzines that had been donated for scanning into their archives. Last time I looked at their site they were still working though these a month after the con.

John D. Berry

I was more jet lagged than you might expect when I arrived at BWI Thurgood Marshall Airport. Eileen and I had just gotten home the night before from a week of genuine vacation in Hawaii, so the overall time difference was six hours.

Rob Jackson

And it has got going brilliantly! Wonderful atmosphere, and great food. Breakfasted on Liz Phillips's home-made scones, clotted cream (also home-made) and jam just now. I don't usually have a cream tea for breakfast…. One of the scones was ginger flavour.

Graham Charnock

I keep the ITB page open in the hope there may be proof of something happening at Corflu, but I guess they must all be having too good a time to worry about me.

John Purcell

I worry about you all the time, Graham.

Steve Jeffery

So Grant Canfield and I convened in the lobby before negotiating the complexities of the Metro (as it turned out it was a straight run) into central DC. Despite the (surprisingly small) White House at one end, and the imposing edifice of the Lincoln memorial at the other, the park itself (actually parks, the National Mall including Constitution Gardens and West Potomac Park) was almost familiar if you've ever tried to cross London using only the green bits.

Despite a notice on the Vietnam Memorial information booth

warning us not to feed the wildlife, the thing that I noticed most was the almost complete absence of squirrels, whereas in London they'd be half a dozen swarming round your feet begging at the drop of a peanut. (Brits tend to be suckers for anything cute and furry, and blissfully ignore the Do Not Feed notices, or are less fastidious about dropping food crumbs. Or any sort of litter for that matter. Rockville itself was cleaner than almost anywhere in the UK, and especially Oxford, whose streets and pavements often resemble a spilled litter bin of bottles, nightclub flyers and food packaging (and indeed food).)

I did eventually see one lone squirrel on the walk back, but it's odd how you miss things you expect to see.

Elaine Stiles

I had agreed to be the con registrar, but that turned out not to be so easy because neither the phone nor car GPS and passersby in the general vicinity of the hotel (including a man who worked for the parent company) could locate it. By the time we stumbled upon it, Michael was handling registration along with his other responsibilities.

Rob Jackson

People moseying off to have fun in central DC, or going for a long walk to buy lots more wine then stopping on the way back for lunch at a Japanese hibachi place, and things like that don't lend themselves to being filmed. Also, you (Graham) pretty much told us not to bother with trying to broadcast anything after 6 pm UK time unless it is an official programme item.

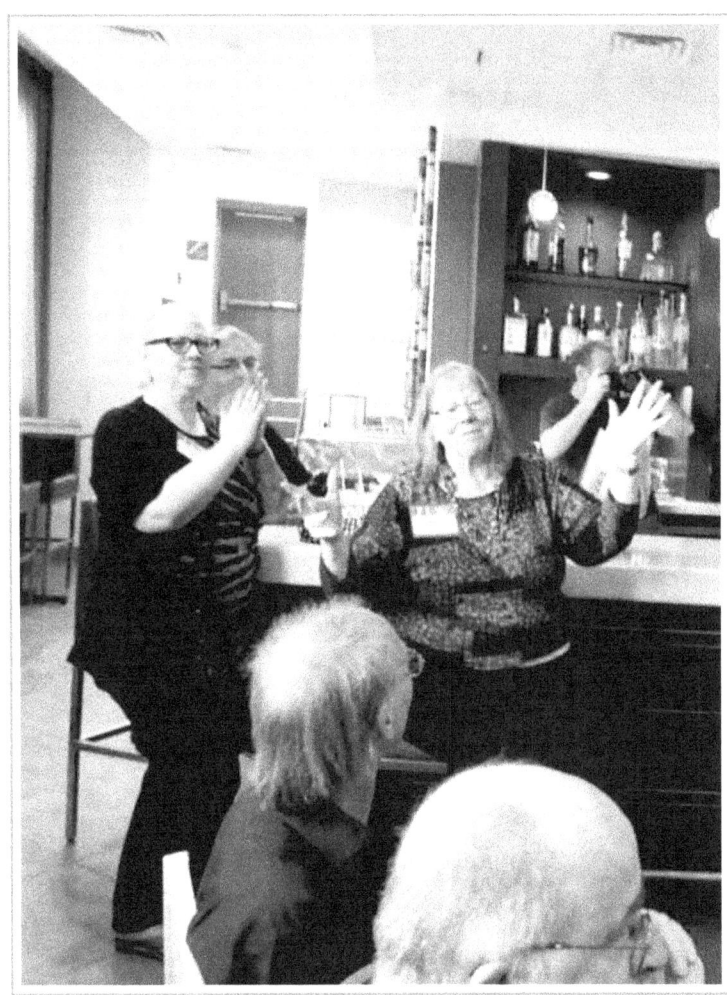

Lynn Steffan, Sandra Bond, Geri Sullivan (MW)

Later I took the laptop up to the con suite, plugged the webcam in and found that a You Tube link worked. Nothing official was due till 6 pm EDT, or 11 pm UK summer time – the Opening Ceremony in the hotel restaurant on the ground floor. That was the only event held there; the main con hall was on the lower ground floor.

News from the consuite: Nigel arrived OK late the previous night and was quickly into fun mode, and Dan and Lynn were greeted with hugs from pretty much everyone in the room.

The Opening Ceremony was in the hotel's foyer bar. A couple of unfortunate non-con hotel guests were innocently sitting at the bar and initially waited things out as the room got more crowded round them, but once Michael started addressing the multitude, discretion had to be the better part of valour and they left.

The eventual GoH was Jim Benford. Both Murray Moore and Dan Steffan had to be passed over as they had been GoH's before and the names hadn't been checked.

The Golden Samovar Russian restaurant where John D B, Karen, Mike Ward, Steve Jeffery and I ate was pleasant and we had a genuine Russian wait person seeing to us.

OPENING CEREMONIES

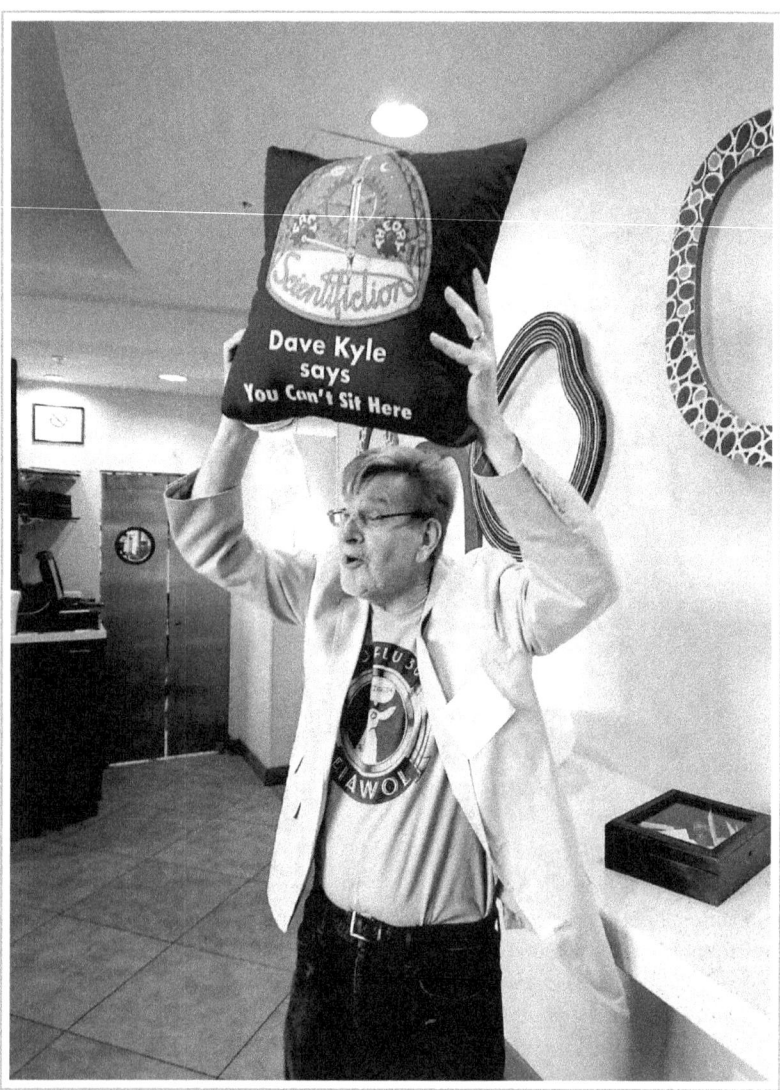

Michael Dobson with the official Corflu Guest of Honor Pillow, which was (eventually) given to Jim Benford (NR)

Steve Jeffery

I'm slightly shamed that – along with many others – I chose to opt out of the Corflu GOH draw this time, the opt out donations providing a very tidy pot for the eventual 'winner' (after several false starts where the names of previous GOH's were successfully drawn out of the hat, only to be discarded as ineligible. At some point I suspect this tradition will have to be revised when it becomes evident that the only people in the draw are those who know they can't be chosen). Finally, though, Jim Benford emerged as the lucky recipient, to be greeted with cheers, sighs of relief from those whose names were still in the hat, and the proceeds of the opt-out fund which he generously went on to donate back again during the auction. An economics graduate could have a field day untangling Corflu's weird closed-loop economy.

Martin Morse Wooster

The first day of Corflu had the opening ceremony, where a sacred box is unearthed that included a crusty bottle of correction fluid or "corflu." The convention chooses a guest of honor by pulling a name from the box, but you can opt out of the honor with a $20 donation. The winner was Jim Benford, who got all the donation money, which he reportedly spent at the fanzine auction on Saturday. His other prize was a pillow, designed by Alison Scott, which says "Dave Kyle Says You Can't Sit Here" and has the badge of the Science

My stodgy dumpling things were late arriving due to a confusion about how many main courses we ordered; we had chosen one extra main as a shared starter.

The portions were all huge, so by the time mine arrived I had had rather a lot of everyone else's – but my conscience wouldn't let me leave that much. Maybe that's why I flaked out earlyish that evening – too much carbohydrate. Nothing to do with the Georgian wine at the restaurant or the lovely beers at Geri's tasting at all. Oooh no.

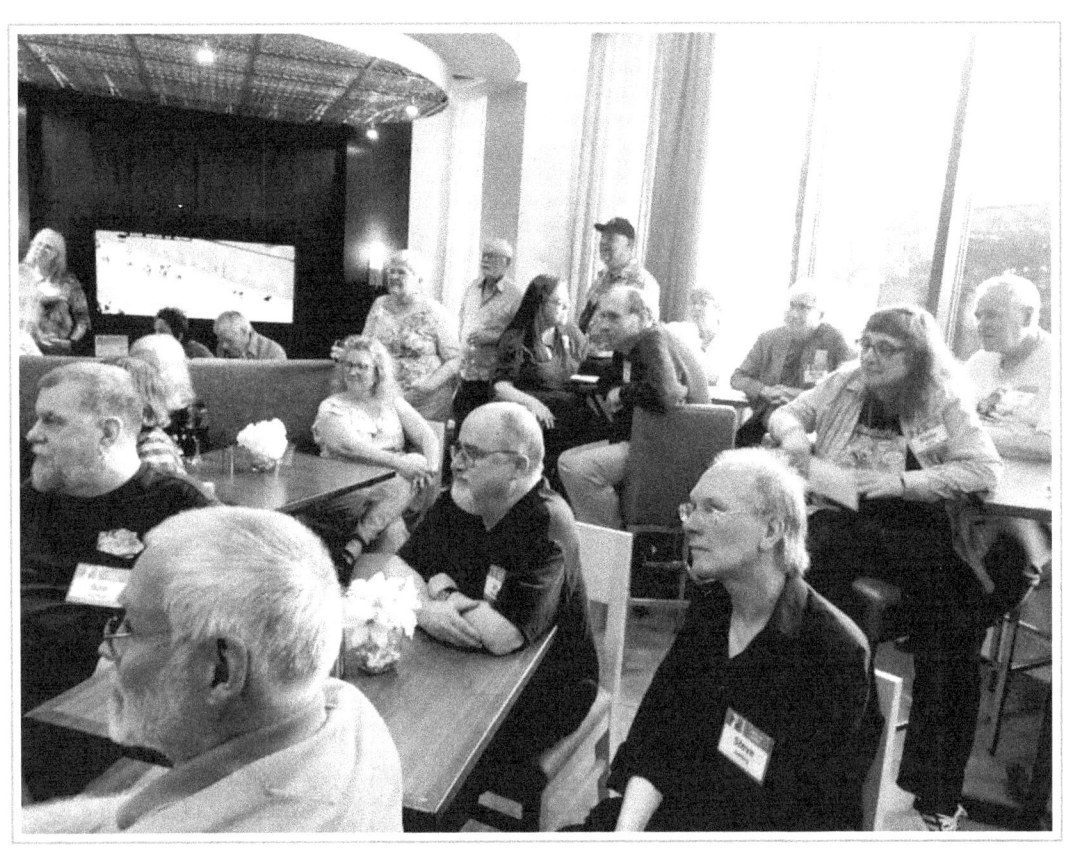

Miscellaneous Corfluvians (MW)

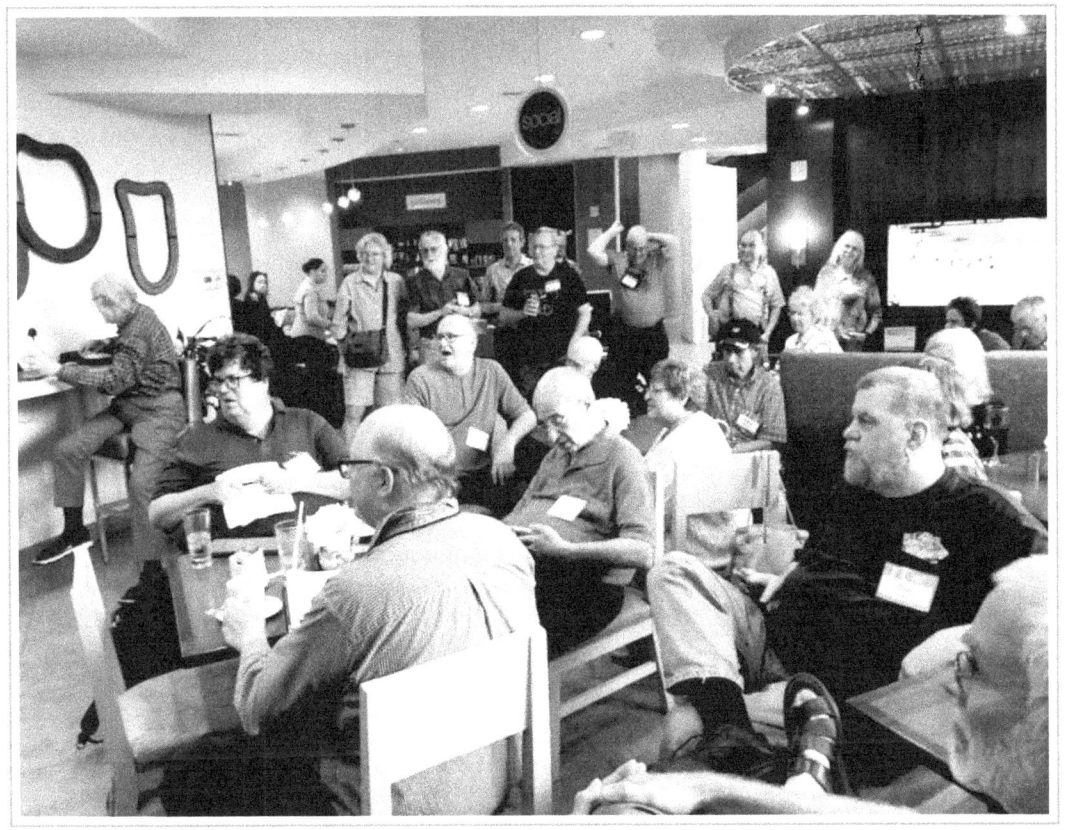

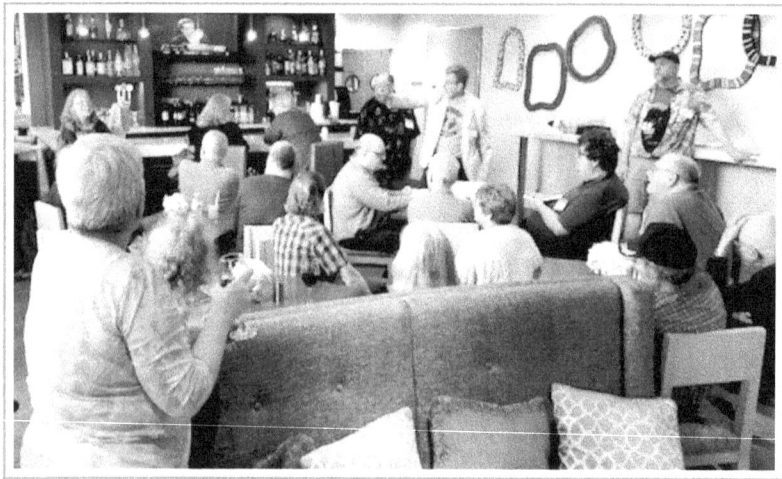
Corflu Opening Ceremony continues...and continues (CP)

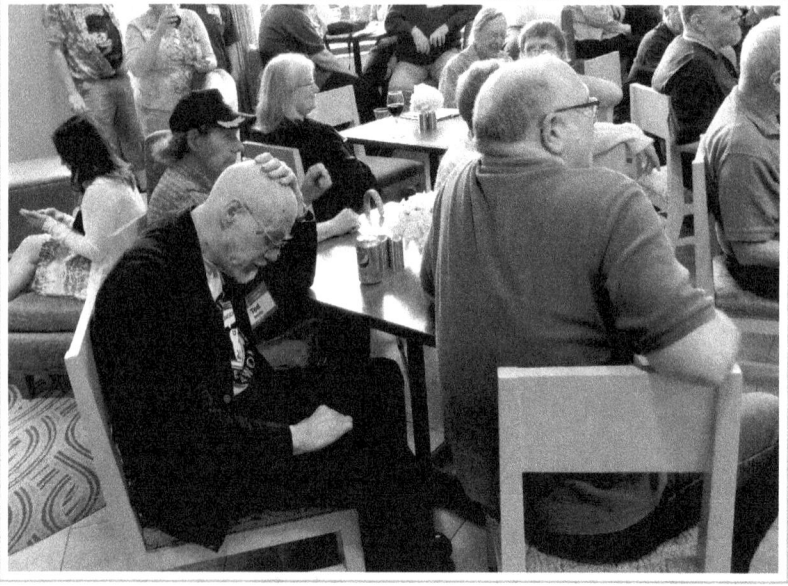

Fiction League of the 1930s.

Grant Canfield

Since you asked for personal reminiscences from attendees, here is the story of My Corflu Fainting Spell.

It happened Friday about a half hour before the official Opening Ceremony. I had just left Dan and Lynn Steffan's room, where a few of us had been getting sercon. A bunch of fans were sitting around in the lounge area outside the con suite, and one of them called my name. I had known Chris Couch for years through fanzines and electronic media, but this was my first time meeting him in person. We were leaning against the wall, chatting, when things suddenly went all white for me. The next thing I knew, I was half kneeling, half sitting on the floor, sort of leaning against Chris, who was also kneeling.

I looked up and saw a bunch of faces looking at me with concern and worry. I said, "Did I just faint?"
Nigel Rowe said, "Oh, yes."

After resting for a few minutes, I said, "I think I better go to my room and lie down for a while."

As I walked away -- or according to witnesses, as I staggered or wobbled away -- I heard someone say, "Did Grant Canfield just faint?"

Then Curt Phillips was walking with me, holding my elbow. He got in the elevator with me, and asked if he could accompany me to my room. I thought that was an excellent idea. In my room, Curt told me he was an RN, and quizzed me about my symptoms.

I was pretty sure I knew what had happened to me. It wasn't hard to figure out. Steve Jeffery and I had ridden the Metro into DC that morning, and had walked around the White House, the Executive Office Building and the Ellipse, then into the Mall, where we visited the Washington Monument, the WWII Memorial, the Reflecting Pool, the Lincoln Memorial, and the Vietnam War Memorial, then back to the Metro Center station to ride back to Rockville.

That was more walking in one day than I usually do in a month, and my back was killing me so I had taken a couple of hydrocodone pain pills. (I later remembered that it was actually three of them, way beyond my accustomed one pill every three or four days or so.) I also told him that I had taken my meds that morning with just a glass of water, instead of with breakfast as I usually do, and that I had had nothing to eat all day, and my only intake had been a couple bottles of water as we were walking around the Mall. (As an aside, I must note that I never saw Steve take so much as a sip of water the whole time we were in DC. I started thinking of him as "The Camel.")

Making it worse, I also admitted that I had gotten high with a few friends as soon as we returned to the hotel. So, I was obviously dehydrated, my electrolytes were depleted due to no food, I was overdosed on strong pain medication, and I had gotten buzzed. And I'm a 73 year old cardiac patient who should have known better, but I had broken all the rules anyway. What a maroon.

Curt was great. He checked my pulse and blood pressure, fetched me a bowl of fruit and some energy bars from the con suite, and generally exhibited a degree of consideration and caring that went a long way toward easing any anxiety I felt about the whole situation. He suggested I rest up after eating and rehydrating, which I did, skipping the Opening Ceremony.

I was much better later in the evening, other than being embarrassed about fainting in public. But I was grateful that if it had to happen, it happened among a group of smart, concerned friends. And I was particularly grateful that Curt was there. His empathy and care, as well as his professionalism as a nurse, was a godsend. Let it be known far and wide that that dude is a great guy of the highest order, and a true mensch.

So that's the story of how I happened to faint at Corflu. My profoundest thanks to Curt Phillips, and to everyone else present for their concern and attention. Other than that incident, I had a great time!

Martin Morse Wooster

Members got quite a lot of stuff. Dobson edited a 163-page fanthology of members' writings,

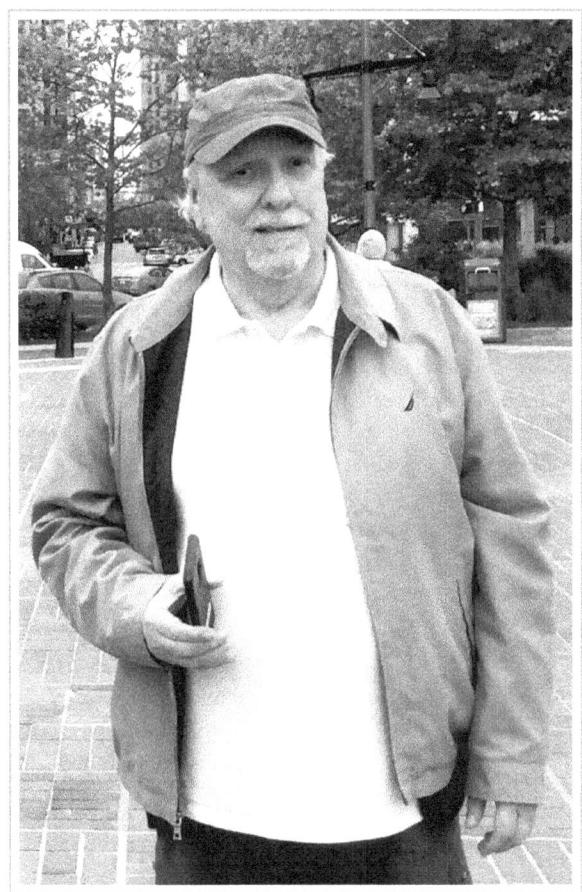
Grant Canfield (RJ)

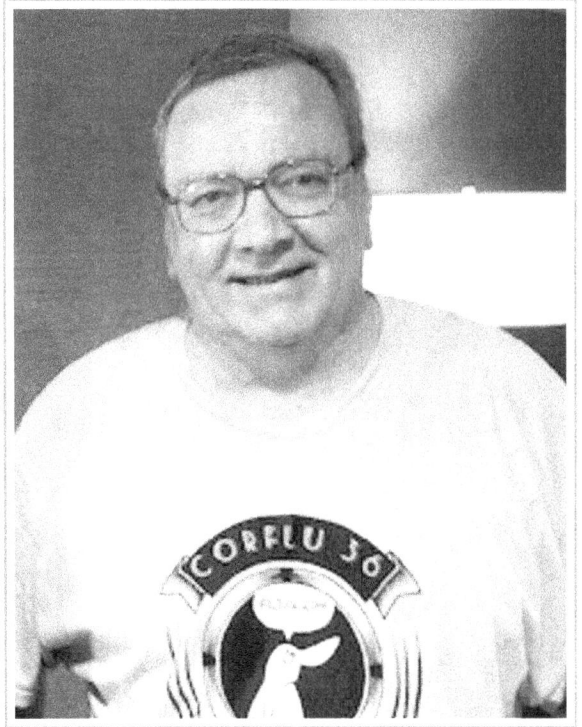
Curt Phillips (RJ)

which is also available on Efanzines. Some mossbacks grumbled that Dobson used CreateSpace as his publisher, but I thought the book was well done. Also included in the members' packet was *Thy Life's A Miracle: Selected Writings of Randy Byers*, a 135-page anthology edited by Luke McGuff.

But that wasn't all! We also got a framed print by Dan Steffan, in a limited edition of 90, which showed a nude Japanese woman with creatures on her back that resembled those of British artist Arthur Thomson. It was a very handsome piece of art, and I will put it on my shelf next to the Star Wars thingie I got at Nationals Park.

John D. Berry

This Corflu, for me, feels like even more of a family reunion than usual, if only because there were so *many* old friends there. I found myself pondering just how many of those people I have known for fifty years or more. Ted, of course, and Steve. Greg and Jim Benford. Colleen. Jay Kinney, Christ Couch, Craig Hughes, Mike Ward. And lots of others I've known for almost as long.

Martin Morse Wooster

I spent much of the time in the con suite listening to stories about 20th century fan legends. I heard about the Scottish fan who, after losing a feud with everyone else in his club, dropped out only to appear in the pages of a tabloid completely nude except for a hand coyly placed over his manhood. The headline of the piece about the fan was 'IT'S ORGYTASTIC."

"Do you mean this guy discovered orgy fandom?" I asked.

"No, it was more like orgy con-dom," said my source, who added that the fan liked showing up at the orgies he organized in a gorilla suit, because women liked sitting on his lap and stroking his fur.

But the story too good to check was whether two Arab sheiks offered to buy Baltimore fan Lee Smoire at Discon II in 1974 for two camels. This claim would be absurd and ridiculous about any other fan than Lee Smoire, who stories cluster around like gaudy barnacles. I cite it to add to Lee Smoire's legend.

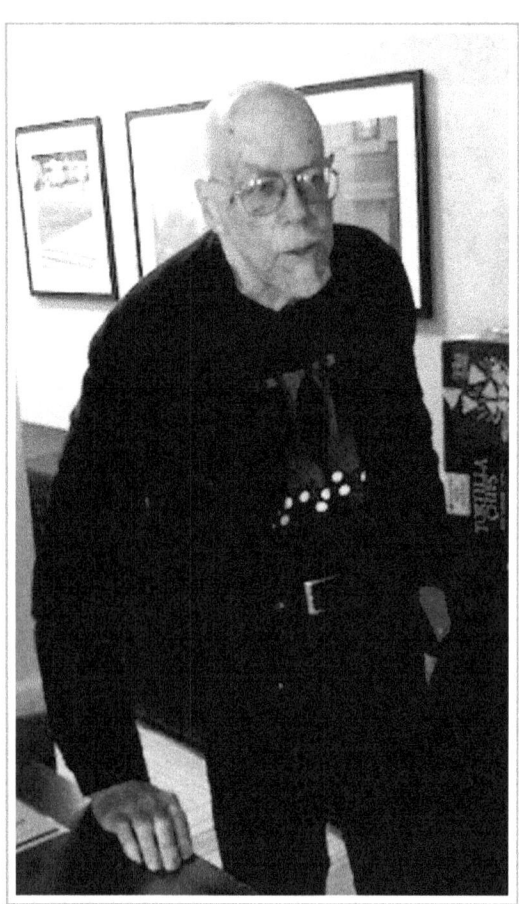

Ted White (CP)

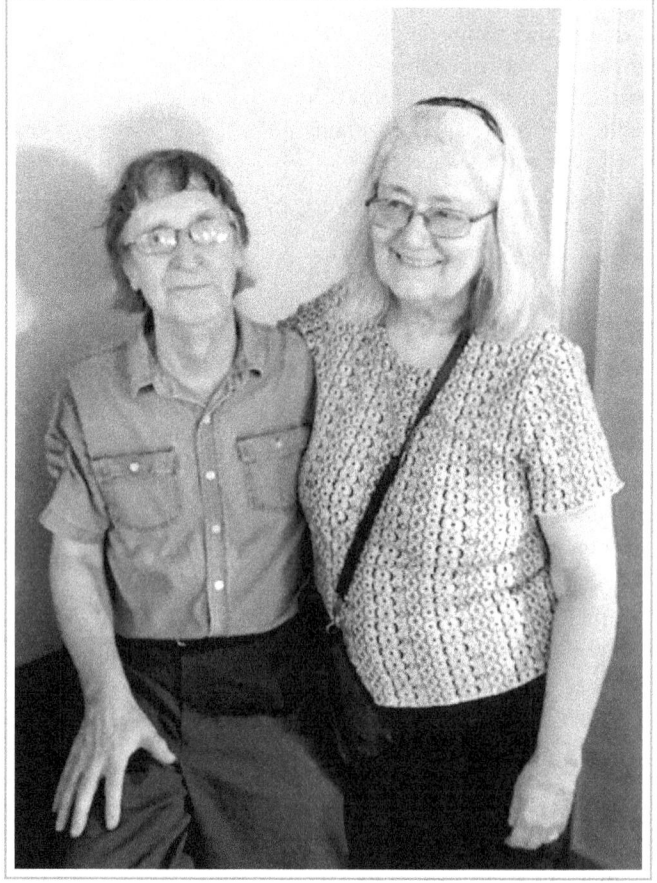

Bill and Mary Burns(CP)

BHEER TASTING

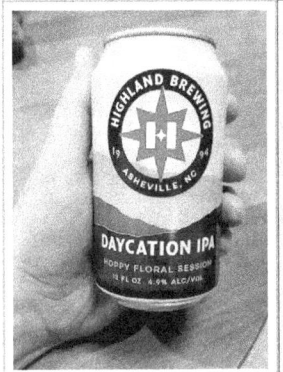

Around 6p on Friday evening, the consuite opened. Big news for the evening was the Bheer Tasting, sponsored by our very own TAFF winner, **Geri Sullivan**!

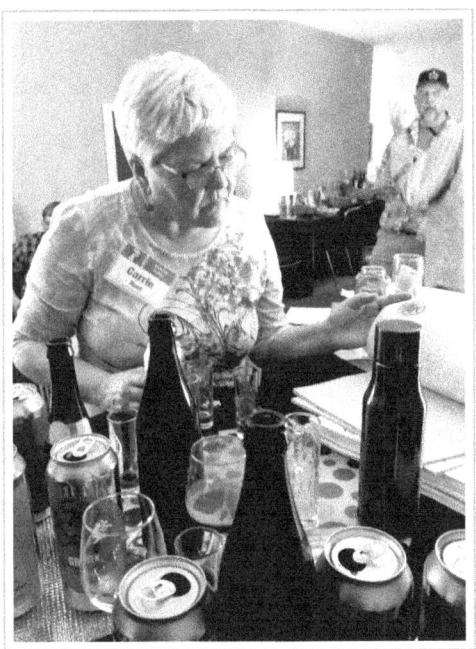
Carrie Root (GS)

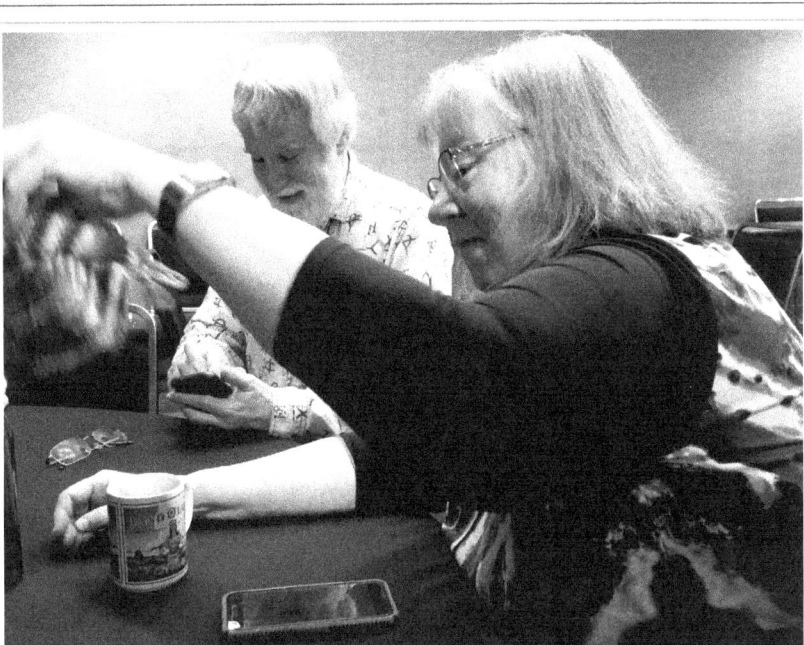
Geri Sullivan (CP)

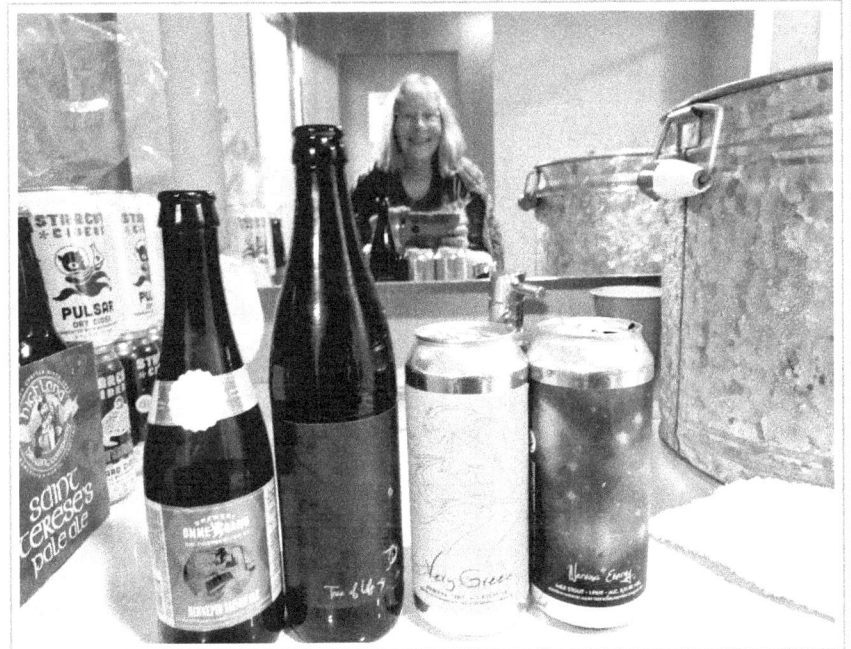
Geri Sullivan (GS)

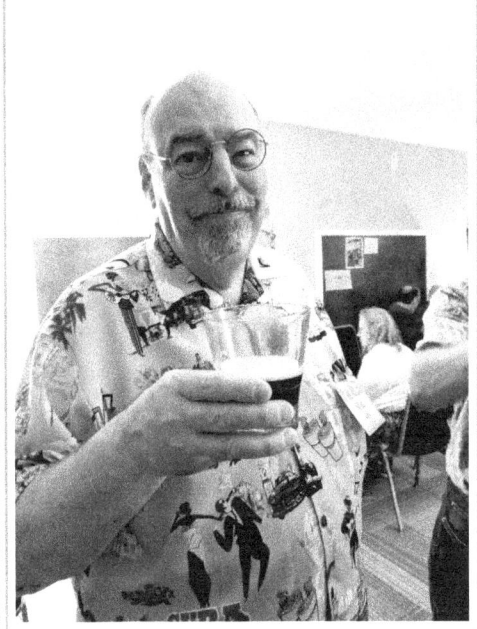
Rich Coad (GS)

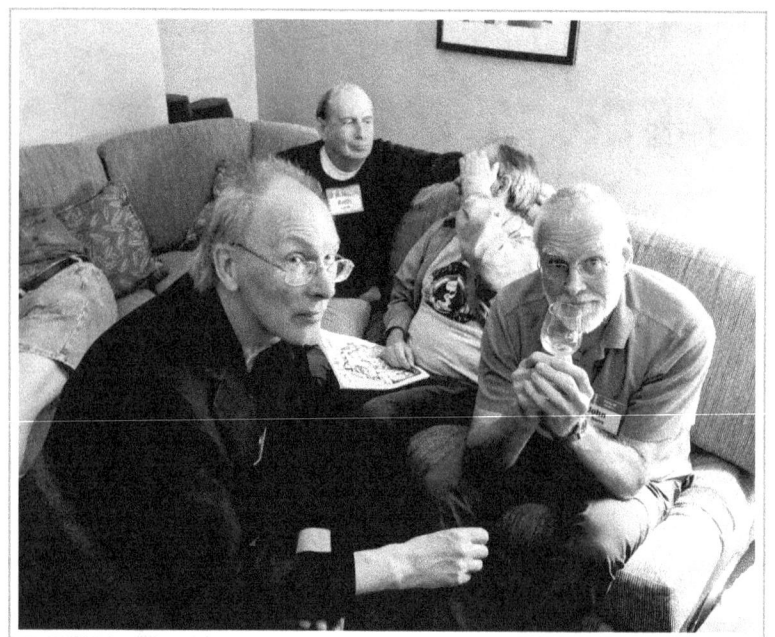 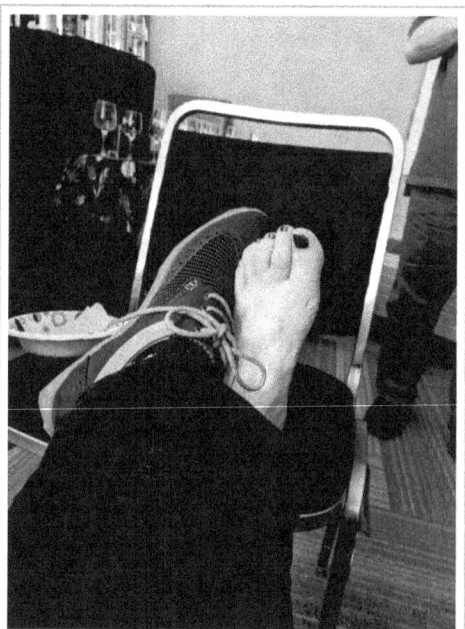

From left: Mystery Body, Steve Jeffery, Keith Lynch, Victor Gonzales, John D. Berry.   Right: Mystery Foot (GS)

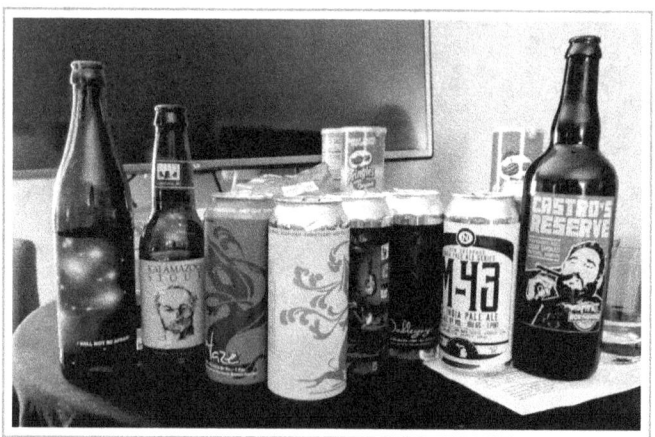

Before + After (GS)

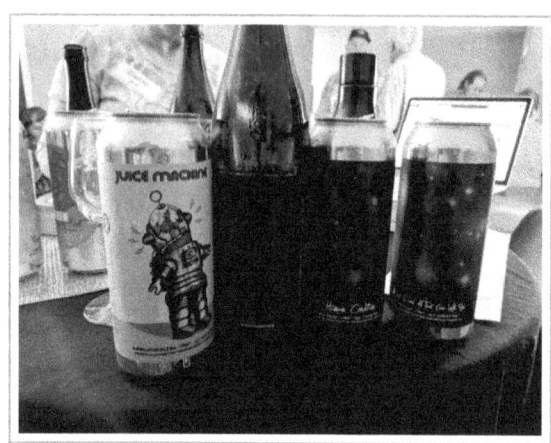 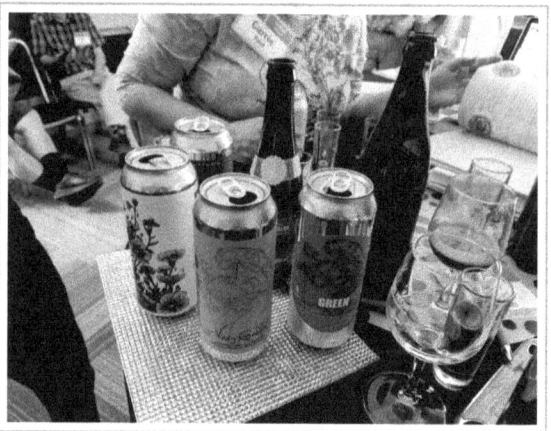

WHAT FANS DO AT CORFLU

#1 Have Dinner with Friends

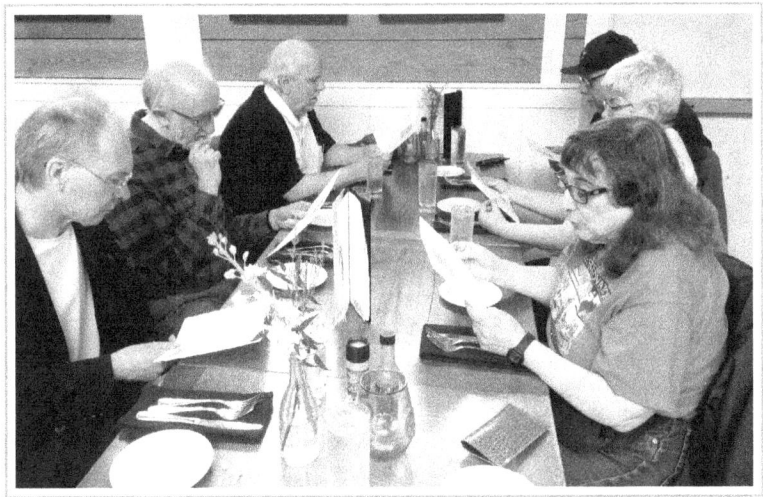

Steve Jeffery, Rob Jackson, Grant Canfield, Andy Hooper, Carrie Root, Elaine Stiles (SS)

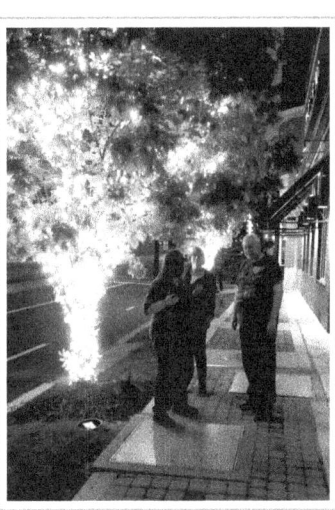

Spike, Pat Virzi, Ian Sorensen (RJ)

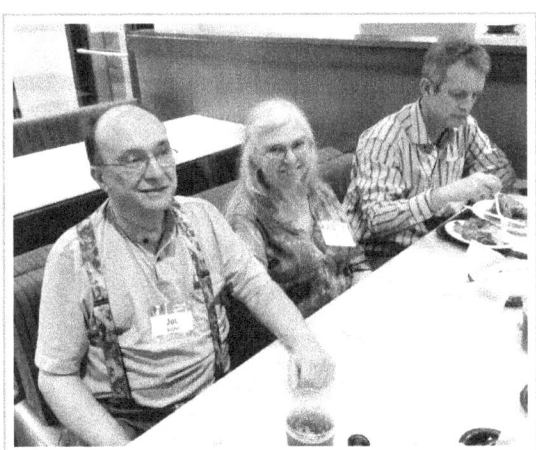

Joe Siclari, Edie Stern, Nigel Rowe (SS)

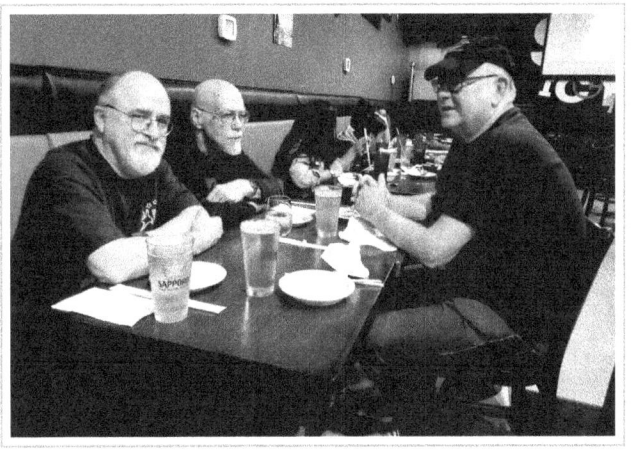

Jay Kinney, Ted White, Frank Lunney (GC)

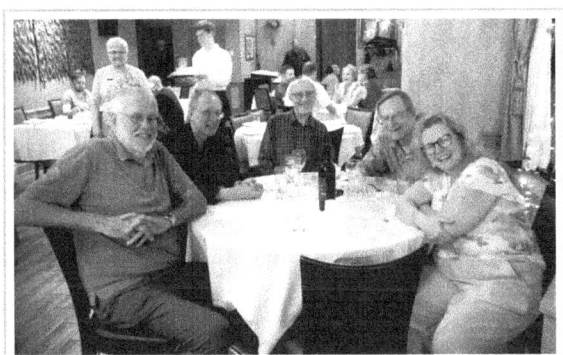

John D. Berry, Steve Jeffery, Rob Jackson, Michael Ward, Karen Schaffer (RJ)

#2 Relax in the Hotel Lobby

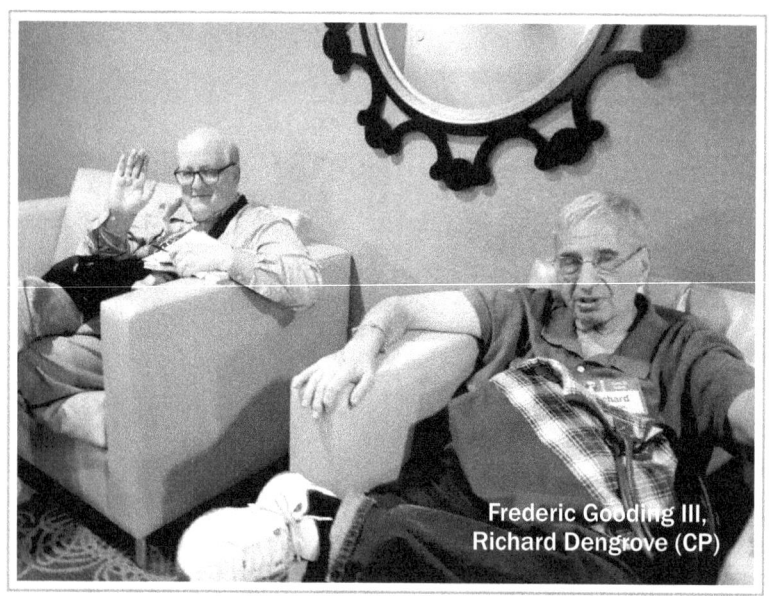

Frederic Gooding III, Richard Dengrove (CP)

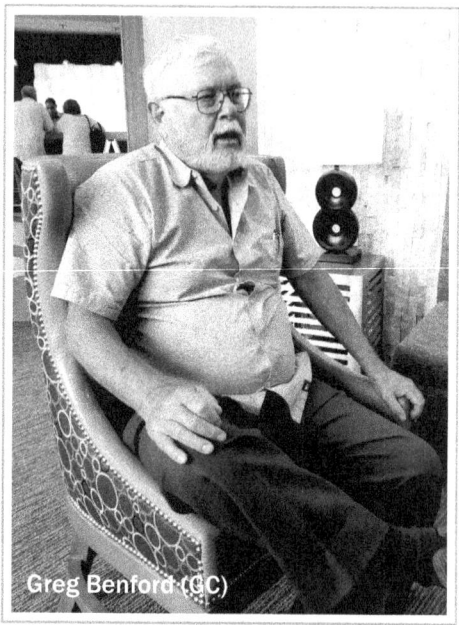

Greg Benford (GC)

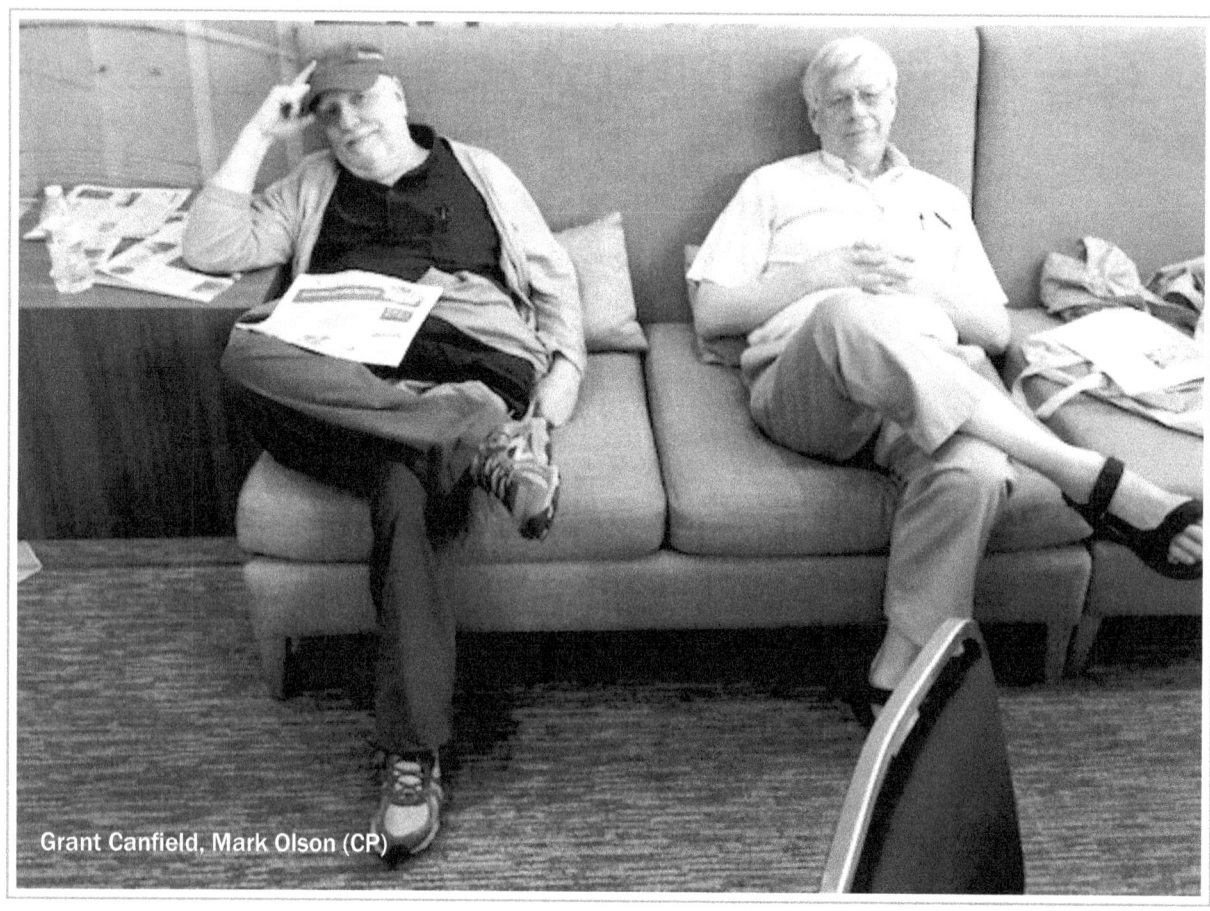

Grant Canfield, Mark Olson (CP)

#3 Scan Old Fanzines

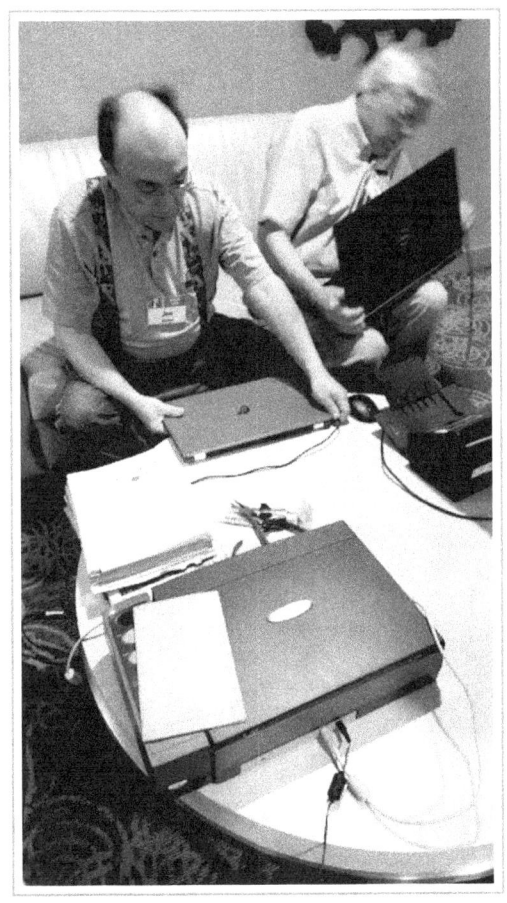

Scanning station for fanac.org. Joe Siclari, Mark Olson (CP)

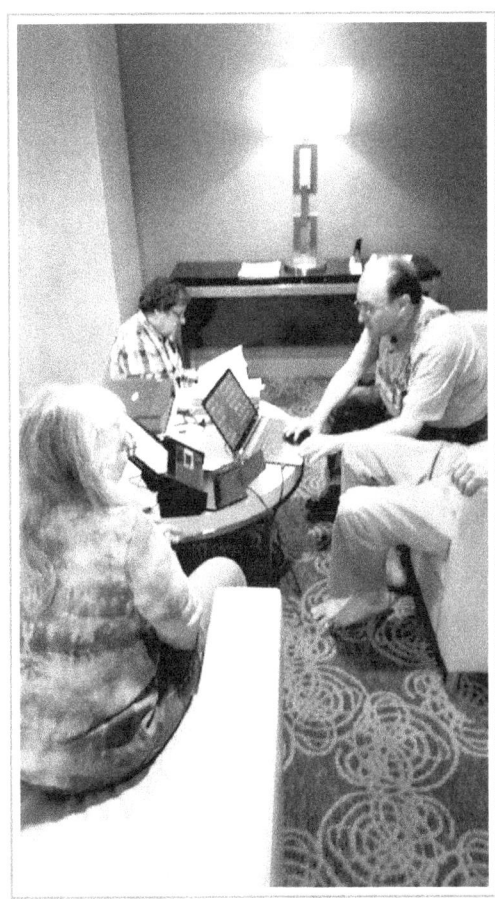

Edie Stern, Chris Couch (not scanning), Joe Siclari (CP)

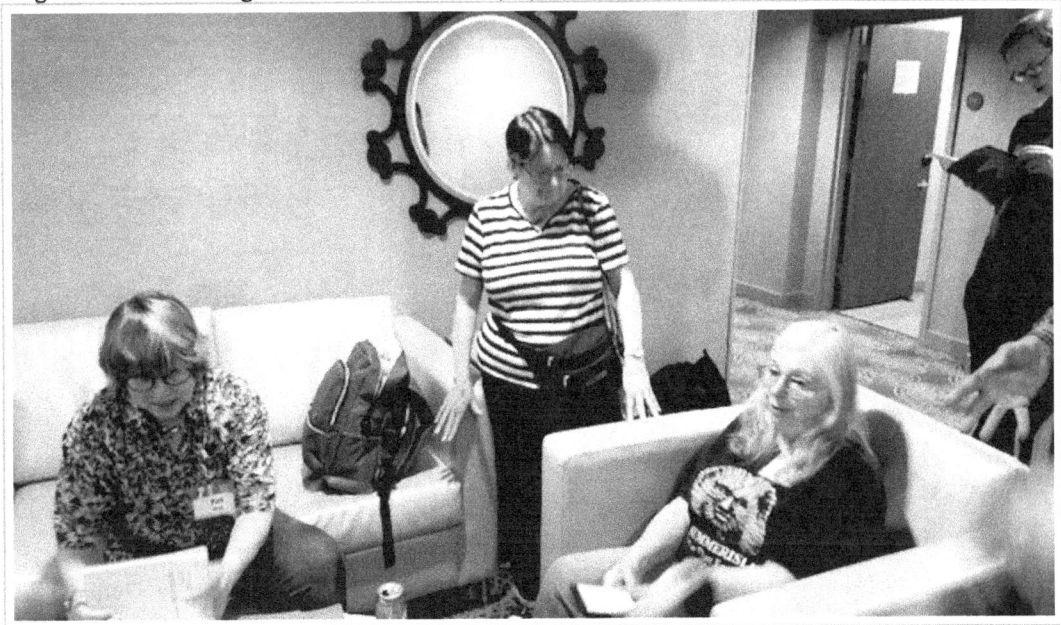

Pat Virzi, Nikki Lynch, Edie Stern (CP)

#4 Hang Out in the Consuite

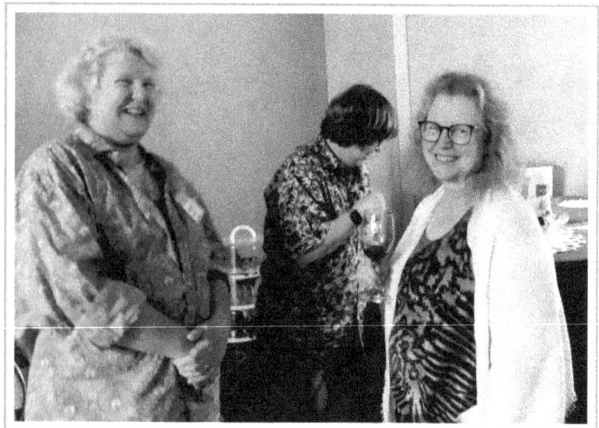

Jeanne Bowman, Pat Virzi, Karen Schaffer   **Alan Rosenthal, Rich Coad**

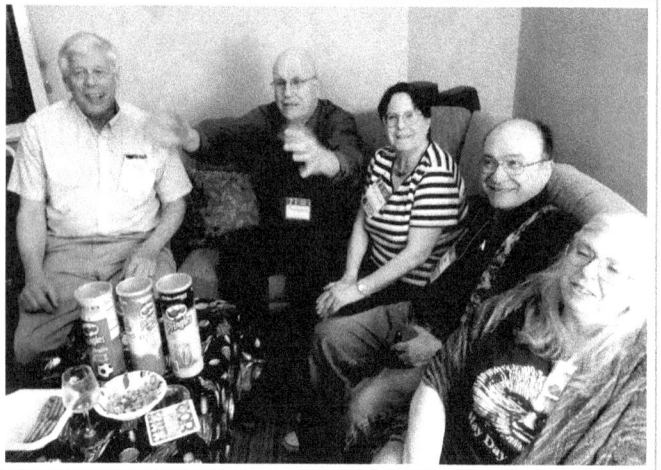
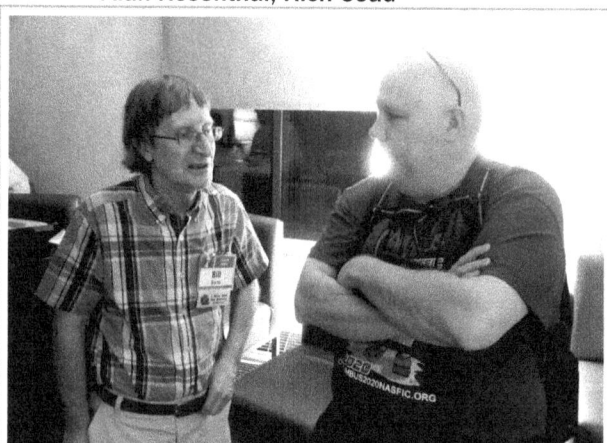

Mark Olson, Rich Lynch, Nikki Lynch, Joe Siclari, Edie Stern   **Bill Burns, Mowgli Assor**

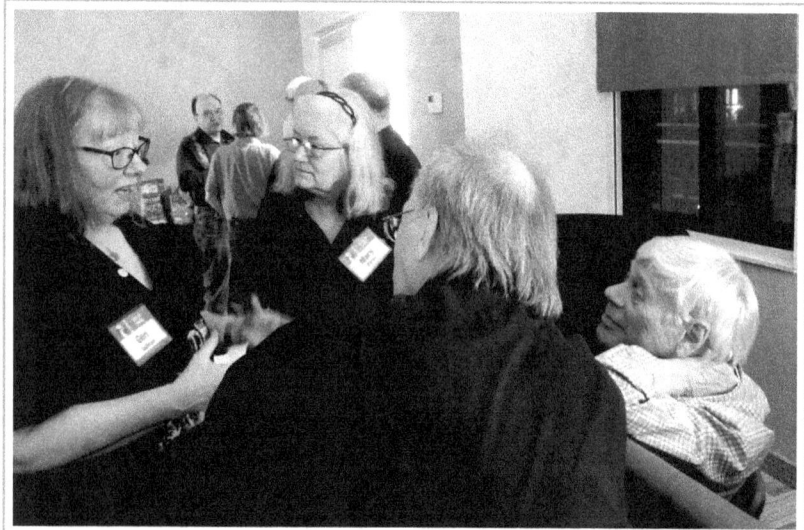
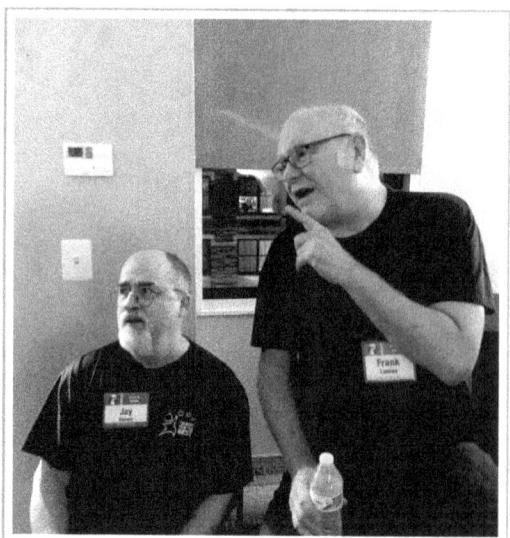

Foreground: **Geri Sullivan, Mary Burns, Steve Jeffery, Mark Olson.**
Middle ground: **Tops of heads of Jay Kinney and Frank Lunney**
Background: **Joe Siclari, Bill Burns, Murray Moore**

Jay Kinney, Frank Lunney

(all photos this page RJ)

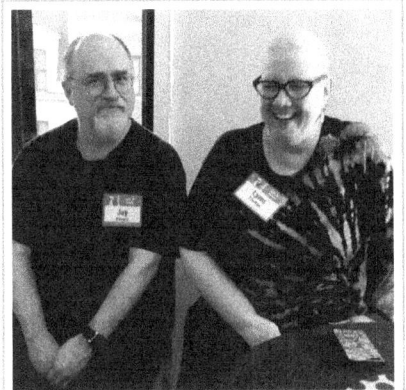
Jay Kinney, Lynn Steffan (SS)

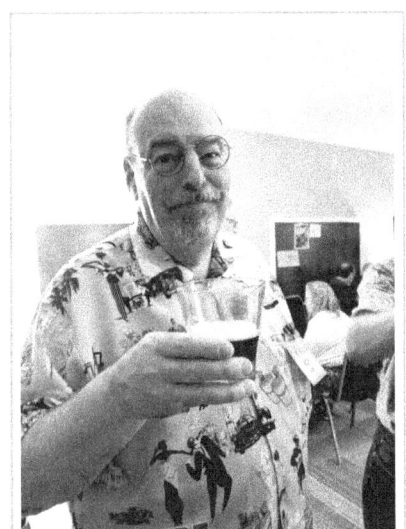
Rich Coad (GS)

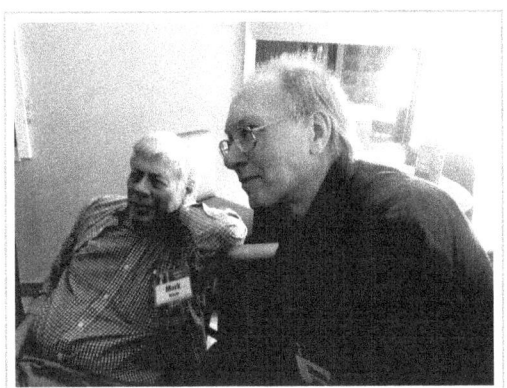
Mark Olson, Steve Jeffery (RJ)

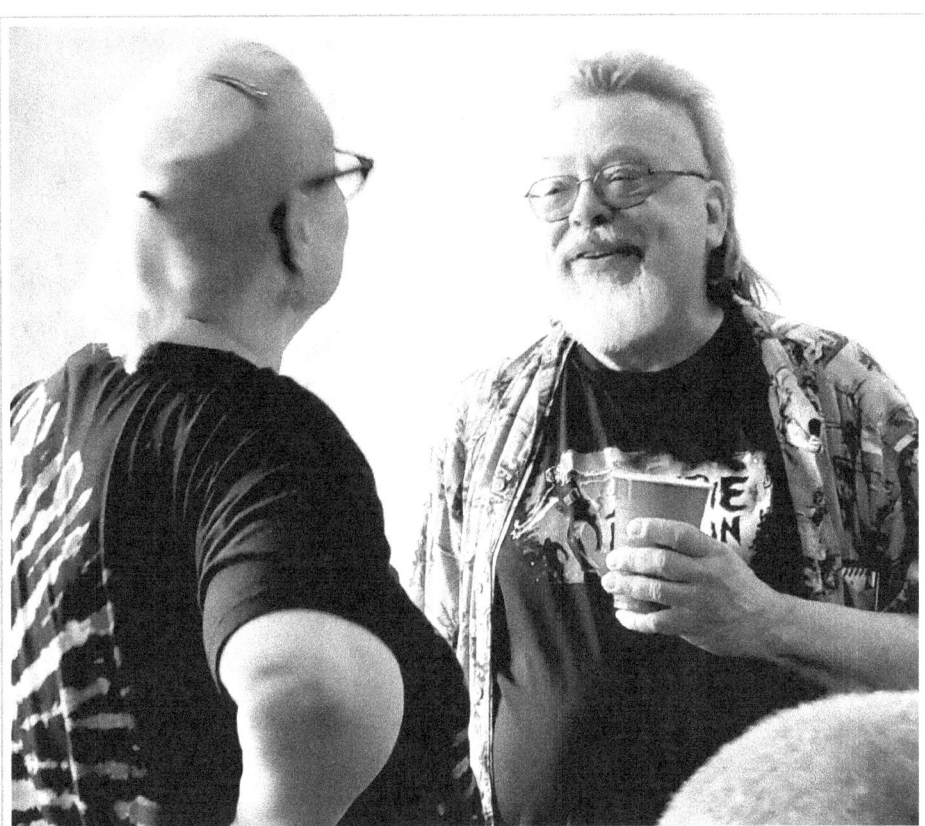
Lynn Steffan, Steve Stiles (GC)

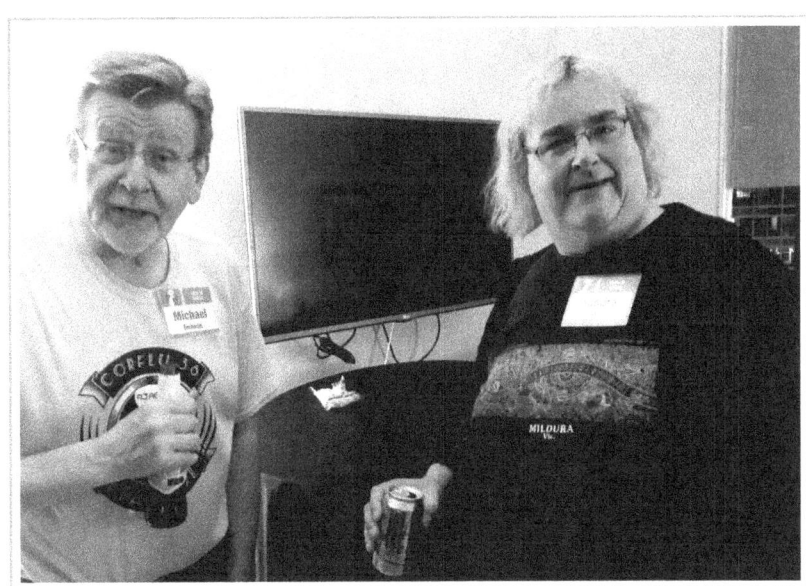
Michael Dobson, Sandra Bond (RJ)

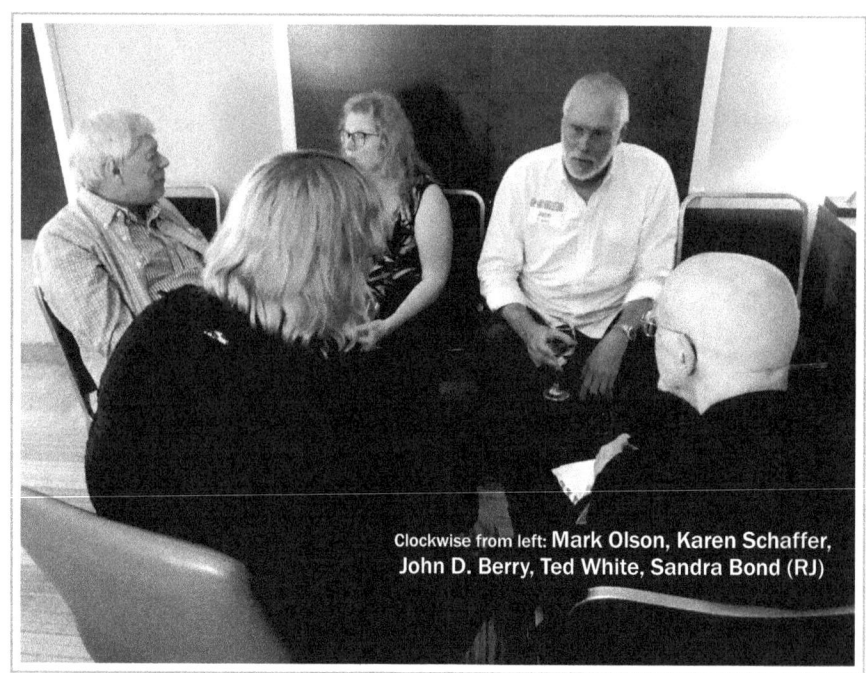

Clockwise from left: **Mark Olson, Karen Schaffer, John D. Berry, Ted White, Sandra Bond** (RJ)

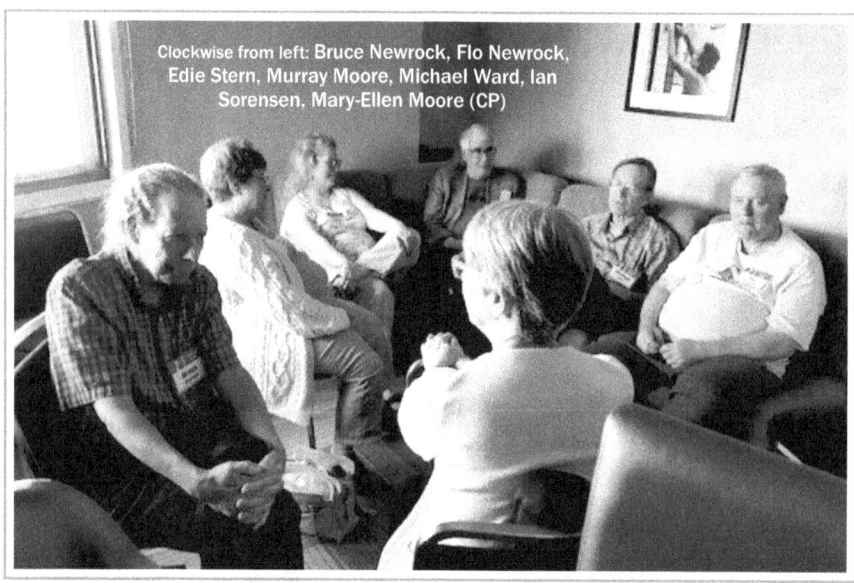

Clockwise from left: **Bruce Newrock, Flo Newrock, Edie Stern, Murray Moore, Michael Ward, Ian Sorensen, Mary-Ellen Moore** (CP)

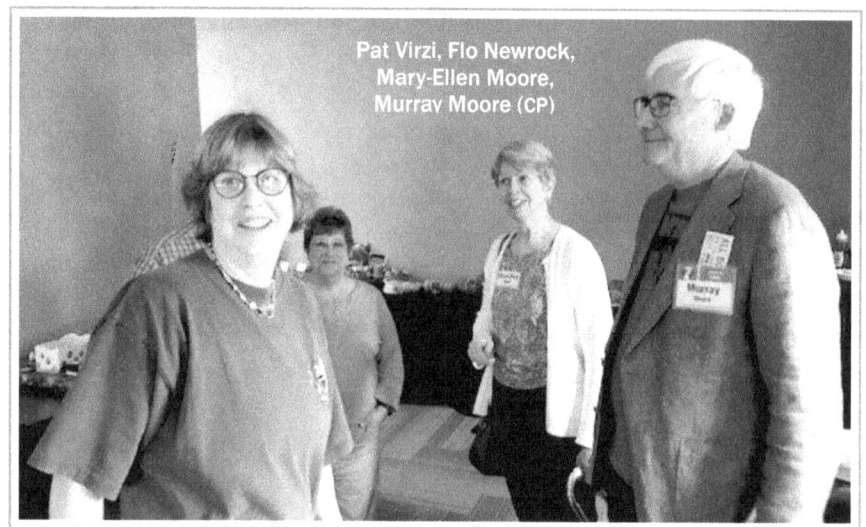

Pat Virzi, Flo Newrock, Mary-Ellen Moore, Murray Moore (CP)

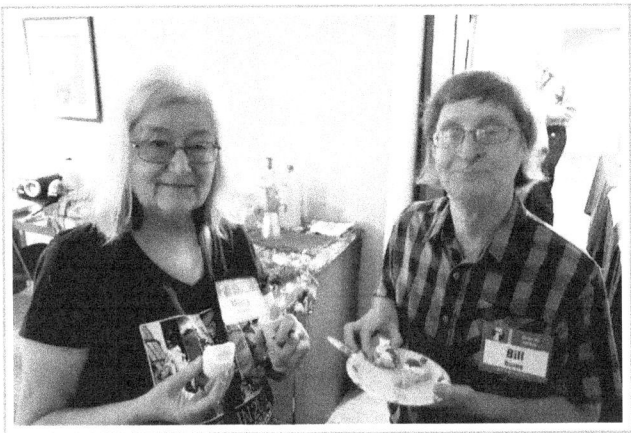
Mary Burns, Bill Burns (CP)

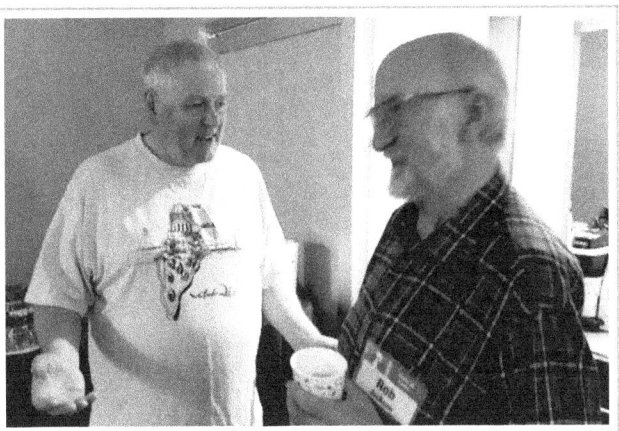
Ian Sorensen, Rob Jackson (CP)

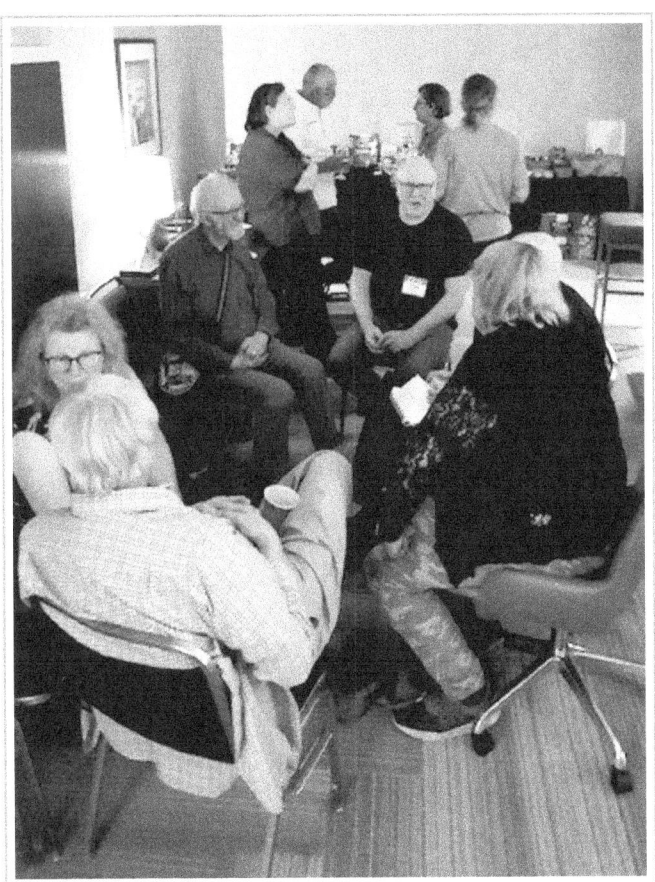
Clockwise from bottom left: Mark Olson, Karen Schaffer, Rob Jackson, John D. Berry, Bill Burns, Michael Ward, Ted White, Sandra Bond (CP)

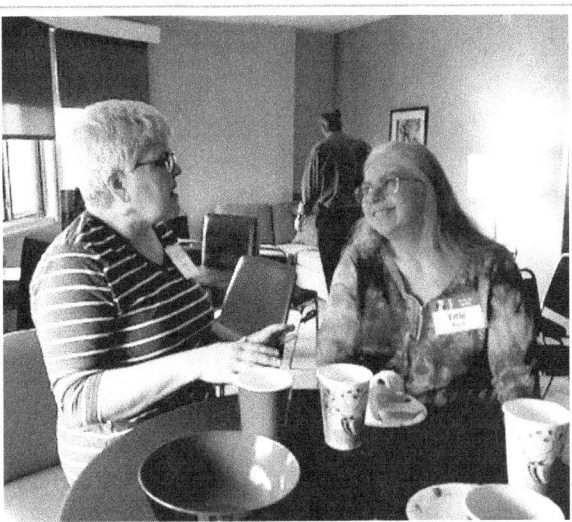
Carrie Root, Edie Stern (CP)

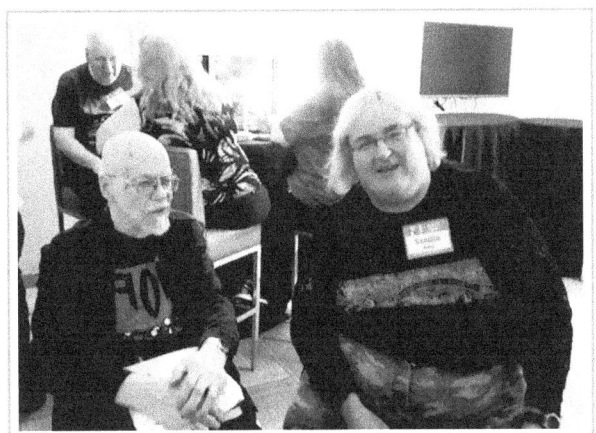
Foreground: Ted White, Sandra Bond. Background: Ian Sorensen, Karen Schaffer (CP)

#5 Read or Just Zone Out

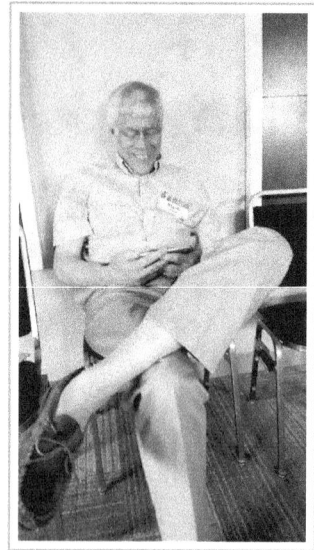
Mark Olson (CP)

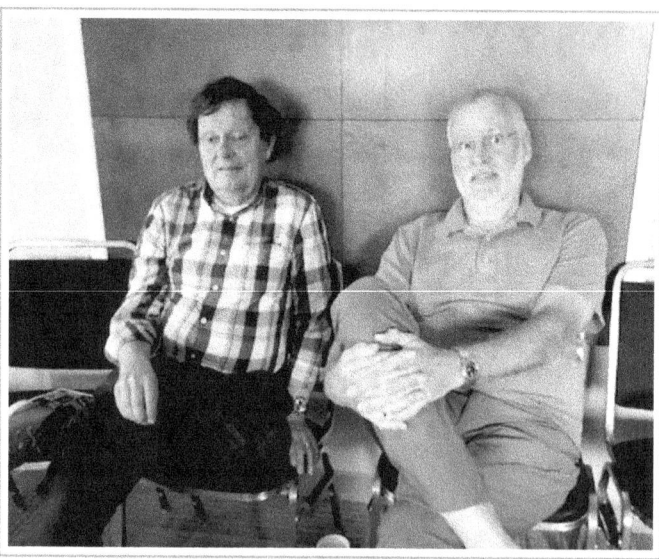
Chris Couch and John D. Berry (CP)

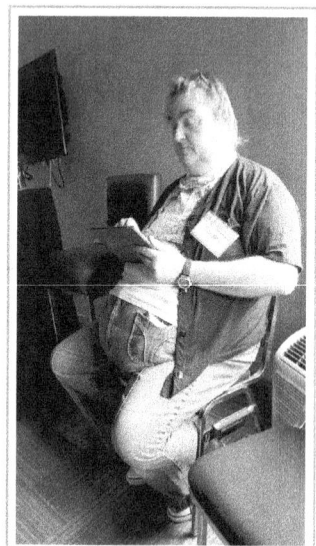
Sandra Bond (CP)

#6 Have Tea Parties

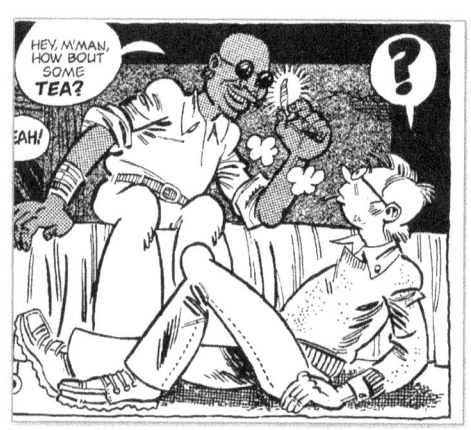

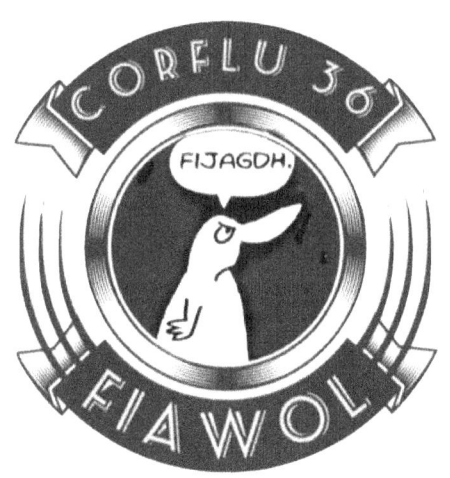

The Program

Saturday 4 May 2019
Daytime

CORFLU PANELS SUNT OMNIS DIVISA IN PARTES TRES

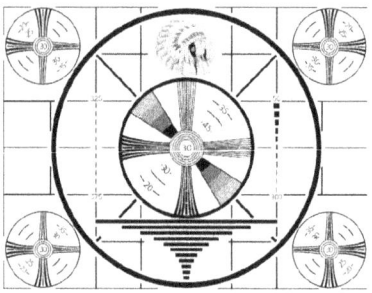

12:00 Noon
Our Programming Day Begins

Opening remarks by Michael Dobson, primarily regarding the absence of a microphone.

12:05 PM — 12:50 PM
PANEL: A Bheer Can Tower to the Moon and Other Fannish Memorials

A discussion of different ways to collect and preserve fannish material, including libraries, anthologies, online storage, and facsimile editions. No bheer cans were harmed in the making of this panel.

PARTICIPANTS

Susan Graham, special collections librarian for the Sapienza/Coslet fanzine collection at the University of Maryland Baltimore County.

Luis Ortiz, publisher of Nonstop Press (nonstoppress.com), editor of *The Science Fiction Fanzine Reader: Focal Points 1930-1960*.

Joe Siclari, chairman of the Fanac Fan History Project, dedicated to preserving information about science fiction fandom, including a database of fanzine scans.

Michael Dobson (moderator), former Smithsonian staffer who worked in preservation-related areas; interested in using new printing technology to make facsimiles of classic fanzines.

12:50 PM — 1:00 PM Break

1:00 PM — 1:50 PM
PANEL: The Void Boys Speak and (Unfortunately) Sing

The history of the legendary focal point fanzine *Void*, as presented by three *Void* Boys and special guest Luis Ortiz, who is working on a *Void* anthology.

PARTICIPANTS

Greg Benford, co-founder of *Void*

Jim Benford, co-founder of *Void*

Ted White, became editor and publisher of *Void* later on.

Luis Ortiz, publisher of Nonstop Press (nonstoppress.com), editor of the upcoming *Void* anthology.

TRIGGER WARNING: May include a rendition of the Void Boys Song.

1:50 PM — 2:00 PM Break

2:00 PM — 2:50 PM
PANEL: Rotsler Award Winners

Four leading fan artists (some of whom who have received one) discuss the various winners of the Rotsler Award.

PARTICIPANTS

Steve Stiles, moderator, Hugo-winning fan artist, underground cartoonist, and well-known *bon vivant*.

Grant Canfield, legendary fan artist who gave up the lucrative field of cartooning in favor of architecture.

Jay Kinney, co-creator of the underground comic *Young Lust*, expert on Western esoteric traditions.

Dan Steffan, Rotsler Award winner, underground and fanzine artist, creator of the Corflu 36 limited edition art piece.

2:50 PM — 3:00 PM Break

3:00 PM — 6:00 PM Auction

A Bheer Can Tower to the Moon
Saturday 4 May 2019 12:00 pm

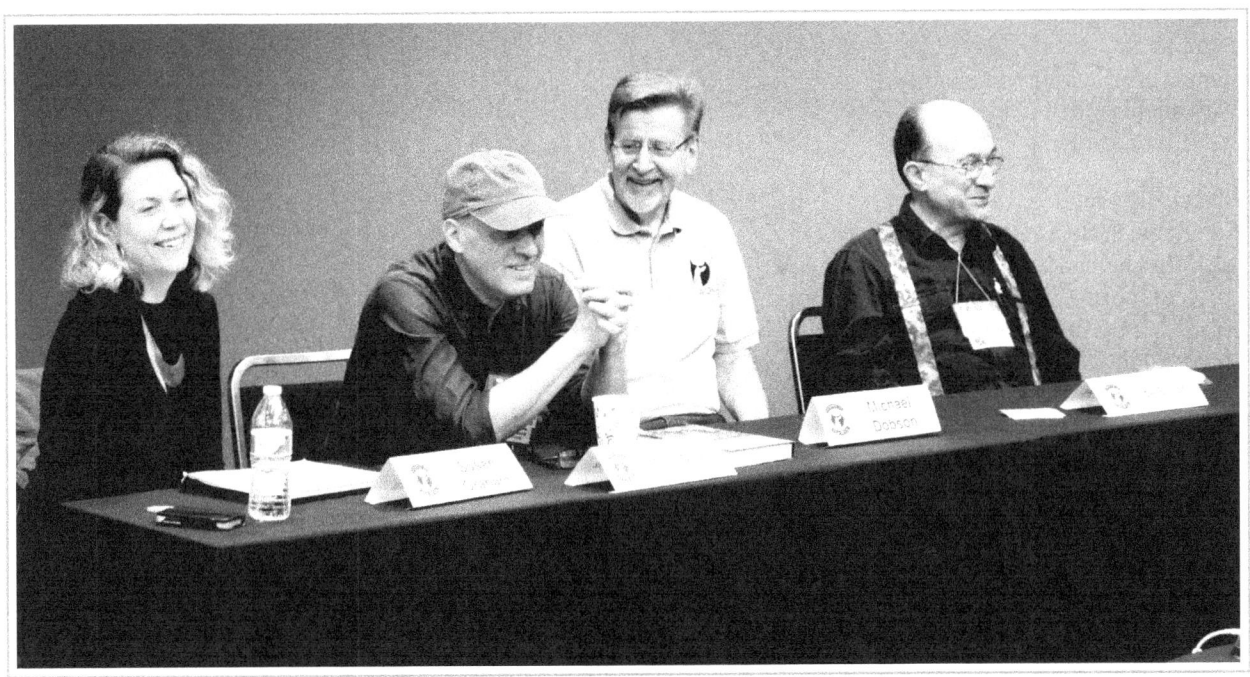

Susan Graham, Luis Ortiz, Michael Dobson, Joe Siclari (LS)

Hampered by a lack of microphone and a workable PowerPoint link, the panel got off to a slow start, but each of the participants had a great story to tell about an aspect of preserving fan history. A good discussion followed.

John D. Berry

During the panel on preservation of fanhistory, a poll of the audience asked what decade you had first gotten involved in fandom. The vast majority named the 1960s or the 1970s. None named a decade later than the 1980s.

Martin Morse Wooster

Saturday's program included three panels and I went to two. A panel on archives featured Non-Stop Press publisher Luis Ortiz, who has just published an anthology of fanzine writings from 1930-1960, Michael Dobson, University of Maryland (Baltimore County) archivist Susan Graham, and Joe Siclari, head of fanac.org.

Susan Graham said that her library bought the fanzine collection of Walter Coslet in 1973 and subsequently acquired the fanzines of Peggy Rae Sapienza, who was a graduate of the school. These fanzines included many from Sapienza's first husband, Bob Pavlat, a famed collector.

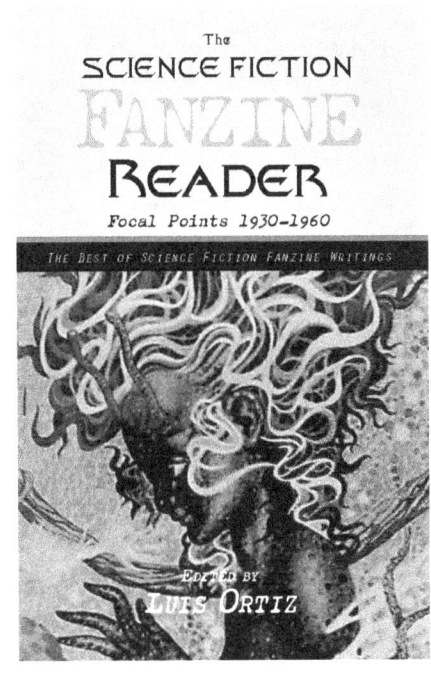

They've also gotten some Frank Kelly Freas art and some papers, including manuscripts by Isaac Asimov, Roger Zelazny, and Lawrence Watt-Evans. They're still organizing their zines, but their website https://lib.guides.umbc.edu/fanzines has a finding aid and essays on feminist fanzines of the 1970s, fanzines' role in society, and the Atlanta Science-Fiction Organization fanzine Cosmag.

Fanac.org scanned 2,000 pages of fanzines at Corflu. Siclari said that he had gotten research requests from unexpected places. They helped out the recent documentary on Ursula K. Le Guin, for example. And when the family of fan H.F. Koenig asked for copies of Koenig's fanzines, they donated a copy of the family genealogy to Fanac.org.

There are also reports of what happened to Harry Warner, Jr.'s fanzine collection. It is apparently in one piece and is being stored at Heritage Auctions in Dallas. No one knows what Heritage plans to do with Warner's collection.

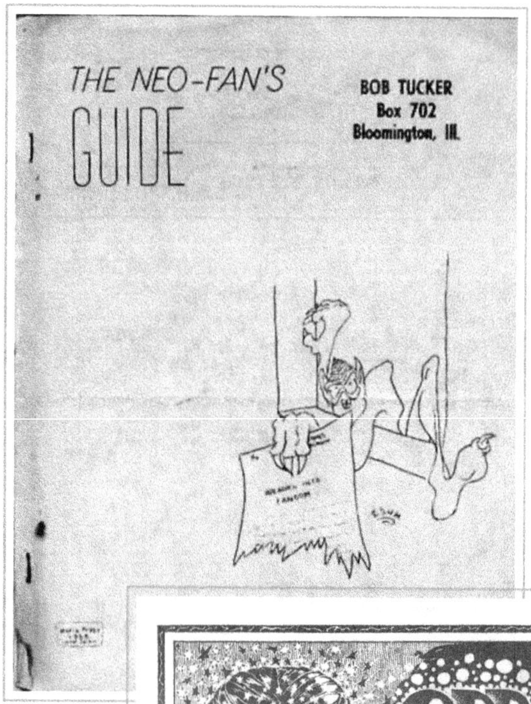

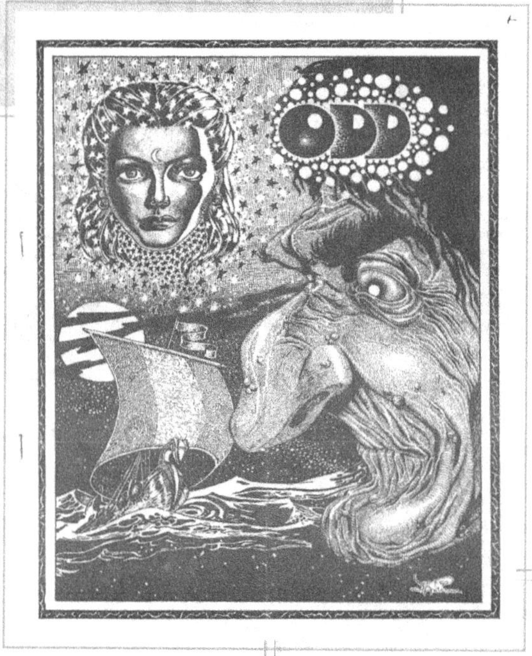

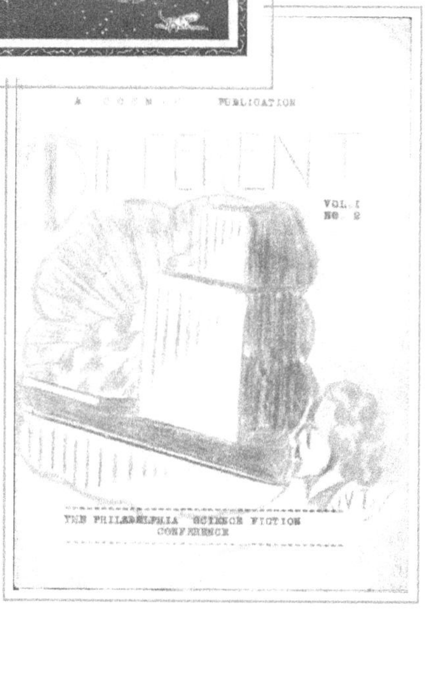

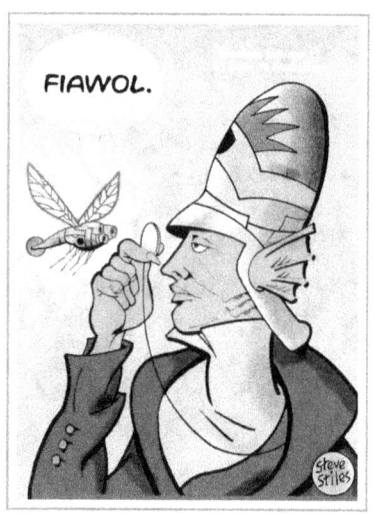

Facilitating Fan History Research
The Coslet-Sapienza Fantasy & Science Fiction Fanzine Collection at UMBC

By Susan Graham

I was very honored to be at Corflu 36. I'd like to thank Michael Dobson for reaching out and inviting me to join the panel on fanzine preservation. I guess I'm what you would call a Neo-Fan! I don't have a long history with sci-i or fantasy, but I have grown to love sci-fi fans and fanzines. I'm still learning, and there's so much to learn! So thank you for being a part of my learning journey.

The Special Collections at UMBC

We have a really wonderful photography collection, with over 2 million photographs from the beginning of photography to the present day and around 8 million photos from the Baltimore *Sun*. Our Maryland history collection is rich in Baltimore history, and includes the Baltimore *Sun* archives and Maryland folklife collections. We collect the archives of UMBC, which document the university's history. Our rare books collection is an eclectic mix of items with artists' books, the history of science, and lots of occult, spiritualism, and paranormal psychology. We also have 18th and 19th century graphic satire, Utopian thought and radical literature, and the Alternative Press Center collection. We also have thousands of comic books as well as original comic artwork!

And of course, we have science fiction collections. These collections are built mainly by donation of gifts in kind, but are also supported by an endowment created by Rita Seplowitz Saltz. They are comprised of the Azriel Rosenfeld Science Fiction Research collection, which contains thousands of books, criticism and reference works, bibliographies, journals and other periodicals, pulp magazines, and graphic novels. We also have numerous manuscripts by authors including Isaac Asimov, Roger Zelazny, Brian Daley, and Lawrence Watt-Evans. Our collections include original sci-fi and fantasy art and cover art by Frank Kelly Freas, and posters.

The Coslet-Sapienza Collection

Last, but certainly not least, we hold the Coslet-Sapienza Fantasy & Science Fiction Fanzine Collection. The Coslet-Sapienza fanzine collection is comprised of tens of thousands of fan-produced magazines. It is named after Walter Coslet, who collected fanzines over the thirty-five years from 1937-1972, and whose collection UMBC purchased in the 1970's; and after Peggy Rae Sapienza, a science fiction fan, fanzine publisher, and organizer of sci-fi cons, who donated her collection and that of her late husband, Bob Pavlat.

The Coslet-Sapienza collection includes titles from the 1930's to the

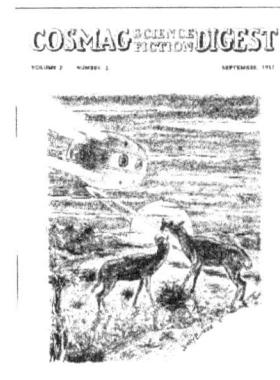
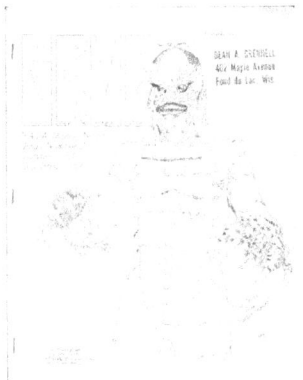
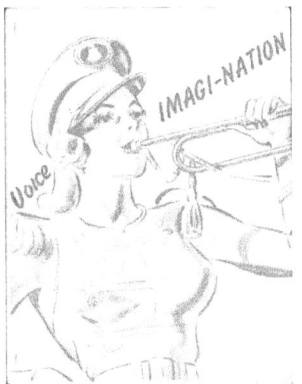
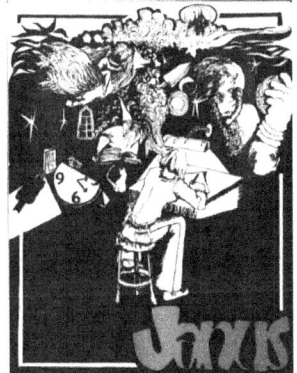

2000's, with long runs of the Fantasy Amateur Press Association (FAPA) mailings, and examples of early writing from Writers who would later become prominent in the field. For example, we have the fanzine where Ray Bradbury first story appeared, we have his own self-published fanzine, *Futuria Fantasia*, and we have the pulp magazine in which his first story was professionally published. So, you can really track a writer's progress through the ages. There are so many different things to research using the fanzines, and it's a great way to study science fiction fan culture.

Supporting Research and Scholarship

What we do is facilitate research and scholarship by preserving fanzines and providing access to them. We act as an east coast repository of of sci-fi and fantasy fanzines. We rehouse them in acid free folders and they are stored in our temperature and humidity controlled space. We assist scholars with their projects, such as looking up information in the fanzines and providing scans to authors such as Chris O'Brien who wrote The Forrest J. Ackerman oeuvre and helping with research for specific articles in fanzines for David Schultz who is writing a bibliography of the writer Clark Ashton Smith.

We also teach a lot of classes including history, art, media and communication studies, and try to use fanzines for some of our activities. Additionally we have put up displays and exhibits with duplicates at the local public library in Catonsville to raise awareness of the fanzine collection. About 10 years ago we created an online exhibit explaining to people what fanzines and pulps are. It looks a little dated now, but it has served us well.

A real turning point for us came during the summer of 2018, when we were involved in the Interdisciplinary CoLab. Modeled after an interdisciplinary research program at Duke, and supported by the office of the Provost, the Interdisciplinary CoLab pilot brought together groups of students from different disciplines to study various topics. Each group had a set of goals to achieve, and received training in narrative-based humanities research practices.

Our group focused on sci fi fanzines and fan culture and was headed by Media & Communication Studies (MCS) professor Don Snyder, and included Ashley Mitchell (Biochemistry), Rebecca Wireman (MCS & Gender & Women's Studies), and Marzuq Hakim (Computer Science). The students worked together for four weeks, each bringing a different perspective. Marzuq was the only one originally interested in sci fi, and Rebecca was the only one who had heard of zines, although feminist zines. before.
In preparation for the CoLab, I put together a research guide all about sci-fi fanzines. It gathers information on fanzines in general, our collection, as well as other collections, other online resources, and scholarly and reference resources about fanzines and fandom. It now includes the CoLab students' final project. Here's a screenshot with the page that includes other fanzine resources online.

My colleague Lindsey Loeper and I taught the students archival literacy and how to work with these primary sources. I chose some from the collection to introduce them to the format. We later showed them how to use the Omeka online exhibit software. They ended up creating an awesome and informative exhibit that includes info about our collection, about fanzines and sci-fi fandom in general, and about how fanzines were produced. I highly recommend that you watch the digital story videos that students produced.

A curator from the Drawing Center in NYC, Giampaolo Bianconi, reached out to me and asked for help with his exhibit *As If: Alternative Histories from Then to Now,* that displayed speculative fiction that is "working towards utopian, reactionary, or simply ambiguous ends, the artists, writers, and amateur science fiction enthusiasts

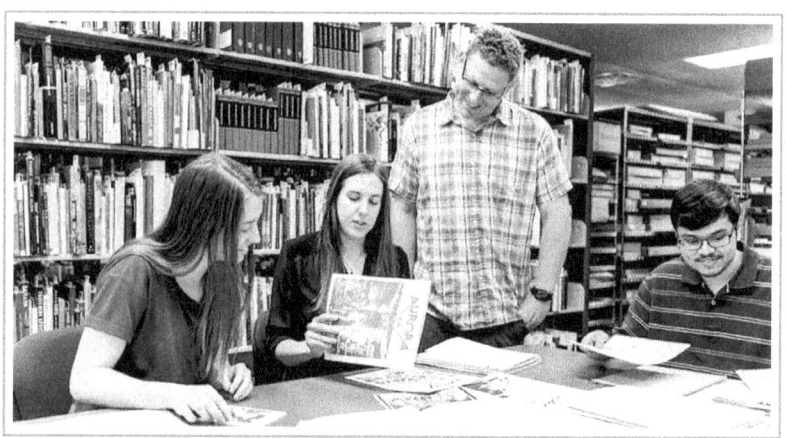

Interdisciplinary CoLab

in this exhibition use the playground of history as a foundation on which to construct alternatives to the stark realities of the present—whether amplifying its inherent contradictions or imagining a better world." They ended up borrowing several items, including lots of fanzines for the show, including titles such as *Xero, G sharp,* and *Futurian War Digest.*

Last fall, Don, the students, and I presented at the Mid Atlantic Popular and American Culture Conference, spreading the word about the CoLab students project and our collection. This spring, Don brought his MCS 499 class into the archives for several sessions and had his students each chose one title of a fanzine and analyzed it as a document, examining the structure, its unique features, and contents. They also wrote a reflective essay presenting a research question that would be a possible focus in a longer semester project; and gave a presentation about their fanzine.

I asked Don for some feedback from his students and he said: "The excited conversations often took place around discussions about images. The students were also very interested in the language of the zines, and how they seemed to create a pre-texting form of shorthand. There was also some feedback connecting the zines to a kind of subreddit, where fans could share their love of an object." Lindsey and I continue to use fanzines in our instruction sessions. We had another MCS class come in and we split them into groups, with each group examining an issue from *Imagination, Futurian War Digest,* or *Triton*. Then they watched the CoLab students' corresponding digital essays about those fanzines and discussed what they learned.

Looking Toward the Future

Don is continuing researching with the fanzines. He's looking at FAPA mailings from the mid-20th century to find discussions of McCarthy and the Red Scare. Due to the momentum in interest in the fanzines and more staff in our cataloging department, I'm also in talks with our catalogers to catalog our fanzine collection. We'd do serials catalog records for the items and a finding aid for the FAPA and other APA mailings and for the convention materials. We also have some original artwork from *The Acolyte*, including drawings and different logo attempts, which would be great for people to know about.

We accept donations and are always happy to talk fanzines!

Connect with us:

- Susan Graham, Special Collections Librarian, sgraha1@umbc.edu

- Beth Saunders, Curator and Head of Special Collections, bethsaunders@umbc.edu

- Special Collections
- https://library.umbc.edu/speccoll/

- Coslet Sapienza Collection
- https://library.umbc.edu/speccoll/publications.php#c11

- CoLab exhibit https://umbcspecialcollections.omeka.net/exhibits/show/cosletsapienzafancoll

- Sci Fi Fanzines Research Guide https://lib.guides.umbc.edu/fanzines

- INSTAGRAM @umbcspecialcollections

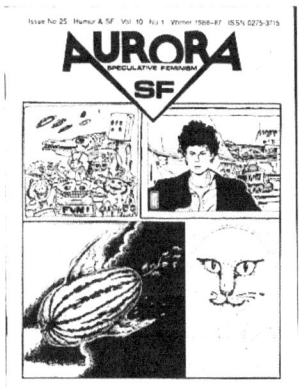

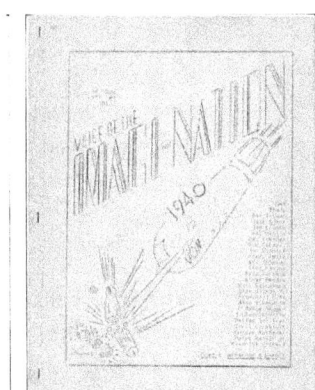
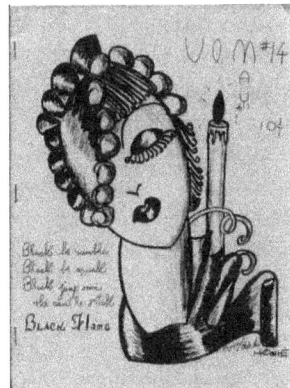

THE VOID BOYS SPEAK AND (UNFORTUNATELY) SING
SATURDAY 4 MAY 2019 1:00 PM

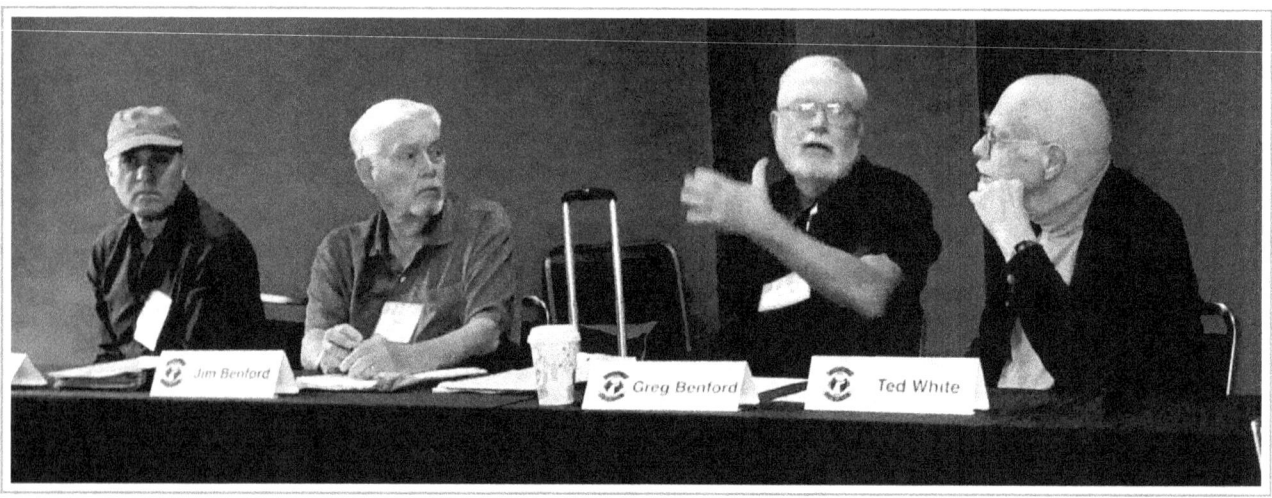

Luis Ortiz, Jim Benford, Greg Benford, Ted White (LS)

The Void *boys showed a cover gallery of classic covers, including their famous multi-page covers, and talked about the story behind each issue. Luis Ortiz, who is doing a* Void *anthology as noted previously, heard the inside story, but did not (contrary to rumor) run screaming from the room.*

Martin Morse Wooster

The second panel was on *Void*, which included the zine's editors, Greg Benford, Jim Benford, and Ted White, and Luis Ortiz, who is working on an anthology of pieces from the zine. *Void* began in 1955, with teenage fans Greg and Jim Benford as editors. When the Benford brothers moved from Germany to Dallas, Tom Reamy became an editor.

The Benfords put out 13 issues of *Void* between 1955-58. But Jim Benford decided to give up fanac for college. Another catalyst for change was when Kent Moomaw, a columnist for the zine, killed himself on his 18th birthday rather than be drafted. In 1958 America was at peace, so there was about a 20 percent chance he would be drafted.

Void then moved its headquarters to New York City, and continued with editors including Greg Benford, Ted White, Pete Graham, and Terry Carr. It lasted another 14 issues through 1962 with a final issue published in 1967.

Both Greg Benford and Ted White said that writing for *Void* inspired their professional careers. Greg

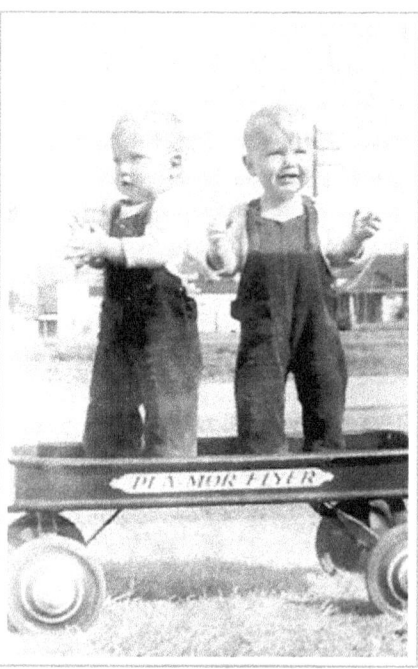

The Benfords started publishing fanzines early.

The Void Boys Song

We are the VOID boys
We make a lot of noise!
We sing songs of fandom,
Hitting out at random,
For we are all co-editors of VOID!

Though our subtle prose delights,
We often stage sharp fights,
With lancing wit for twits
To give all fandom fits!
--and keep the dull sercons annoyed!
With all co-editors of VOID!

We publish the finest authors--
Someday they'll fill our coffers
Though feisty critics we'll frequently avoid!
Yet we remain, despite our fame
Throughout all fannish fandom—
Hitting out at random,
For we are all co-editors of VOID!

By Greg and Jim Benford,
with adds by Terry Carr and Ted White

Benford said that his fan writing prepared him to win a contest sponsored by Fantasy and Science Fiction that launched his career as a novelist.

"All of our fanac was fun because of the challenges we met," White said. "I thought Terry (Carr) was a better writer than me, and it was a daily challenge to write to his level." *Void* even had a song, with the music being whatever you'd like.

Robert Lichtman

Just heard the Void Boys song! Nostalgic!

Greg Benford added a few reminiscences later.

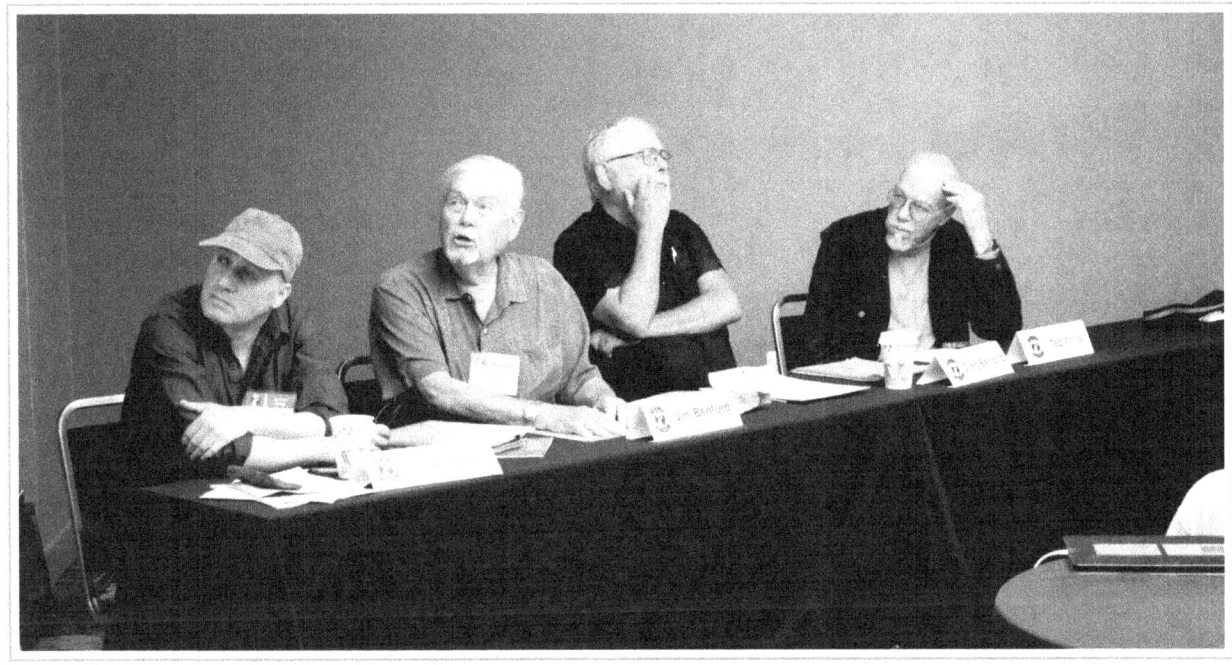

Luis Ortiz, Jim Benford, Greg Benford, Ted White (LS)

Doing Void
Greg Benford

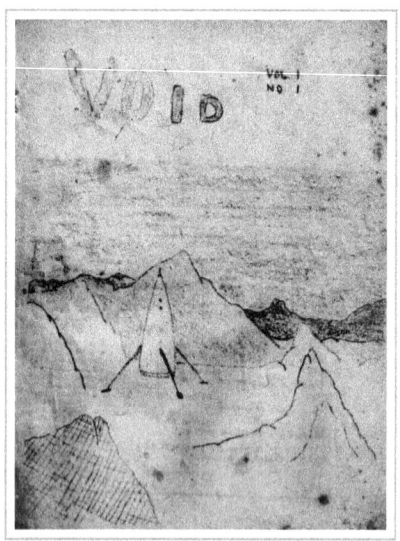

From the beginning, I saw *Void* at age 13 as a way to learn how to write.

The first issues had very short, very bad stories by me, some under pseudonyms, to hide the fact that Jim & I wrote nearly all the zine. I knew I was a kid of early teens who wanted to do what he could not remotely attain then. But maybe in a few more years…

Most learning comes from imitating, I found, for me. So I started imitating the Void Boys style that, without noticing it much, I had actually begun developing in the *Voids* from #8 or so to #13. I tried things out, even rewrote!—first time I ever did. (All earlier *Void* editorials I did on stencil, and much of the articles, too.)

By the time *Void* went to NYC, *Void* 19, I was using Dallas fandom as a source of funny satire, though I was already at the University of Oklahoma.

I wrote all my editorials in first draft with hand corrections, right to the end.

Here's my editorial in #19: http://fanac.org/fanzines/VOID/VOID19-02.html

As I said in my *Boonfark* article, I came to regret this method. I may have worn it out. By the end of *Void*, in 1963 I went with Jim to UC San Diego and have only been back once. Six years or so ago, as GOH at Fencon, I visited our little home there, bringing back many memories. (Dad was commanding the Texas National Guard, before his next combat assignment, but even then colonels didn't make the big bucks. When I

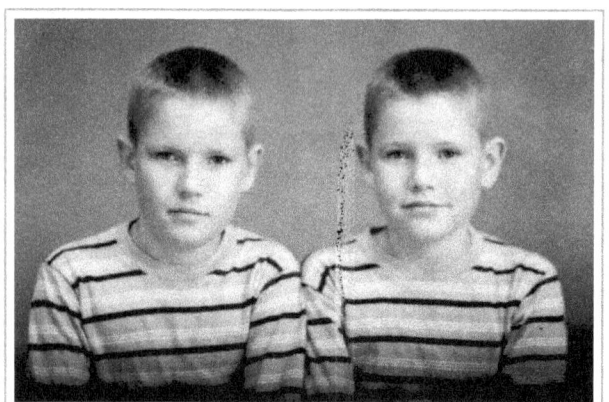
Greg and Jim Benford before fandom

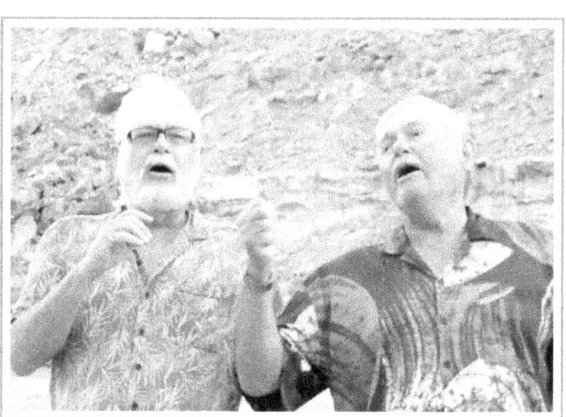
Greg and Jim Benford after fandom

got as job as a researchassistant at Texas in 1959, I made more per month than Dad!)

Ted made *Void* a marvel of fmz production—art, graphics, multi-page covers, etc. I got Willis and Shaw and others to contribute. Then Terry Carr came and the Void boys mannerisms peaked. *Voids* #s 20 to 28 were striking to me.
By 1962 I had honed my style, learned to write in different voices in other fanzines…then focused on physics from 1963 to 1967, getting my PhD.

I met people at University of Oklahoma that seemed super-fannish, too. Across the hall of the dorm room Jim and shared was Jerry Muskrat, husky Cherokee Indian. He showed us a trick in his totally dark dorm room. He could on command fart and light it, so suddenly the room got bright for an instant. Then again, and again. In three different musical notes. Yellows, greens and blues, not a mere methane burn red. Never seen that since. If he'd been a fan, I would have written him up. But he could read only marginally, especially not 'that rocket stuff'—and flunked out in a semester..

Fandom flowed on and I still read the sf mags. In 1964 I read in F&SF an announcement of a little contest, to write a story of 1000 words around a poem by Doris Pitkin Buck about unicorns and Univacs, the early big computers.

Sitting in the grad class in statistical physics, I had already read the text chapters ahead, on using Grand Canonical Ensemble methods. I had worked the problems, too. Jim and I always used this method: work ahead, ask questions as the teacher presents material. You look bright, because you can keep up—indeed, since you're a week ahead, can ask questions that lead naturally to what the prof wants to show next. Also, sit in front, engage the prof by eye, nod.

But I was bored…and suddenly the idea for a story with unicorns and Univacs at play, came to mind. I started writing it by hand, pretending to be taking notes. I used a fake sophisticate voice set in San Francisco, entirely phony but enough for veneer. Got 500 words done before the lecture was over. Asked the prof (who later won a Nobel) a pointed question, got the answer I expected.

Went back to our appointment, Jim & I made dinner, and I finished the story. Next day, typed it up. Sent it in to F&SF.

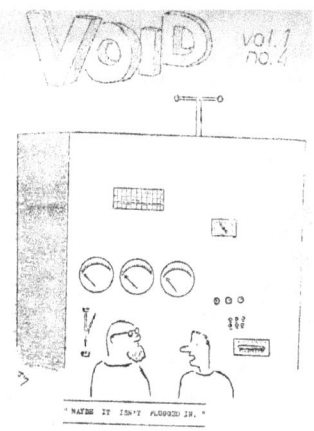

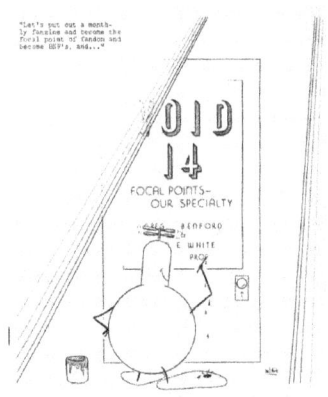

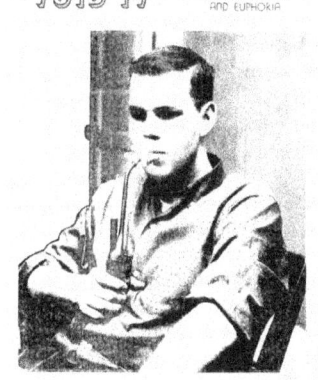

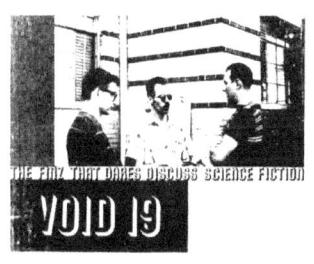

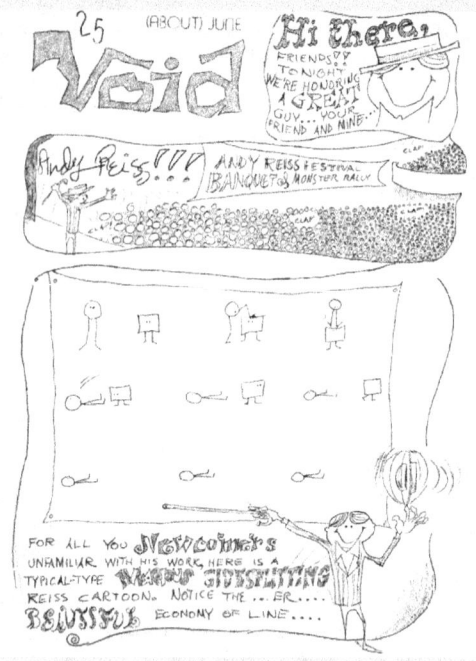
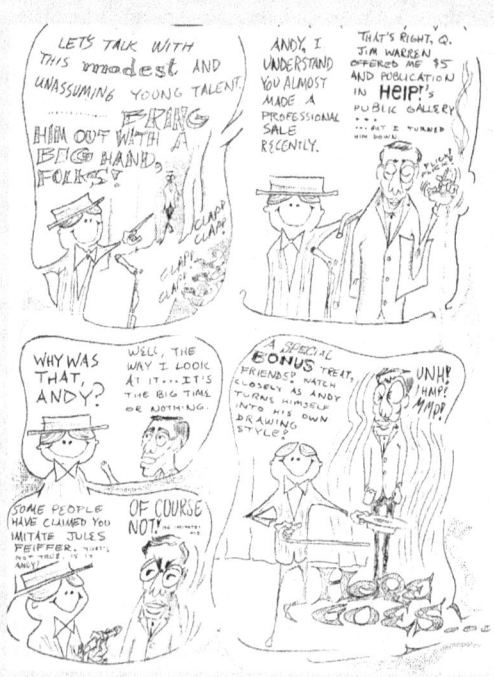
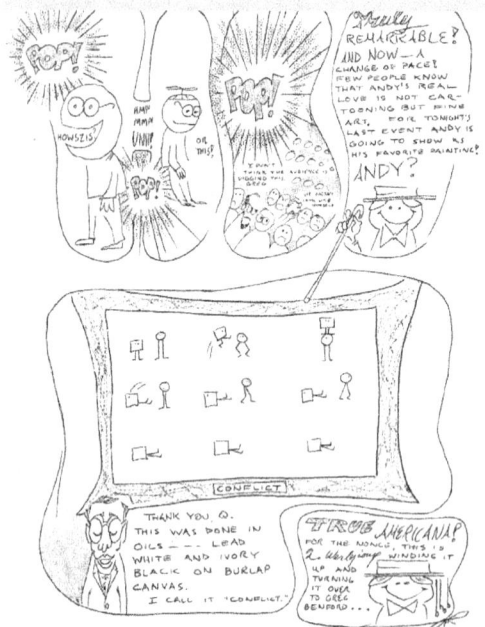

Multi-page cover of *Void* 25

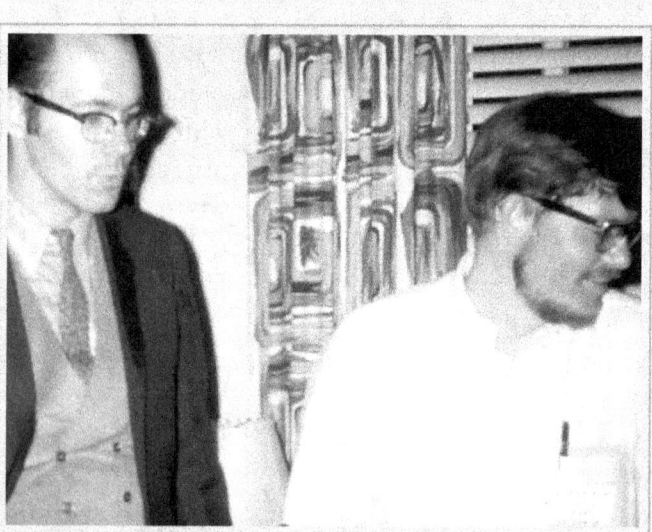

Ted White and Greg Benford

Months later, I won the contest: $20 from the 2 cents/word rate, plus a lifetime sub to F&SF. It still comes, 55 years later. I used the $20 to buy some stock later, a stock I still own. Dunno what happened to Doris Pitkin Buck.

"Stand-In" was my only fantasy story out of 230, so far. The New Wave debate sprung up in US fandom, urging me on to think what sf could be. I wrote a long tribute to Campbellian sf for Donaho's *Habbakuk* and began integrating the science I was learning into stories. In reviewing early *Voids* I found the kernel of a time signaling idea in a 2-page story I wrote when 14—decades before writing *Timescape*. Hard sf became in some of my stories autobiographical, fetched from my career.

Fandom and *Void* and physics made my adult world, it seems.

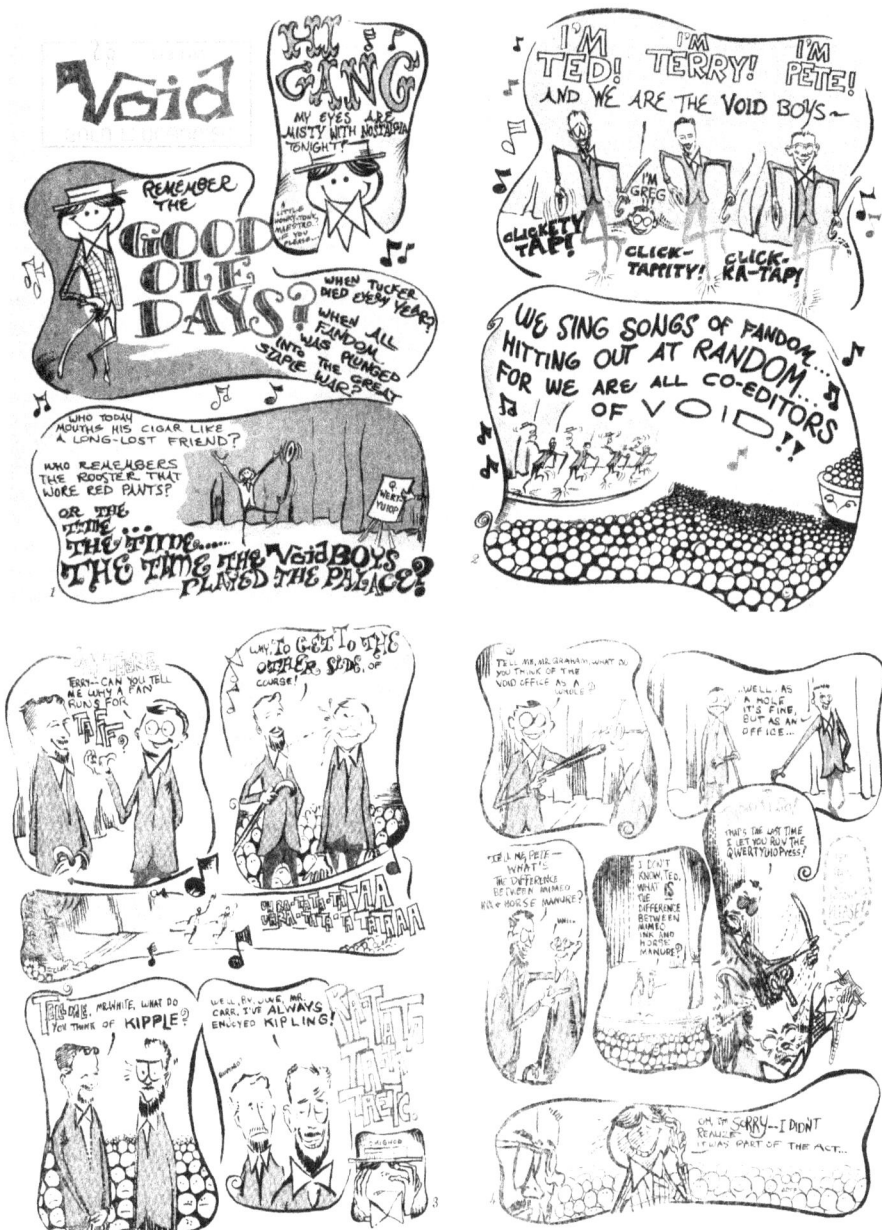

Four-page cover of *Void* 28

Rotsler Award Winners
Saturday 4 May 2019 2:00 pm

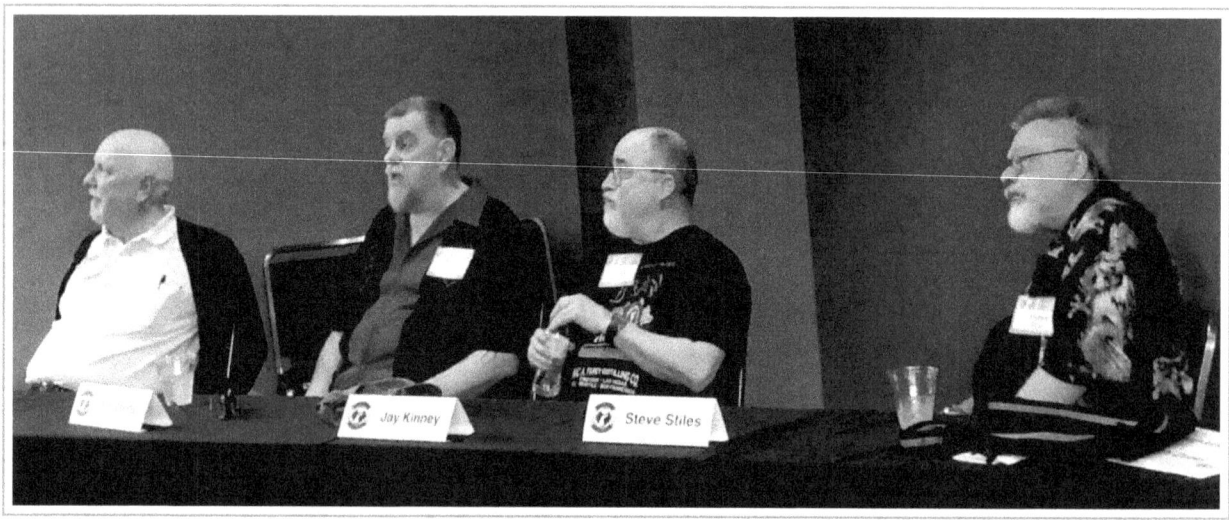

Grant Canfield, Dan Steffan, Jay Kinney, Steve Stiles (BB)

Steve Jeffery

As a (long lapsed) fan artist it was nice to see the panel and slide show hosted by Dan Steffan with Steve Stiles, Jay Kinney and Grant Canfield on the work of various fan artists, many of whom were familiar (or in Rotsler's case, near ubiquitous) but others less so. Especially pleasing to see work by Taral, and to nod agreement with Steve Stiles comment that Taral can draw "the only skunk I'd really like to fuck" (or possibly, along with Taral, want to be).
Although while I admire Taral's erotic-cute renditions of his furry avatar, Sondra Maar, I still can't quite fathom his seeming obsession with *Fraggle Rock*.

The panelists watched a PowerPoint presentation Steve had put together with art from the various Rotsler Award winners, and then they commented on the art. I asked if they had any additional thoughts.

Jay Kinney

Urk! Well that panel and much of the Corflu is all kind of a blur and I don't know if I have much to add beyond what I said on the panel itself.

Grant Canfield

I really can't add anything to what Jay said.

So we'll let the art speak for itself: Rotsler Award Winners:, followed by a few by Rotsler himself. http://www.scifiinc.org/rotsler/ NOTE: There was no award given in 2011.)

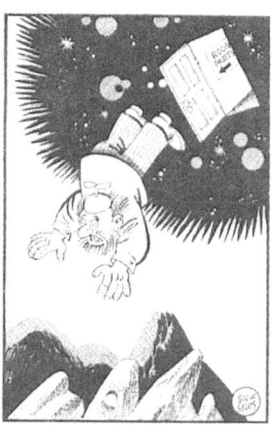

Steve Stiles (1998)

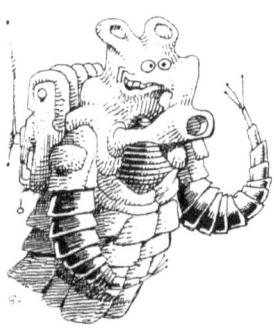

Grant Canfield (1999)

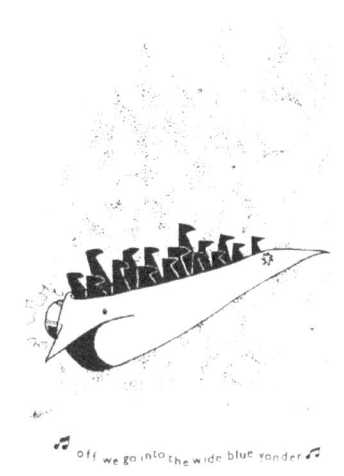

Arthur Thompson (ATom) (2000)

Ray Nelson (2003)

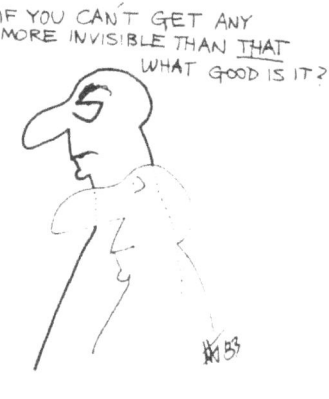

Alexis Gilliland (2006)

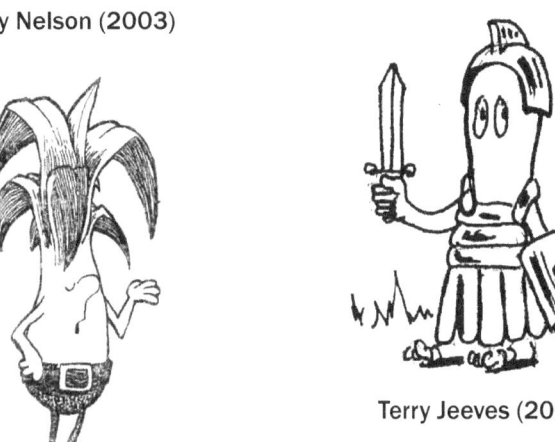

Brad Foster (2001)

Harry Bell (2004)

Terry Jeeves (2007)

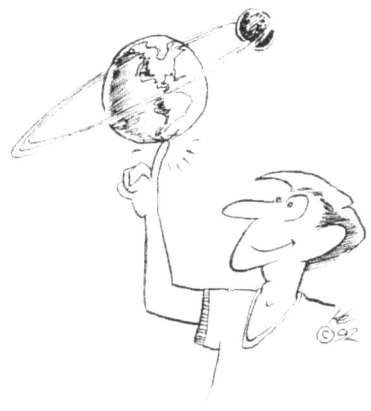

Kurt Erichsen (2002)

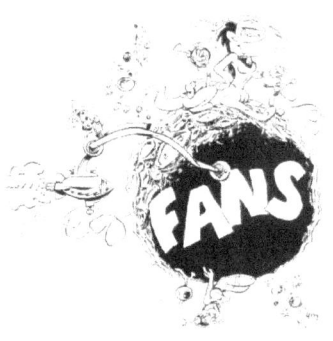

Mark Schirmeister (2005)

Taral Wayne (2008)

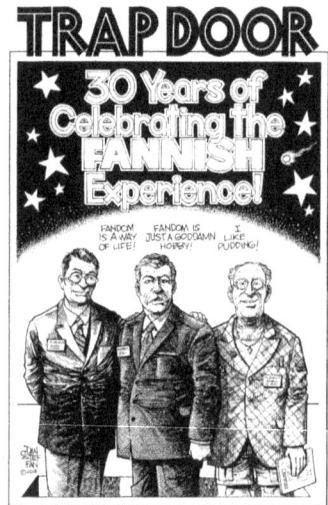
Dan Steffan (2009)

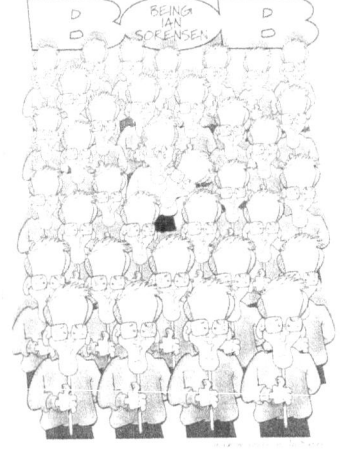
Jim Barker (2013)

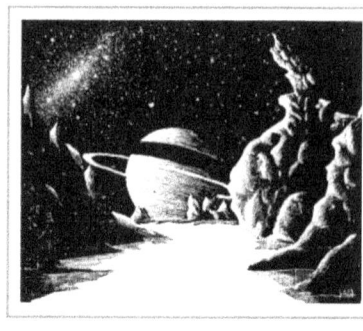
Ditmar (2016)

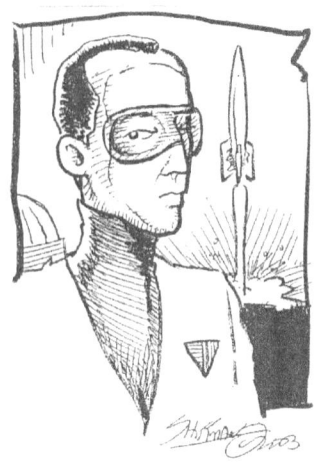
Stu Shiffman (2010)

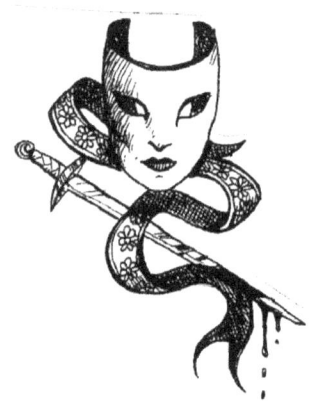
Sue Mason (2014)

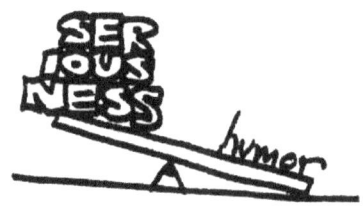

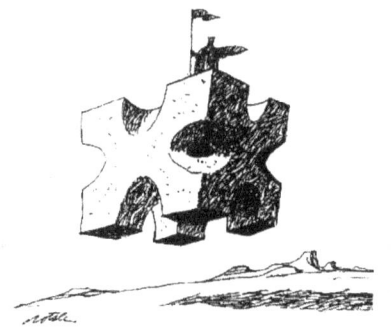

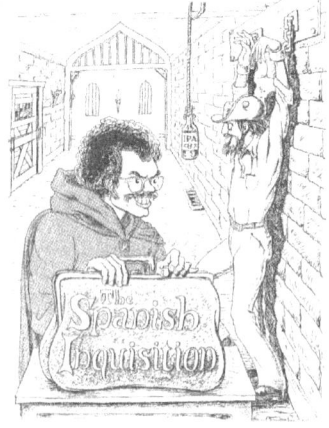
Ross Chamberlain (2012)

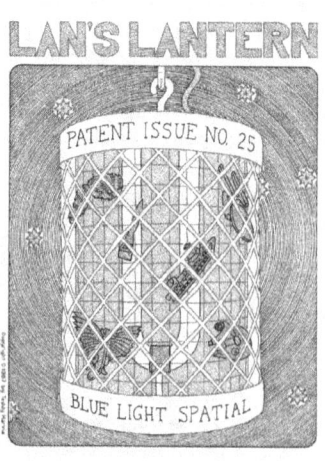
Teddy Harvia (2015)

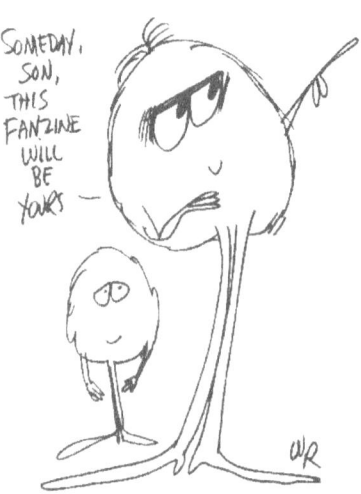
Bill Rotsler

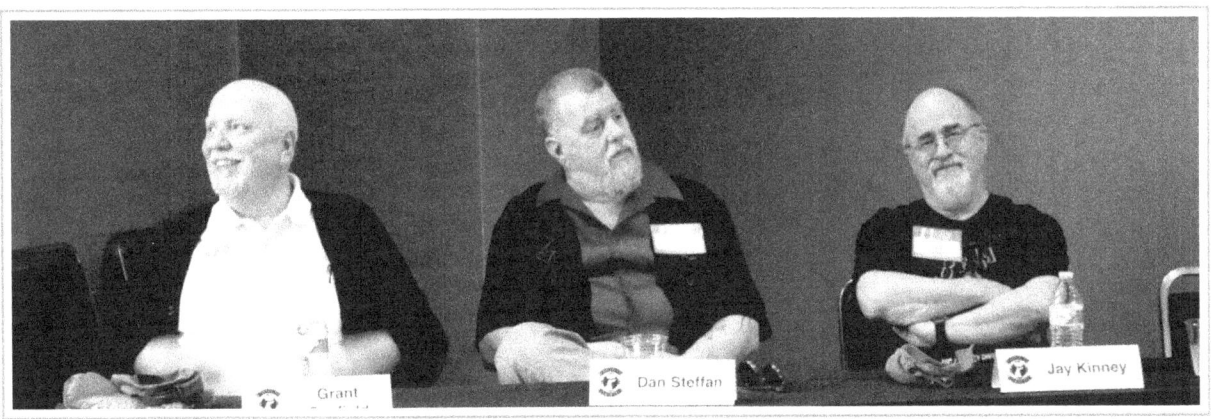
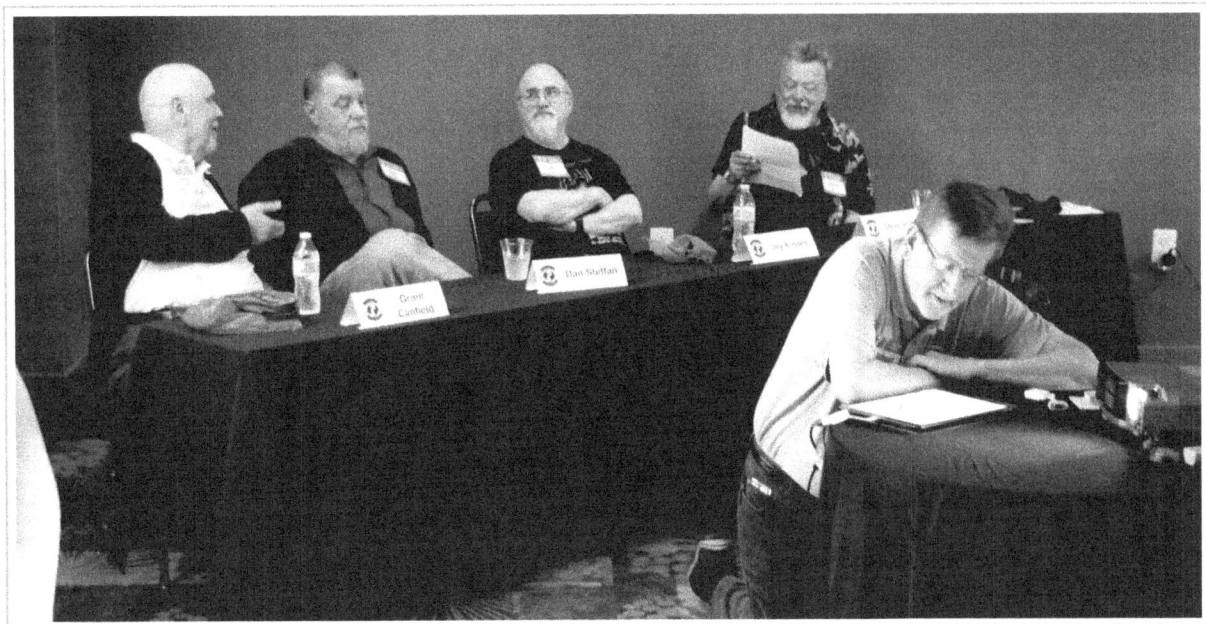
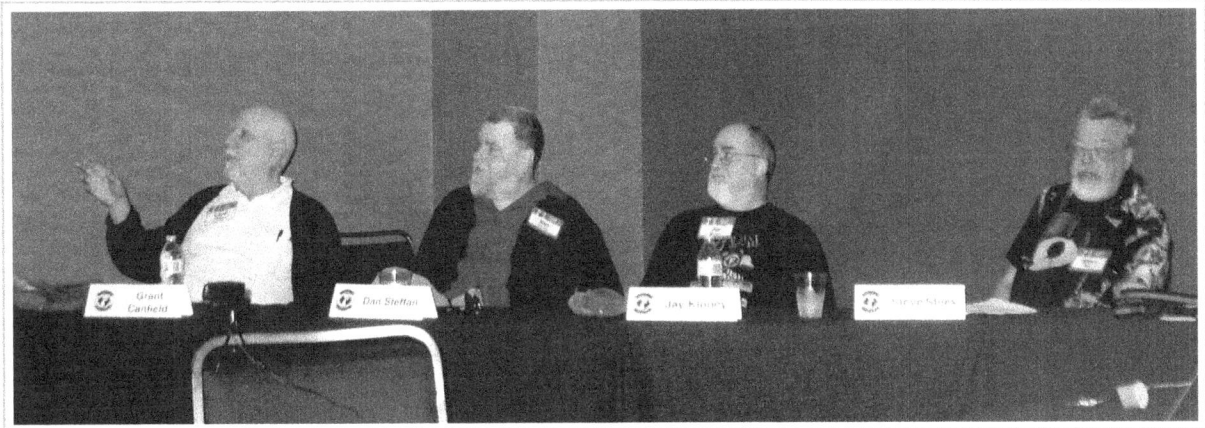

Top: Grant, Dan, Jay (LS).
Middle: Grant, Dan, Jay, Steve (with Michael Dobson advancing slides) (LS).
Bottom: Grant, Dan, Jay, Steve (SJ)

The Auction
Saturday 4 May 2019 3:00 pm — 6:00 pm

Steve Jeffery

After the first few conventions I've tended to avoid auctions on the grounds that our house if already too cluttered with stuff (I have boxes of fanzines I've not looked at in years, sometimes decades, and wonder why I'm still keeping them, apart from laziness and a feeling that I shouldn't just throw them out.)

At Corflu 36, however, Andy's magic fez presided over some spirited and entertaining bidding wars, with collector and archivist Mowgli Assor emerging as a surprise (and surprisingly generous) winner.

I bid for a Tiptree cookbook, to go with the shelf of other cookbooks that I collect but rarely follow apart from using as a very rough guide to ingredients and quantities. This is probably why I have never managed to replicate the same dish twice, although version seems to work well enough.

Unfortunately the Tiptree book didn't contain David Levine and Kate Yule's recipe in Bento for 'nerve gas chicken', which involves incinerating a quantity of pungent spices in a hot pan until the kitchen becomes uninhabitable unless you are wearing a gasmask, and even the hardiest and most recalcitrant cockroaches pack up and leave. (A similar result can be achieved by opening a packet of *blachan*, a Thai fermented shrimp paste, anywhere other than the middle of a large open field. The smell, which is indescribable but never forgotten, can linger for days.)

As the pile of fanzines, books and posters in front of Mowgli got steadily higher, occasional items would be allowed to slip through to other bidders. I added a couple of fanzines and Corflu XXX t-shirt and later added a couple more t-shirts (including one for Corflu Cobalt which I missed buying at the time) from fan fund table in the con

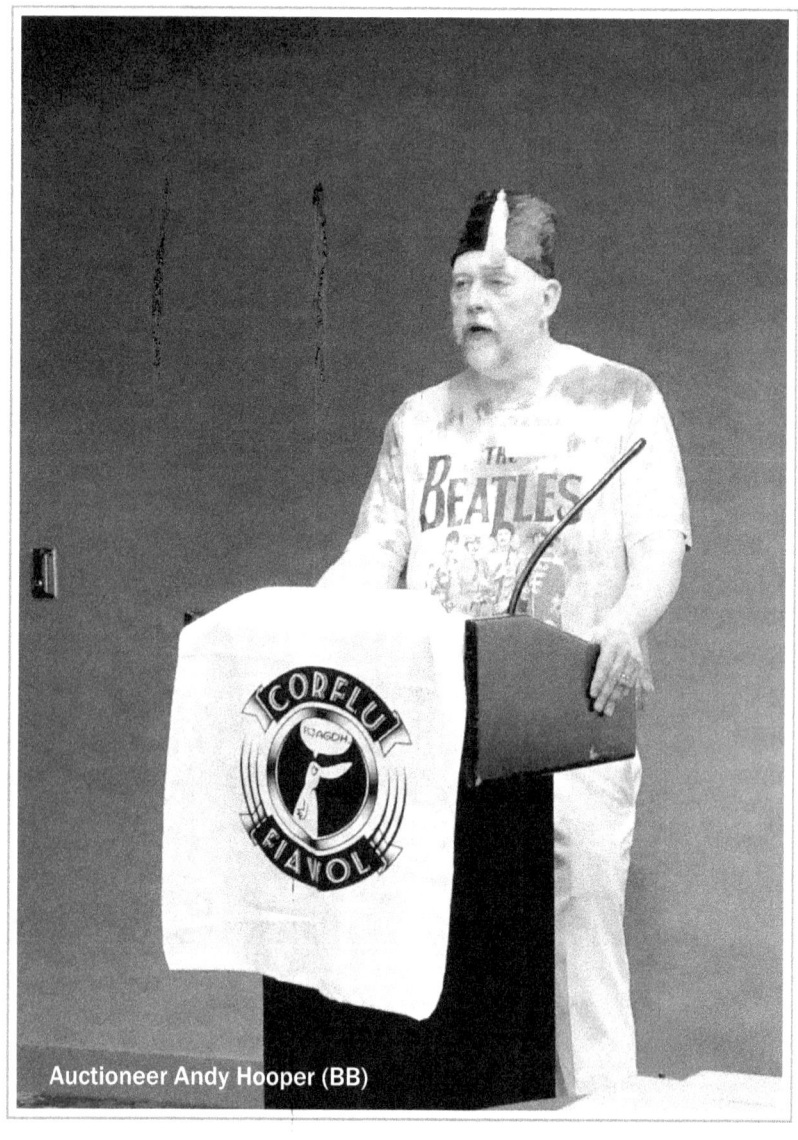

Auctioneer Andy Hooper (BB)

suite, on the basis that (a) they are light to transport back and (b) Vikki keeps threatening to throw several of my favourite t-shirts away on the spurious grounds that they have holes in them. (This same logic, surprisingly, does not extend to Vikki's favourite cardigan, whose sleeves are best be described as a series of holes held together by threads of wool, and whose ongoing raggedness is constantly aggravated by catching on door handles.)

Sandra Bond

[Robert Lichtman] might like to know that a run of the first 23 *Trap Doors* fetched a cool $125.Graham Charnock
Can someone remind me which idiot was crazy enough to pay $100 for an old *Wrinkled Shrew*.

Rob Jackson

I think it was Victor, but I am sure Nigel was in the bidding too. I reran the video of the auction and found it an hour and 20 minutes in (after much skipping) – yes, it was Victor.

Bill Burns

Here's some results from the auction Saturday:

Total: $1503 to be distributed to:
    TAFF: $150
    DUFF: $60
    Corflu 36: $559
    The Corflu 50: $574
    Fanac.org: $160

We sold 89 of the 120+ items put out. Thanks to Mowgli Assor who accounted for almost half of that!

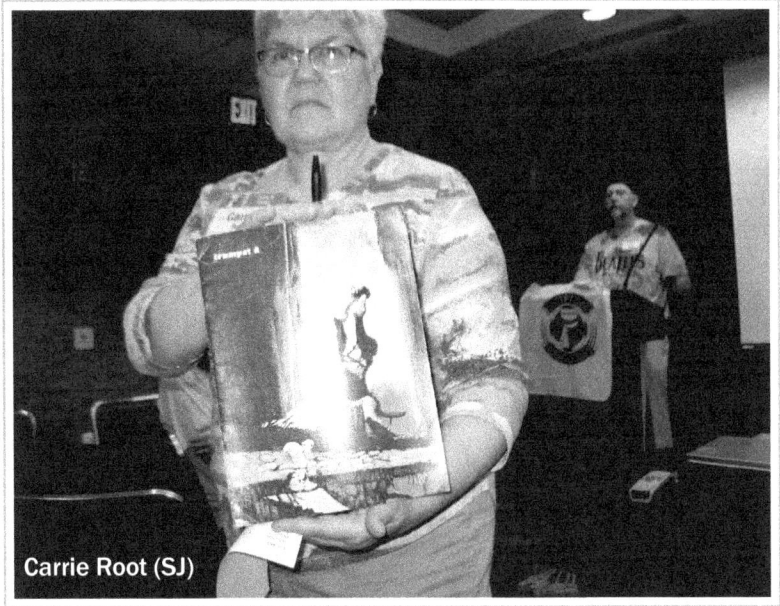
Carrie Root (SJ)

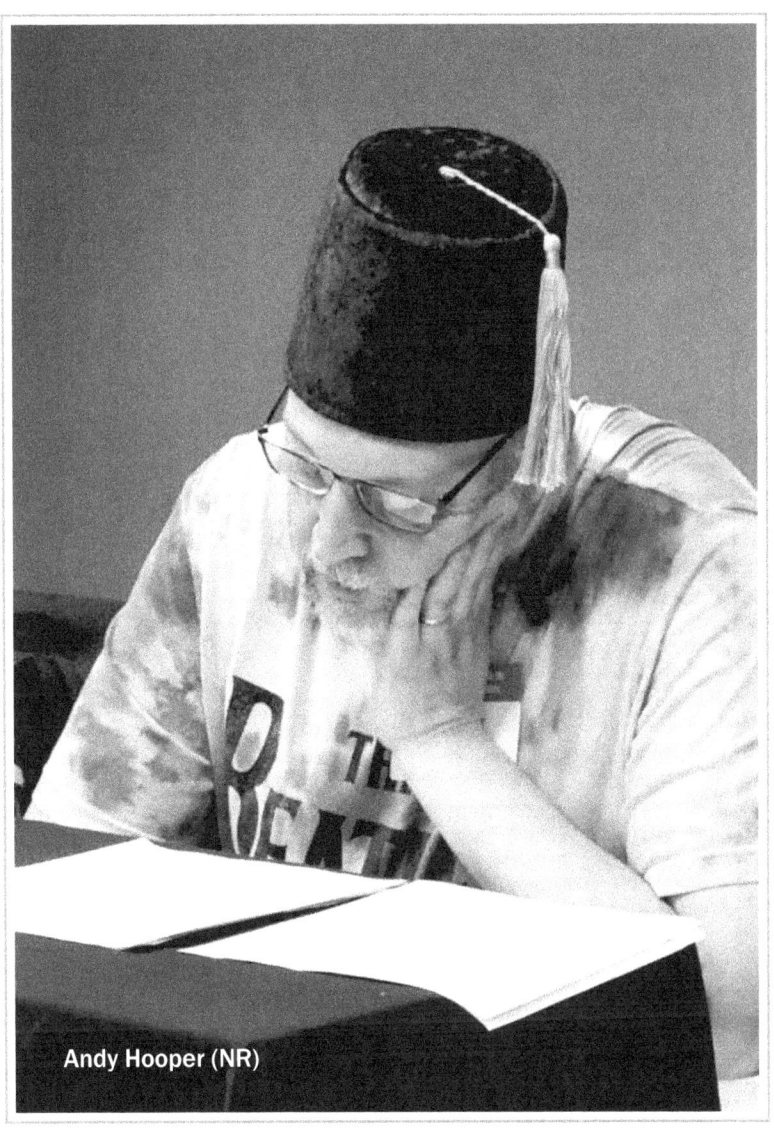
Andy Hooper (NR)

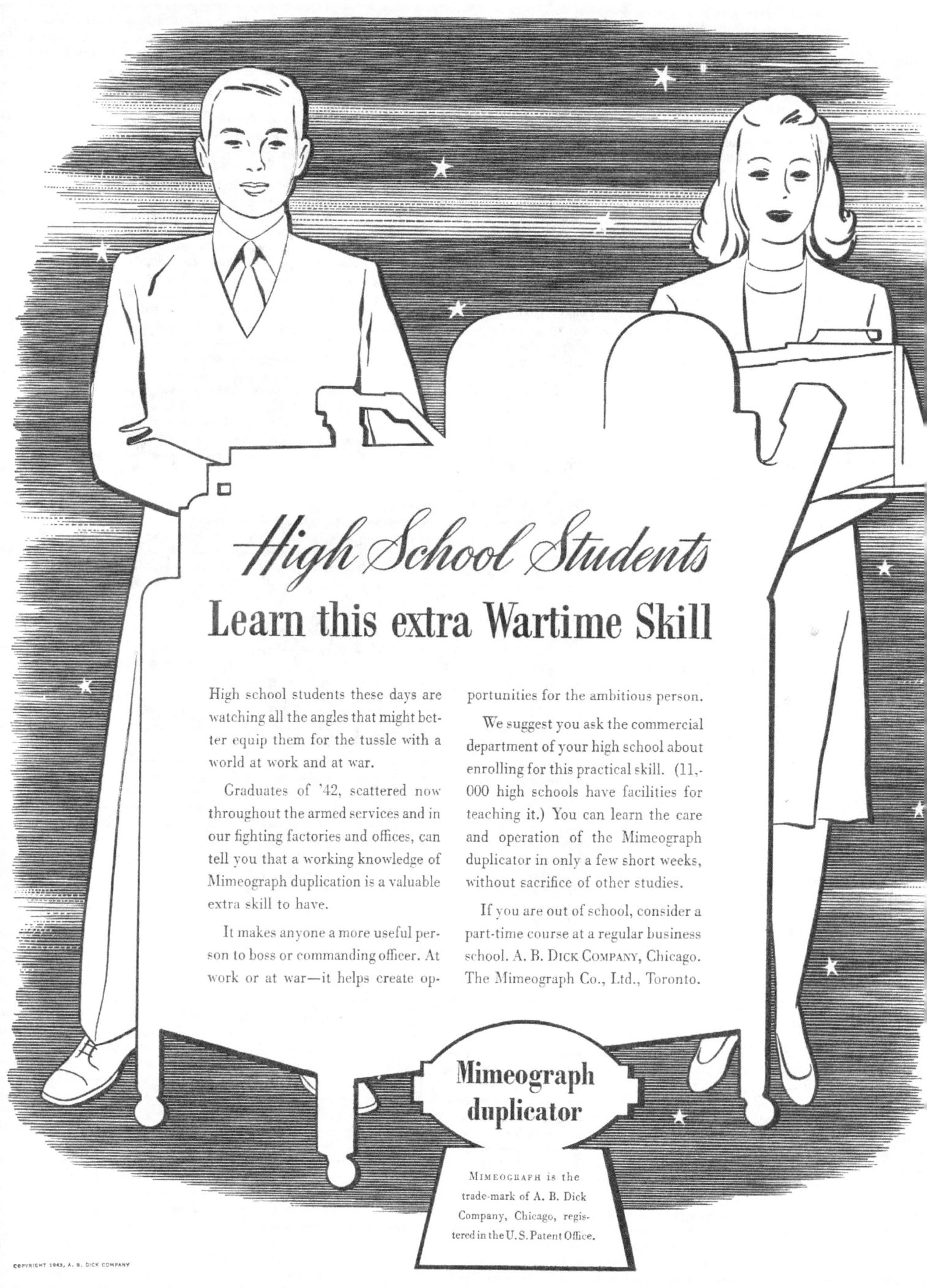

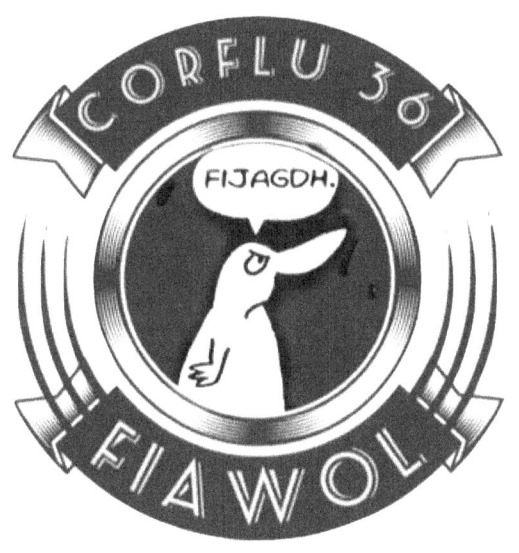

CORFLU AFTER DARK

Saturday 4 May 2019
Evening

Just a Minac (Game Show)
Saturday 4 May 2019 8:00 pm — 8:50 pm

Just a Minac is a fannish version of the BBC Radio 4 game show, in which panelists talk for sixty seconds on a given subject "without hesitation, repetition, or deviation." It's harder than it sounds.

Rob Jackson

The evening started with a burger and beer at World of Beer, with Geri, Sandra, Pat V and myself. Great choice of beers and good food, served fast enough that S&ra and I were back in good time for "Just a Minac." That also featured Nigel, JDB and Rich.

It was a good laff for the panellists and the audience, and S&ra compered it brilliantly as ever. Rich was sharpest and won a little trophy Michael had provided, but somehow I managed to umm and err myself into second place. Though unfamiliar with the BBC version, JDB picked up the rules jolly quickly.

Steve Jeffery

I was surprised and immensely cheered by how well Sandra Bond's 'Just a Minac' panel game went across both with the participants and the audience. I thought its appeal, based on a long-running BBC radio show where participants have to speak on a randomly selected topic for one minute without hesitating, repeating themselves or deviating from the topic, might take a bit of explaining but Rich Coad in particular seems to immediately channel the spirit of

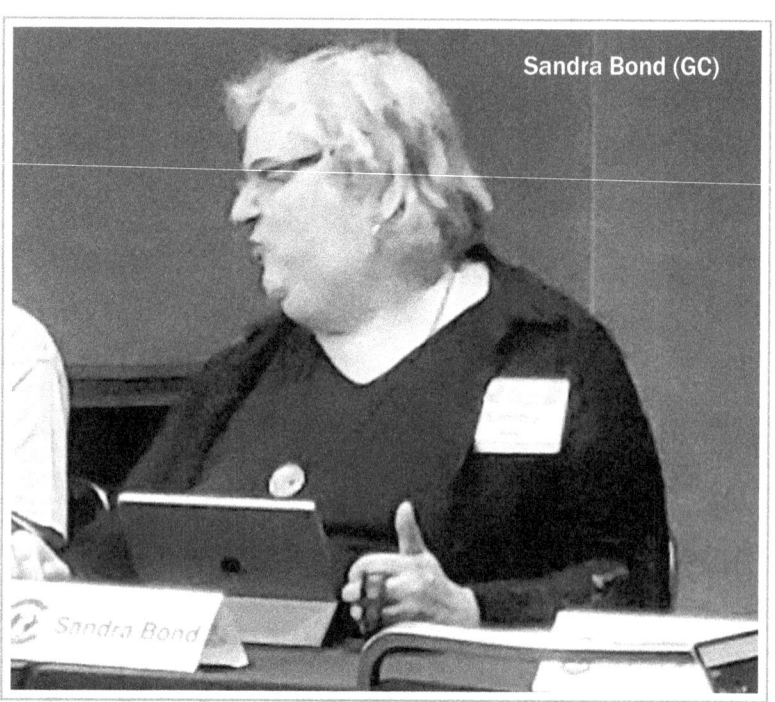

Sandra Bond (GC)

Just a Minac

Hosted without hesitation, repetition, or deviation
by **Sandra Bond**

With your panelists

John D. Berry

Rich Coad

Rob Jackson

Nigel Rowe

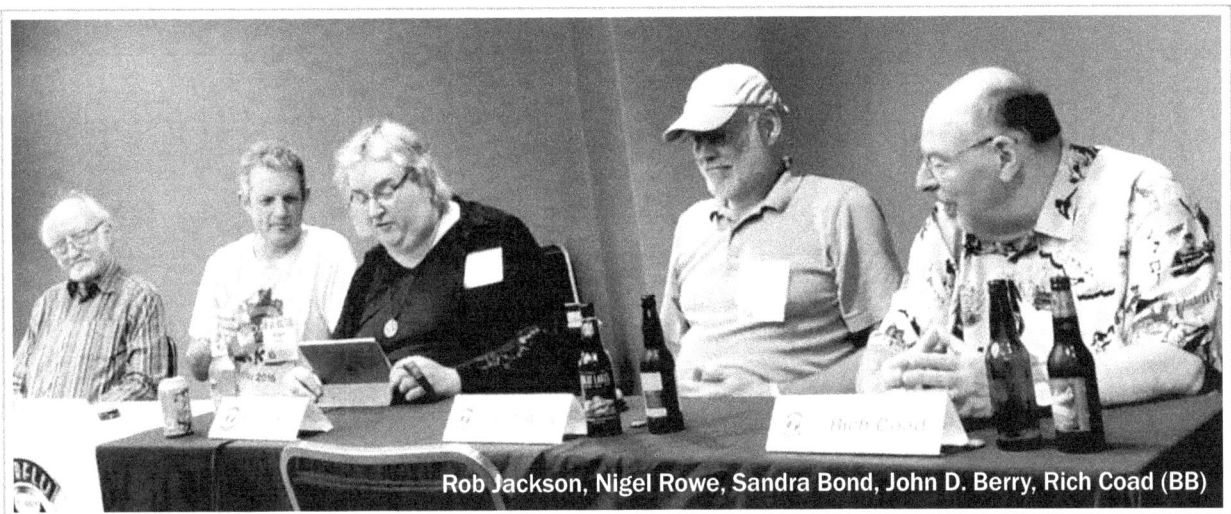
Rob Jackson, Nigel Rowe, Sandra Bond, John D. Berry, Rich Coad (BB)

the show's champion player, Paul Merton, by challenging his opponents with only three seconds left on the clock, at which point all you have to do is repeat the title of the topic (this is allowed) to win the point.

I admit I was in stitches though a lot of his as the challenges got more and more outrageous and desperate. (And if you've ever hear Merton's arch rival Giles Brandreth, this is purely in the spirit of the game, in which – as someone once said of academic disputes – the rivalry is elevated in direct proportion to the triviality of the outcome.)

Martin Morse Wooster

Saturday night had two program items. The first,. "Just a Minac," organized by Sandra Bond, was the fannish version of the British game show "Just a Minute." The idea is that the contestants—John D. Berry, Rich Coad, Rob Jackson, and Nigel Rowe—would give one-minute speeches, delivered "without hesitation, repetition, or deviation," on topics such as "The Nine Billion Names of God" or "My Favorite Beer." This was not as easy as its sounds, and I thought it was agreeably silly. Nigel Rowe seemed the most creative contestant to me, but Rich Coad was the winner.

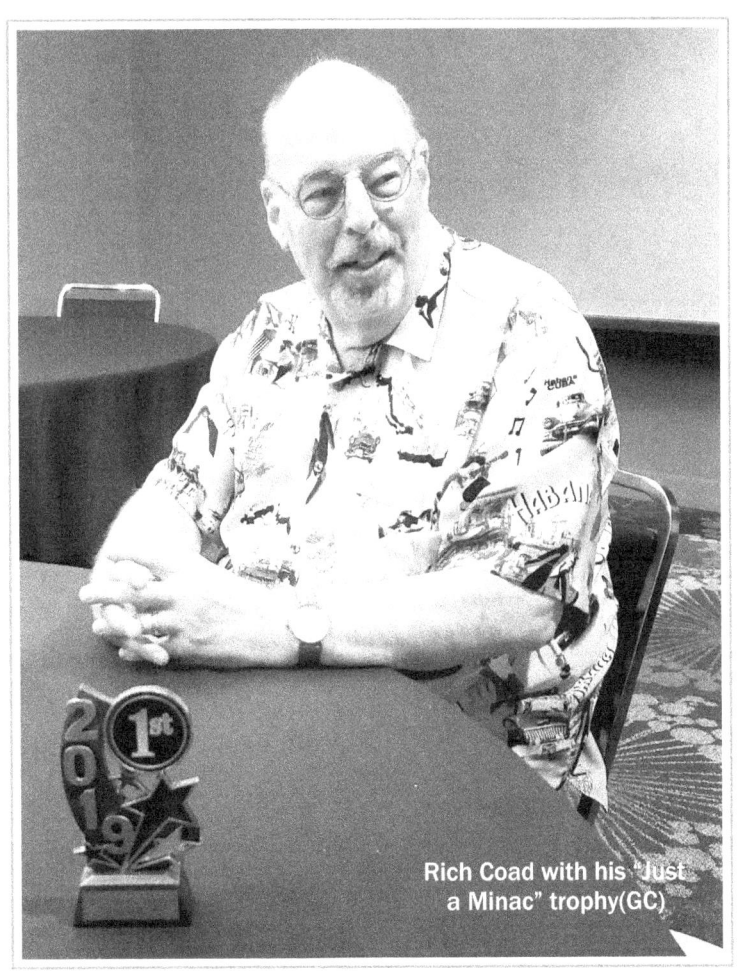
Rich Coad with his "Just a Minac" trophy(GC)

TIME CHUNNEL (A PLAY BY ANDY HOOPER)
SATURDAY 4 MAY 2019 8:00 PM — 8:50 PM

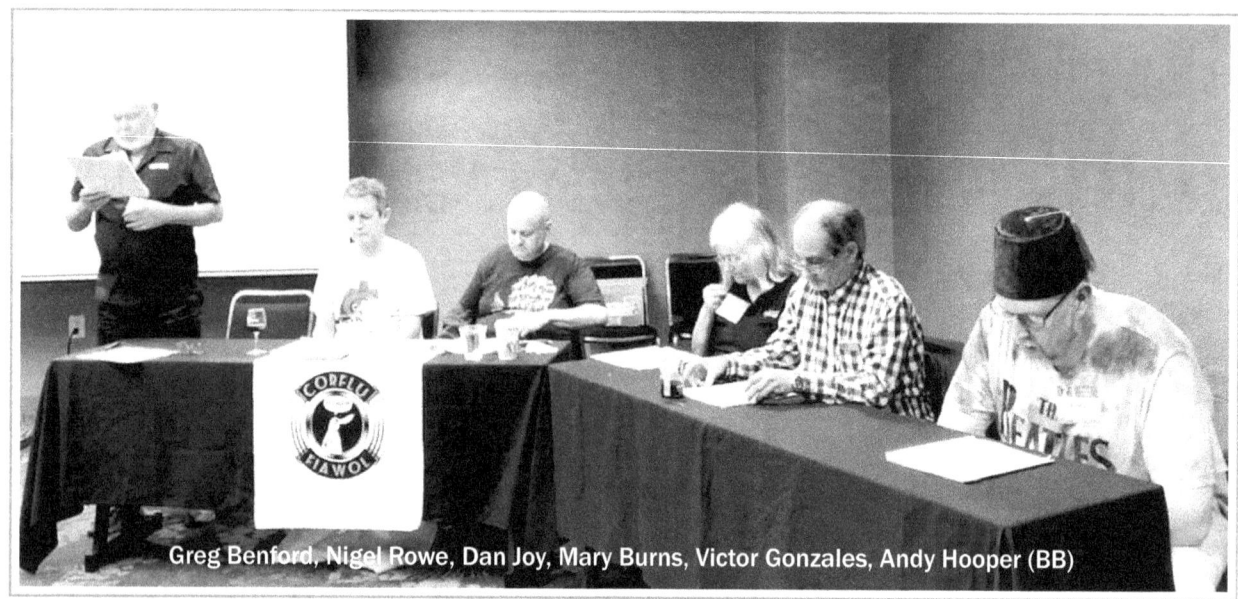

Greg Benford, Nigel Rowe, Dan Joy, Mary Burns, Victor Gonzales, Andy Hooper (BB)

Time Chunnel

A Play of
No Fixed Duration

By Andy Hooper

Written on the Occasion of Corflu 36, May 2019

Cast

Howard Barkenhorst, a clueless fan

Nolan Gondorff, a US Fish & Wildlife Agent

Linda Zigler, an MI-6 contractor

Emil Fossé, an irate French Truck Driver

Carolyn Forbes-Hill, girlfriend from another world

Howard Prime, a fan from another world.

THE TIME CHUNNEL

Howard

My name's Frank Barkenhorst. I carry a badge. My partner is Sgt. Claude Degler. We work the feud and heresy squad out of the Rampart station – the boss is Captain Tucker.

No, that's a lie. This isn't CRUDNET.
My name's Jommy Barkenhorst, and I'm an able spacer aboard the space cruiser *Derwood Kirby*. We're patrolling the space lanes between Titan and Toledo, keeping an eye our for ice pirates and organleggers.

No, that's also a lie. My name's Howard Barkenhorst. I'm a sock puppet. I work for a medium sized social media troll farm, making up posts for people too busy and wealthy to write their own. I have about fifteen different on-line identities, enough to start my own apa. Two of my clients are rival pop singers in Korea, so I send my self insults across the International Date Line. But what I'm really about are fanzines – science fiction fanzines, grainy, smudgy, fusty old slabs of paper, cranked out of mimeographs by ambitious teenage kids of any age or era. And I like modern fanzines too, data files I can blow up to any size, and slick laser-printed journals are all good too. Fandom is a virtual way of life.

If none of these introductions seem believable to you, then I'm already sunk; nothing about this story is as plausible as space-time pirates or giant electric penguins. But if, like me, you have long had a sense that our world is somehow imbalanced, misaligned, as if someone put the batteries in the wrong way – you might find the arrival of two strangers at the door a chance for some sort of explanation.

Nolan

Mr. Barkenhorst? My name's Nolan Gondorff. This is my associate, Linda Zigler. We're researchers at the University of California at Riverside. You've heard of the Eaton Collection?

Howard

Of course. I've sent them copies of all my fanzines – STFREF, VERSO, HAMSAM, CALABASH, SNEETCH ON THE BEACH…

Linda

We know you're an enthusiastic archiver. It's clear that you really… live with your collection.

Howard

Um, yes. Yes, there are a lot of fanzines in the house. Not all of them are my collection, of course; some are from other fans who left them in my care. I imagine your pile of unsorted boxes is even bigger.

Nolan

We're actually here because we're very interested in some fanzines that were published quite recently. Is there…do you actually have a pile of current fanzines?

Howard

Jesus Christ, did Gary Farber send you? Current zines are in this black mag rack. And this green one. And a couple are there on the end of the table.

Linda

Are they sorted by…?

Howard

Australian and British A4 zines, full-sized American zines in the black rack, smaller zines in green. Issues of VANAMONDE are underneath that Christmas Cactus, to catch spills.

Nolan

So what are we…?

Linda

Australian. In the black rack. Presumably – oh, crumbs.

Nolan

You, um, you haven't even opened this one, Howard.

Howard

I know. It's terrible. Here, I have an opener. (a beat) Hmm.

Nolan

PSYCHOBILLY POTAROO. I believe it's a marsupial, Like an enormous, long-tailed shrew….

Howard

Yes, I see that.

Linda

Published by Roger Weddall, from Carlton, Victoria. Published this March!

Howard

Huh…

Nolan

Howard, Roger Weddall died 29 years ago.

Howard

Yes, but that isn't necessarily an impediment to publishing! Terry Carr, Charles Burbee, Walt Willis – they get published almost as frequently as when they were alive!

Linda

But here's another interesting case. You opened this one. JETERMANIA #6 by Martin Smith. There are photos in this one – look Martin's lost all his hair. And here's a picture of his wife, and their three kids in front of their home in the Bronx.

Howard

Martin Bloody Smith.

Nolan

He's not from Croydon any more. And, just for the record, also…

Howard

Dead. Dead as a Puffin. Dead as flared trousers.

Linda

But you haven't mentioned it to anyone, or asked who was responsible?

Howard

Well, it's a Hoax. It's a trick, a gag! Quick, tell me Horrible Old Roy Tackett is about to pop out from behind that door! I mean, someone else could easily be named Martin Smith, fer Godssake! People publish things as tributes, memorials – John Henri Holmberg went around calling himself Carl Brandon Junior when he first entered fandom. Someone else could call themselves "Roger Wedall" because just they loved leather pants. Who are you two? Does the Eaton Collection have X-files?

Nolan

So, technically, we're special students at Riverside – and I actually have a badge, but it's from the Fish and Wildlife service. But Linda consults for a company that's a front for MI-6 in Canada.

Linda

I'm an independent contractor. But MI-6 believes these science fiction fanzines mean something very important, and we had to contact you about them personally, without involving anyone else.

Nolan

Howard, I got involved in this because I was a zine-head too – I grew up in Oregon with punks and rubber stamp freaks, and got into square dance fanzines when I was at school. I also had a friend who died in 1986, and last year, he starts sending me a bowling fanzine.

Linda

And that wasn't any sort of hoax, either. We know that there have been other fanzines – fanzines you have questions about.

Nolan

Conventions you've never heard of sending you "past Guest of Honor" offers. Work by artists dated after they supposedly died. That kind of thing.

Howard

It's not my imagination? It's not just that I imagined that they died, or had a dream about it?

Linda

Howard, you know that Roger Weddall is dead. It was a tragedy. No one knew he was even sick. He died very soon after his DUFF trip to America in 1992.

Nolan

But look at what Roger says in PSYCHOBILLY POTAROO: He's excited to welcome a European fan to the New Zealand Worldcon, as the GUFF delegate, because he won the GUFF race in 1995, and lost the 1992 DUFF race to Alan Stewart.

Howard

That never happened. Roger beat Greg Hills to win the 1992 DUFF race, and went to Magicon in Orlando.

Linda

This is good. You have a stronger grasp of reality than I thought. So this is your Philip K Dick moment, Howard, when you find out your misgivings about reality are actually true.

Nolan

We call it "being read in." You're a science fiction fan – you've always hoped that there were alternatives to our reality. And we're here to tell you that there is at least one reality tangential to ours that can be proven to exist. Because it's apparently full of people that want to destroy our world.

Howard

By sending me fanzines? By winning the GUFF race in 1995?

Linda

The fanzines may be a warning from someone who feels differently. Or they may be a mistake, we don't really know. But they've given us a chance to study the differences between us. We think – our management thinks – someone like you will know and understand those changes when you see them.

Howard

So, do I – send Roger a letter of comment? In Carlton? You can't send email to the alternate reality?

How does the mail get to the right living Roger, and not the dead one in our world?

Linda

Through the Chunnel.

Howard

The Chunnel? The Channel under the English Tunnel?

Nolan

In 1998, some scientists from Hatfield investigated a phenomenon called "chronoelongation," reported by drivers who routinely used the tunnel to cross between Kent and Calais. Sealed chronometers arrived at the opposite end of the tunnel showing significantly longer periods of time had elapsed than clocks that had been synchronized to them before the trip.

Linda

And they got permission from the Ministry of Defense to build a machine based on a design by Bob Shaw. It was supposed to measure and synchronize fluctuations in time. When they switched it on, part of the Tunnel wall fell away – revealing an identical machine, with an identical team or researchers running it. The two worlds became connected.

Nolan

At first they were terrified, of course, and cut traffic to a trickle. But after a while, the scientists on one side formed a working group with the scientists from the other, and some limited exchange began to occur. And it was determined that unless a certain amount of traffic was routed into another reality, the waiting times in Folkestone would become impossibly long. The only way the Chunnel can work is if some percentage of traffic is detoured into to another world.

Howard

So. Yes. Um. Couldn't you ask Bill Nye to do this?

Nolan

Good answer. I don't know what Bill Nye does on the other side. That's the thing you have to understand: it's not just another world, it's a nearly- world, with another version of you, and me, and almost everyone we know.

Linda

And they may look the same, but they're not the same. There are differences. They had a slightly different Stalin, and a different Roosevelt. They had a different war, and made a different United Nations at the end. Their Doris Day never sang "Que Sera." Their Elvis never went into the army. In their world, Keith Moon is the poet laureate of Britain.

Howard

So how can that be the same?

Nolan

All those differences added up to the same team of scientists and the same Bob Shaw time machine.

Linda

And there is an agreement to keep the worlds as separate as possible – to prevent immigration between them. We don't ask them for help, and they don't ask for ours.

Nolan

And we've never tried to put anyone into the other world before.

Howard

Before what?

Linda

Your life in the other world is not very different. You'd spend a lot of time reading fanzines, and telling us what they tell you.

Howard

And does the other me – move into my life?

Nolan

(*Laughing*) No, no, that would be pointlessly complicated, don't you think? No, we'll make him a sudden and irresistible offer that will keep him in a different hemisphere.

Howard

And am I going to work their version of Snapchat and Twitter all day? Will my phone still be in network?

Nolan

Perhaps not exactly. Tell me, Howard, how are your typing skills? You've had experience composing directly to stencil, right?

Howard

(*Narrrating*) Spin a schoolroom globe, and trace a glowing line over the pole to illustrate my flight path from Springfield to Heathrow. From there, a coach ride to scenic Swindon, and a rendezvous with my escort to the other world, His name was Emil; he chain-smoked foul, armpit-smelling Gauloises; and his differences with God could never be resolved.

Emil

Are you Howard? Come with me if you like hot chips and warm-hearted Belgian women.

Howard

(*Still Narrating*) Who can say no to that? Cherchez les frites. Emil Fossé was profane, truculent, and equally unhappy on either side of the Channel. He had no faith in God, humanity, technology, nature or dogs, who were too simple to betray you, buy always died anyway. Over the course of our long journey to Calais and back again, he shared his bitter indictments of many people, places and things including Boris Johnson.

Emil

A drunken circus bear in a suit but lacking the judgment or sense of balance.

Howard

Emmanuel Macron:

Emil

A banker with the soul of another banker. Raised agnostic, demanded to be baptized Catholic at age 12, now agnostic once more. A hysteric.

Howard

Hillary Clinton:

Emil

The Queen of the Damned. She must bathe in the blood of super-delegates at the full moon, or wither into dust.

Howard

Queen Elizabeth II

Emil

Lyndon LaRouche was right; she is at the center of the most pernicious narcotics and sex traffic cartel in the Western world.

Howard

Tim Horton's Timbits:

Emil

What, you think I am a child? And an imbecile at that? Take your dirty donut holes and go.

Howard

There were no short-cuts, he assured me.

Emil

There are no short-cuts. I assure you. There is only waiting in this terrible, stinking cab while we creep along on our way to the Chunnel. You follow the lane with the longest wait, the worst inspections, and the most endless backups. You wait until you are sure you must go mad; and perhaps you do go mad, but still you wait. Once you have given up all hope, and want only to die – your crossing may finally begin. And if you have waited long enough, and suffered enough – you may find that you have entered the other world.

Howard

I see why people aren't exactly pouring through the crossing.

Emil

They would if Management let them. If it's bad enough here, how could it be even worse there?

Howard

And is it? Even worse over there?

Emil

The sun comes up. The sky is blue. Man is wallowing in sin in all possible worlds, so why measure who is the more damned?

Howard

But you still don't like the other side.

Emil

Meh. Their cell phones are like house bricks. They still put the word "balsamic" in front of everything.

Howard

That's quaint.

Emil

But they're cunning. They were able to figure out that they hate us long before we started hating them. So they have a huge head start. Almost every bad thing you can think of has something to do with them. Climate change. Donald Trump. Brexit. The bankruptcy of Toys R Us. Pretty much all of it has happened because of those bastards on the other side.

Howard

I wonder if the other Howard is having this conversation with the other Emil while we wait. Your name is actually Richard Shaver, isn't it?

Emil

The Other Howard is naked on a beach somewhere. We're not like them. We don't send people to the Yodel House.

Howard

I really don't think I've been adequately briefed.

Emil

The Yodel House is where they keep the people from our side, while their duplicates from the other side cause mischief over here.

Howard

They do that? What does management say about it?

Emil

Management doesn't answer questions.

Howard

That's not – never mind, how many people from over there are over here?

Emil:

We think it must be nearly 300 now.

Howard

That's a lot more than I was told. And they all replace someone?

Emil

There is an academy, where you learn about your other, where they prepare you to live here, in secret. They call it the Fugghead School.

Howard

The Fugghead School? Is this a piece of faan fiction? Are you a fabulous Burbee-like character?

Emil

Save your existential crisis to amuse me at a later time. When your double is ready to cross over, they capture you and put you in the Yodel House – it's actually a prison – and try to get you to confess.

Howard

What do they want people to confess to?

Emil

That we have a secret plan to conquer them, to destroy them or bring about the end of their World's existence.

Howard

Well, do we?

Emil

It's a secret.

Howard

This is not helping my confidence.

Emil

I don't want you to be confident. I want you to be bitter, and sarcastic and paranoid. Don't be too cheerful or convinced that life is going your way, you'll stick out like – like someone from another world.

Howard

But why should they call it the Fugghead School? What does any of this have to do with fandom?

Emil

It's the difference between our worlds. In our reality, science fiction conquered the world. In the other reality, Fandom conquered the world. There's a difference, you'll see.

Howard

(Narrating again) And we went on arguing and questioning each other for hours, until the effects of jet lag caught up with me. I was asleep when we crossed the Chunnel, woke up enough to show an equally groggy official some papers, then promptly fell back asleep at the beginning of the return trip. The next thing I knew, Emil was shaking me awake in Folkestone, saying that if I hurried, I could make my flight back to America. I hustled to jump aboard another coach to Heathrow, and it was ten minutes before I realized I was on the other side.

How is it different? It's older. They haven't built as many new things, or pre-emptively knocked down as many old ones. When I went to the airport, I had to report to a ticket counter, where they printed a boarding pass for me on something resembling a punch card. There were mechanical calculators in use, and the amazing clatter of typewriters came out of the airline offices. The airport was completely devoid of charging stations. Absolutely no one wheeled around awkwardly on Segways.

So follow that glowing line back over the pole, and touch back down on the blinking dot of Springfield. Nervously taxied back to the house – no Lyft, no Uber, no eCars – and nervously enter with me, wondering what will be the same, what will be in the refrigerator. Modern computer, monitor, and printer all missing of course, replaced with – my God, is that a Sinclair? But that's a sideshow. The main event is a gorgeous IBM Selectric with a midnight blue vinyl dust cover, next to an immaculately maintained Roneo duplicator and a top-flight electrostenciller.

Also, over here I have a wife.

Well, perhaps she isn't technically my wife, since neither of us is wearing a ring, and there is no picture of her in a wedding dress anywhere in the house. When she came down the stairs and kissed me, I did my very best not to look surprised. I wasn't able to even call her by her name until she went to the bathroom and I could rifle through her purse for her driver's license. You're really a spy now. I said. Carolyn Forbes-Hill. We work together and live together, that's going to be interesting. We have the most ridiculous job: Newspapers call us up to check and see if the facts their reporters have reported are true. And there's dozens of papers doing this all the time. We look things up in encyclopedias, we look in file cabinets full of clippings and magazine pages, we even look in the O-E-D. And again: They pay us to do this!

Carolyn

After lunch, I'm going to type out the letter column. If you want to take the issue to the Slan Moot on Saturday, we have to duplicate it tomorrow.

Howard

How many copies am I making?

Carolyn

You promised to do 75 this time, after you ran out before everyone got their copy. You're strong. I know it won't give you Twonk's Disease to make 25 extra copies.

Howard

It's not my arm that worries me, it's the stencil.

Carolyn

Sing the A. B. Dick song!

Howard

I – I don't –

Carolyn

Oh, Howard! You made it up on the way back from the El Paso Worldcon. "To Solve your duplicating problems quick….all you need?

Howard

"Is an A. B. Dick!" But if I recall correctly, you were ogling my Rex Rotary on that trip.

Carolyn

Howard! Not in front of the Galleys!

Howard

(Narrating again) I didn't mention: She writes children's books, too. There's a dingo and a wallaroo and a box jellyfish named Simon, and they have magical adventures together.

Carolyn

And you promised to let John Hertz know if you could toastmaster at Westerclave.

Howard

(Narrating on) So that kind of settles the issue for me: I have to get out of here before the 4th of July, or I'll be forced to make jokes to and about a fandom I only know from a dream I once had. The proliferation of fans that are not dead yet over here is pretty amazing. People like Anna Vargo. Mike Wood. Martin Smith, of course. Seth Goldberg. Susan Wood. Jim Young. Kent Moomaw. Ron Ellik. Vaughn Freakin' Bodé…of course, they tell me he weighs 360 pounds now, but he's alive.

Carolyn

John says he's going to teach us "Bonaparte's Expedition." My bosom heaves with anticipation.

Howard

Also, we do Regency dance. None of those velvet pants have room for my Bonaparte, I assure you. So that's different from anything I'd ever do at "home." Also, we're doing a fanzine called AXION together, and apparently I never published anything called VERSO or CALABASH. Which is frustrating, but maybe I can write those articles all over again. Assuming there is anything left to write about at all – there have been so many more fanzines published here than I know of at home in the other world. 26 issues of SIKANDER. Over 100 issues of FANAC, because the Breendoggle never killed it off, because there was no Breendoggle.

Over here, Walter Breen was a Catholic Priest who never had anything to do with science fiction fans. 28 issues of ENERGUMEN! Malcom Edwards did SIXTEEN issues of TAPPEN! That's THREE TIMES as many as he did on the otherside, in the real world.

But it's like there is a price to pay for all this faanish splendor. This is a story Carolyn told at a party, after the other me apparently told it to her:

Carolyn

Oh, well, you know about the story of how someone died at the first World Convention in 1939? Howard told me all about it. Apparently. there were some technocrats in charge of the convention, and there were some anarchists who didn't care for it. One of the anarchists published a yellow sheet warning about the tyrannical intentions of the technocrats. This kid – he was only a kid, maybe sixteen years old – signs his name to this warning.

So the characters in charge, Moskowitz and the like, accosted this kid, his name was David I think, and they slapped him in the face and sent him out of the hall. And he goes crying to the automat across the street where all the other anarchists were eating their Nesselrode pie before going in to the meeting, and they thrust out their bony chests and marched off to see this Moskowitz character.

A woman named Frances Alberti swung her purse at a kid named Donald Allen Wollheim, and put him in the hospital with a skull fracture. While he was in there, recovering, he caught pneumonia and died. Of course, that's a far cry from actually dying at the convention – it was like six weeks later that he finally died. But you get the point.

Apparently a lot of people refused to ever speak to Sam Moskowitz again, he was hounded from fandom, and ended up promoting quick-setting concrete in trade magazines. But I'm not really positive it was concrete; you'll have to ask Howard.

Howard

That's right, Will Sykora's fiancée hit Donald Wollheim in the brain with her purse at the first Worldcon and he eventually died. Nolan Gondorff comes to see me – he pretends he's a publisher who wants to hire me --, and he pretends to understand why I'm excited, but I know someone in Management will understand.

I start thinking that management is somehow connected to fandom or else I wouldn't be here. I start thinking about famous gafiates on my side of the Chunnel, and correlate some names on this side. Carmody, Bosnyak. Whiteoak. Bergeron. Lafayette Hubbard. No one is immortal, not even here. But that's what a legacy is for.

I should have been connecting these sinister dots, but I kept getting distracted. I had unknown articles by Walt Willis and Dean Grennell to read, and letters to answer. And I was supposed to write a biography of Filthy Pierre Straus, because the Yonkers Worldcon had made him fan guest of honor. The Smithsonian was going to display his filth-o-phone.

So I was caught flat-footed when Gondorff and Zigler came to tell me the game was over.

Nolan

The game's over Mr. Barkenhorst. The other Howard has broken containment, and will be back here within a matter of hours.

Howard

How did that happen?

Linda

He shared two months with the girl that we paid to seduce him, then started having panic attacks and staring for hours at the Tasman sea. He broke up with her using refrigerator magnets, and got on an airplane to Hawaii before she could call us.

Howard

But I'm really not ready. I've made no progress at all on finding the Fugghead School. Or the prisoners in the Yodel House. I haven't even managed to prove that they caused Brexit, or rigged the 2016 Eurovision song contest.

Nolan

Howard, those are strategic concerns. We're interface. We grab the bags, and get out before housekeeping arrives to clean up.

Howard

Is housekeeping on their way here?

Linda

No, Howard, we don't have assets like that over here. But this is extraction, right? If you don't take it you find your own ride.

Nolan

We've got pictures of everything. We still have access to scanners and digital cameras, remember?

Howard

Yeah, but you don't have – my Roneo!

Linda

It's already too late, Howard, I think your fingertips are blackened for life.

Howard

You don't understand! I've been trying to get a mimeograph to work for me for forty years. They NEVER worked right – too light or too dark, sheets stuck together, sheets stuck to the drum, can't feed, won't ink, just won't work! But over here – over here, it's like every mimeo is the Enchanted Duplicator! Stencils don't tear! Ink doesn't clump! Illos don't bleed through!

Nolan

Howard, you won't be able to stay here. Even if you could explain yourself to the other Howard, there's only one bank account in your name. You have the same Social security number. You can't stay in this world, Howard.

Howard

I know, But I'm not ready to go, Look, don't worry about me. I have a passport. I know how to get to the airport. And book a coach ticket to Calais. Don't worry, I'll go – I want to. I kind of miss my sock puppets.

I didn't pack much – just the clothes I brought with me, and some duplicates of titles that I wouldn't be able to get at home. And I wanted to tell Carolyn….something. But how do you tell someone that you're actually her boyfriend's doppelganger, and you're returning to your alien homeworld now?

Carolyn

I don't know, maybe you should just save it for Howard when he gets here. At least that way maybe you won't have to explain the whole thing twice.

Howard

So you knew who I was this whole time? That's kind of…weird.

Carolyn

So you were comfortable, you know, plowing me, when you thought I was fooled into believing you were my boyfriend, but the fact that I was in on it makes it weird now?

Howard

Yeah, I guess I have a lot to think through there.

Carolyn

Your world's not ready for me. Listen. It's easy; I love Howard so much that even a slightly slow version of him turns me on. Sometimes I'd wake up and it would be two or three minutes before I would remember it was you.

So now I'll get to see the two of you together at last. I was right; it's no challenge to tell you apart. Even if you started out the same. Our worlds act on us in a million ways, writing and erasing us again and again. Even if we are identical, we are never, ever the same.

Howard Prime

How did I get such a stfnal pal as you?
Carolyn:
Ooh, Howie! You came back, you came back!

Howard Prime

I promised I would. Oh God, it's boring in Tasmania. How long does it take to count all the mammals that lay eggs? After that, it's pretty much nothing but snooker.

Howard

I'm happy to meet you.

Howard Prime

Well, I know I'm happy to meet you. I'm actually quite a fan of VERSO and CALABASH. I guess you could say I wish I'd written them.

Howard

I guess you could say you did. How did you discover my version of our stuff?

Howard Prime

Oh, you want it to be somebody deep, like Billy Wolfenbarger. But Woody Bernardi was probably the first fan from your world that I met in person. He was lost, or course and I don't know if he ever figured out exactly where he was, but his clothes – his gadgets – those shoes! He was just so obviously a person from another world. After that, I reached out to the drivers on the Chunnel route – anybody interested in science fiction, in fans – they should pay a visit to far away Springfield. After that, I met all the Travelling Jiants: John D. Berry, Art Widner, Christina Lake. It was easy to have them take a few envelopes back with them, to be mailed from home to save postage. Berry was never fooled, but jan howard finder made three more trips, just so he could be my mailing agent.

Howard

I was sorry when he died.

Howard Prime

He's not dead over here. He's 80 years old and deaf as a concrete gnome, but still writing letters. Of course, the version that mailed fanzines to you for me died in 2013. What is it about your world that seems to kill fans at such an early age, Howard? Surely you've asked yourself that question since you've been on this side.

Howard

Maybe, But I don't have an answer.

Howard Prime

Your world is science fictional, Howard, but it isn't fannish. It's full of wonders, but they add up to something mundane. Everyone can publish at any time, but no one bothers to do anything but 144 characters of crud.
And don't tell me I can't judge fairly from here. I couldn't let you come and live in my life without investigating yours. Do you remember when several fans claimed they had seen you at Minicon, but you spent that Easter weekend at home? This became quite a fad, until we almost ended up with two Tuckers at the same Midwescon.

Howard

I'm envious. I only knew one Tucker.

Howard Prime

Are you sure about that? The Chunnel was open for 12 years before your Bob died in 2006. We lost ours in 2009, but I know he made at least one trip to your Bloomington. And you know they insisted on pulling it out, just to see if they were truly identical.

Howard

This is all like a cautionary tale.

Howard Prime

Oh, relax. You've gained a new perspective on two separate realities. And you totally slept with my girlfriend and got away with it. It's not entirely bad to be you, is it?

Howard

It wasn't all bad being you, either.

Howard Prime

So have you decided where we should build the Fugghead School?

Howard

Yes. No. Maybe. I had considered Puerto Rico. But now I think we might have better luck setting up in Las Vegas. A private school for very special children – I think it would fit right in.

Howard Prime

And all just waiting for the right moment to publish. But none of it can happen unless you go back and build it.

Howard

I guess you're right. But you gotta tell me: What does all this have to do with election hacking and Brexit and Hugo bloc voting and sad, skinny puppies?

Howard Prime

Yeah, that's not my department. This may come as a shock after what you've heard, but all those things are all entirely yours. We had nothing to do with your Trump, or your Putin or Teresa May – we just want more books and fanzines about robots and spaceships. It's your world that seems to have lost its sense of wonder about those things. But we can put it back, right?

Howard

One mimeo stencil at a time. All right, I'm going. Time to wire the Sheriff in Laporte, Indiana.

Howard and Howard Prime

(In unison) "The son-of-a-bitch stole my watch!"

Howard

(Back to narration again) So that was a jovial parting. Now, I just had to go through the 56 hour ordeal of returning to the Chunnel, and somehow go through the right lanes that would get me back to my own world. It would be simply unthinkable if I ended trapped up in this paradise where the leaf blower was never invented and people publish on perfectly-working mimeographs.

Emil

That kind of luxury is not for working class heroes like us, Howard. We thrive on the struggle, the fury, and the sheer boredom of existence. What does God have to offer us besides that?

Howard

I'd just like to stop and get something for the road – some Dr. Pepper, maybe some Cheetos.

Emil

Cheetos are a yellow bourgeois illusion, and beneath my contempt. We will stop at the proletarian truck stop in Elgin, and you will buy a bag of pork rinds, like a man. And a cassette tape of music by Leonard Cohen, you desperate simpleton.

Howard

Ah, Emil…I think this may be the beginning of a beautiful friendship.

(The entire cast hums "Le Marseillaise" as they are introduced and take their bows)

Rob Jackson

Andy's play was shorter, more focussed and a bit less abstruse than some of his previous ones, and there was some good audience feedback. Then the con suite – the wine tasting had been earlier, but there was plenty of wine still not tasted, and the vibe was still great. I'd love to have taken more photos, as people were smiling and enjoying themselves nearly all night – but the lighting in there was crap as nearly all of it was from table lamps round the sides so people's faces were guaranteed to be in shadow. Oh well.

Saturday Night's Alright (for Fanac)
Saturday 4 May 2019 9:00 pm — Very Late

Steve Jeffery

Back in the consuite, Geri Sullivan's beer tasting evening included a number of brews that might best be described as intriguing and challenging rather than actually palatable (certainly as session beers) and favoured rather more variants of chocolate flavoured stout than were good for my (by this stage) delicate constitution.

By the middle of the third bottle I was distinctly struggling, both with the taste (imagine trying to drinking a pint of Black Forest gateau) and to stay awake. By 3am I was ready concede defeat and make for bed, but Geri, more imbued to the effects, was having none of it, and forced me awake with cold flannels so that I was one of the lucky few to see Geri's and Pat Virzi's depiction of the benefits of mimeo fibretone as performed through the medium of interpretive dance. Presumably, as we were in the spillover con suite, this was one of the convention's sercon items.

It's probably best to draw a discreet veil over the effects of all this the next morning, necessitating an emergency dash back to my room.

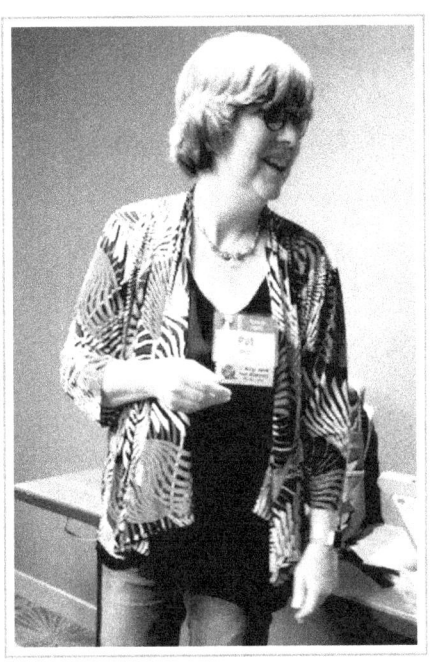
Pat Virzi (CP)

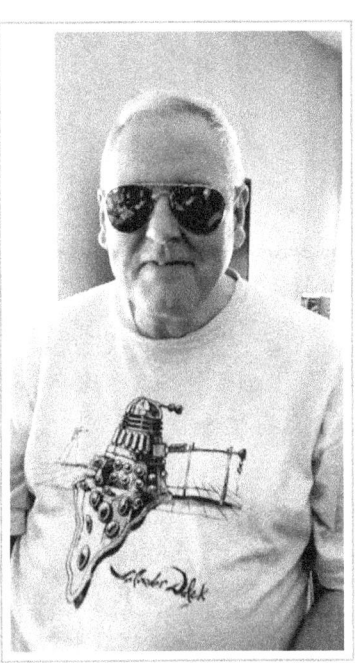
Ian Sorensen (CP)

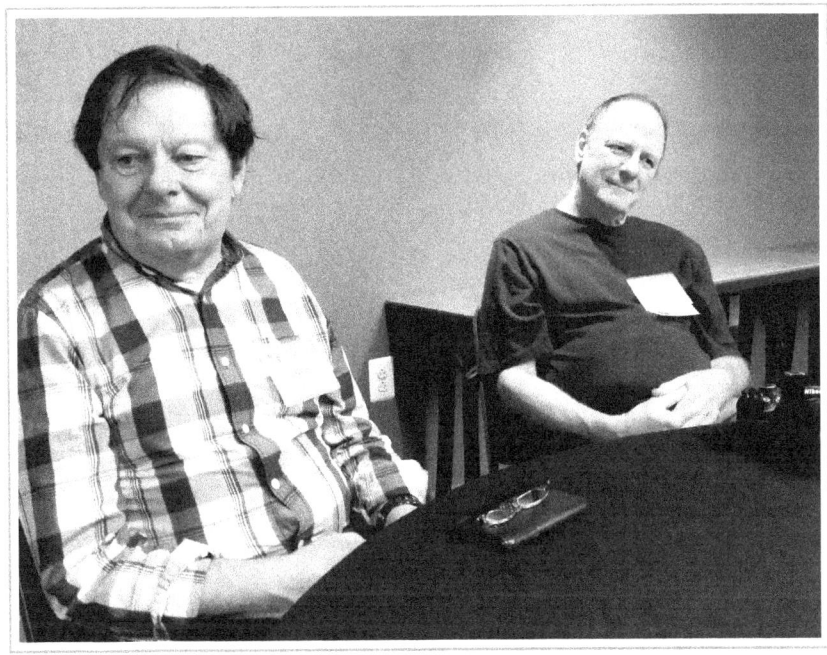
Jeff Schalles and Chris Couch (SS)

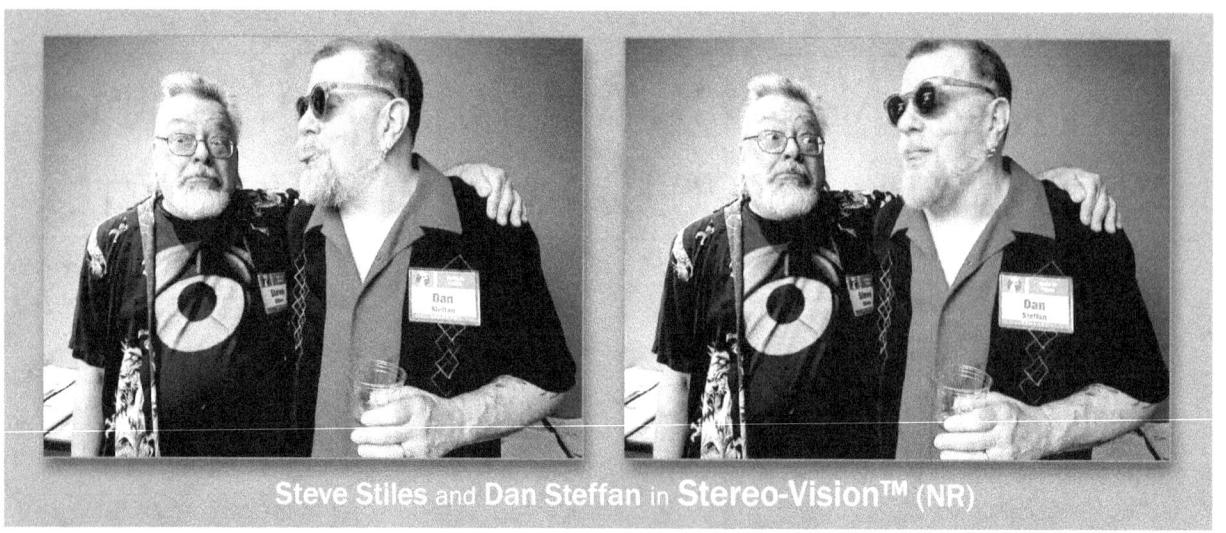
Steve Stiles and Dan Steffan in **Stereo-Vision™** (NR)

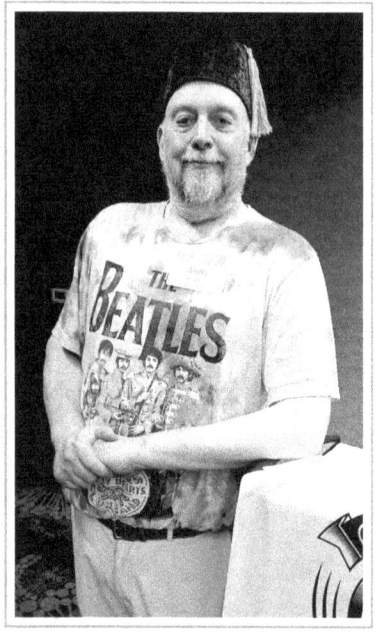
Andy Hooper (NR)

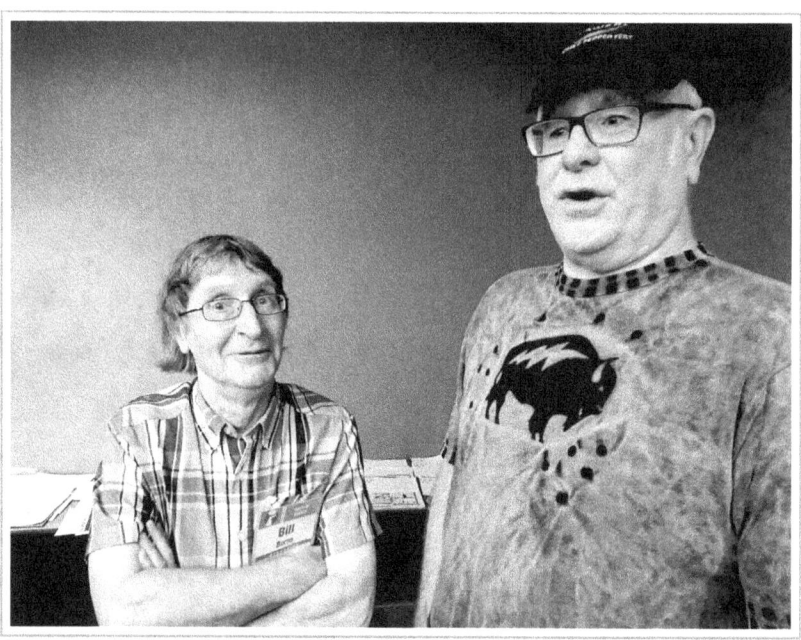
Bill Burns, Frank Lunney (NR)

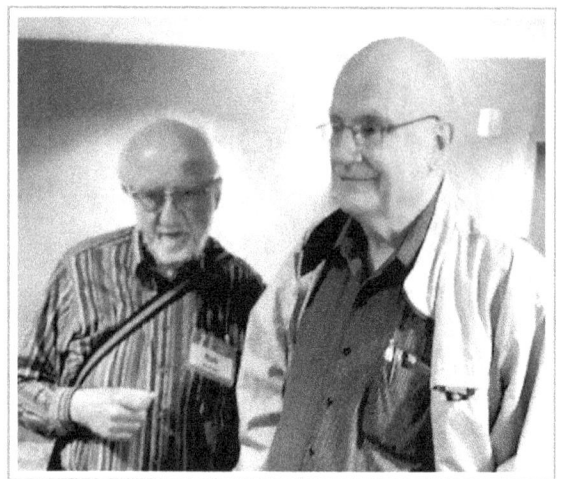
Rob Jackson, Rich Lynch (CP)

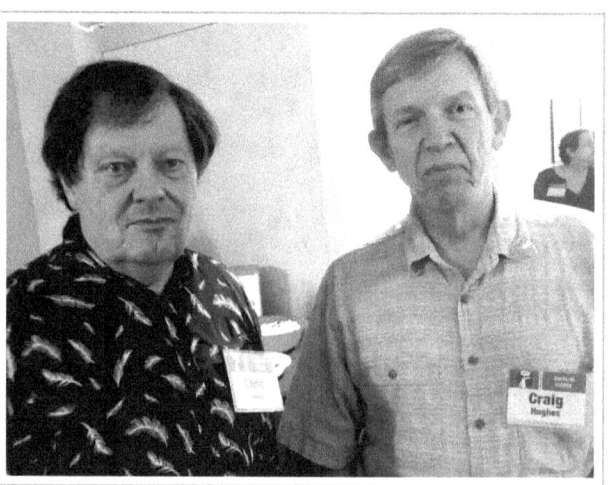
Chris Couch, Craig Hughes (SS)

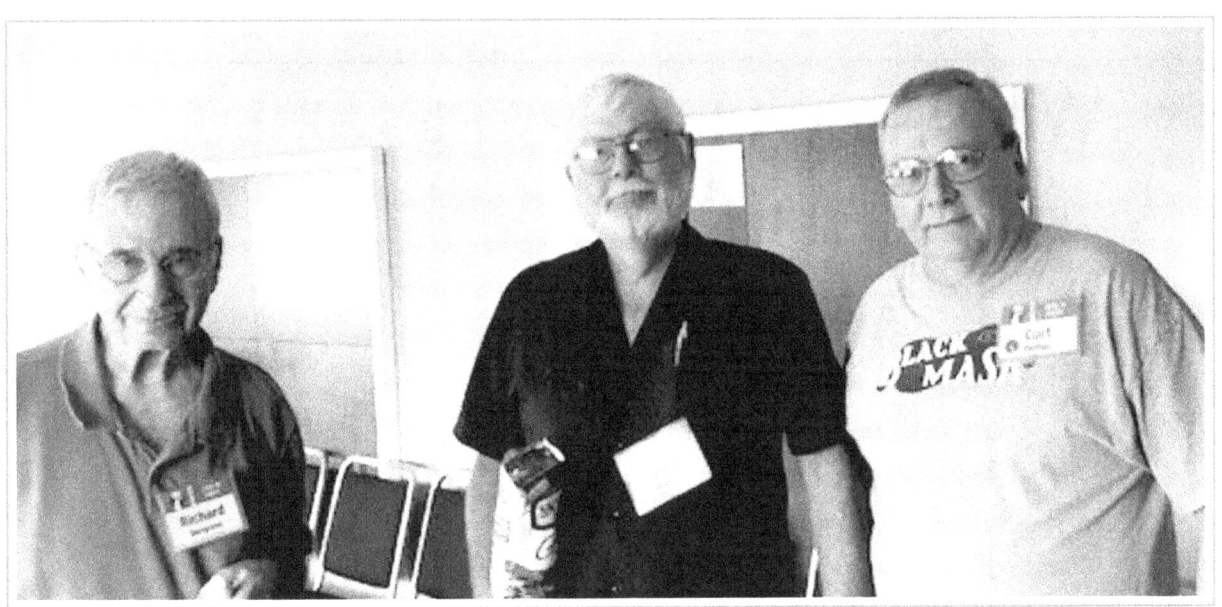

Richard Dengrove, Greg Benford, Curt Phillips (CP)

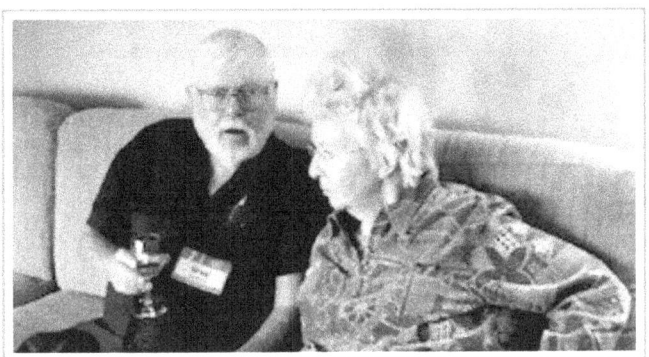

Greg Benford, *Physics Today* editor Gloria Lubkin (CP)

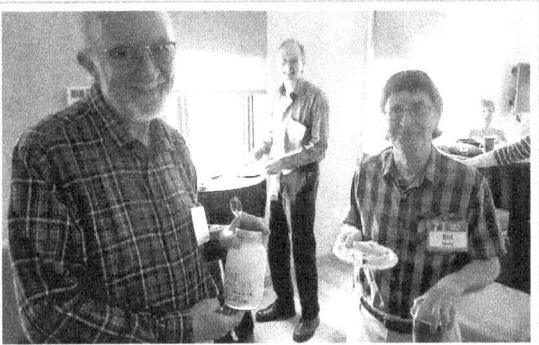

Rob Jackson, Steve Jeffery, Bill Burns (CP)

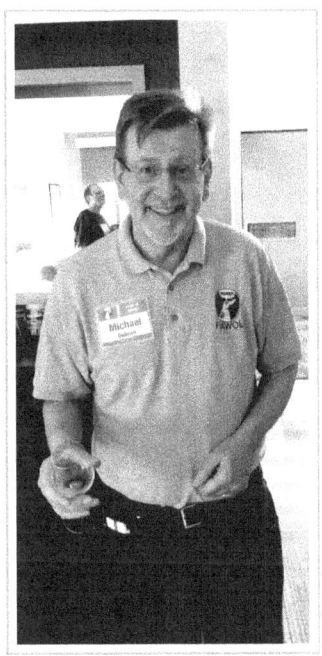

Michael Dobson (SS)

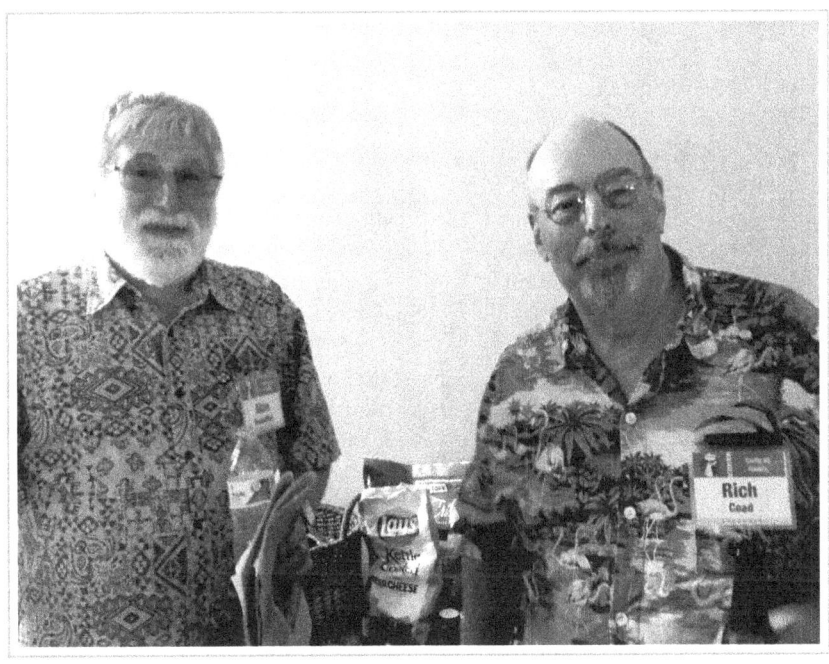

Alan Rosenthal, Rich Coad (CP)

~~Whining~~ Wining in the Consuite
Saturday 4 May 2019 — Late

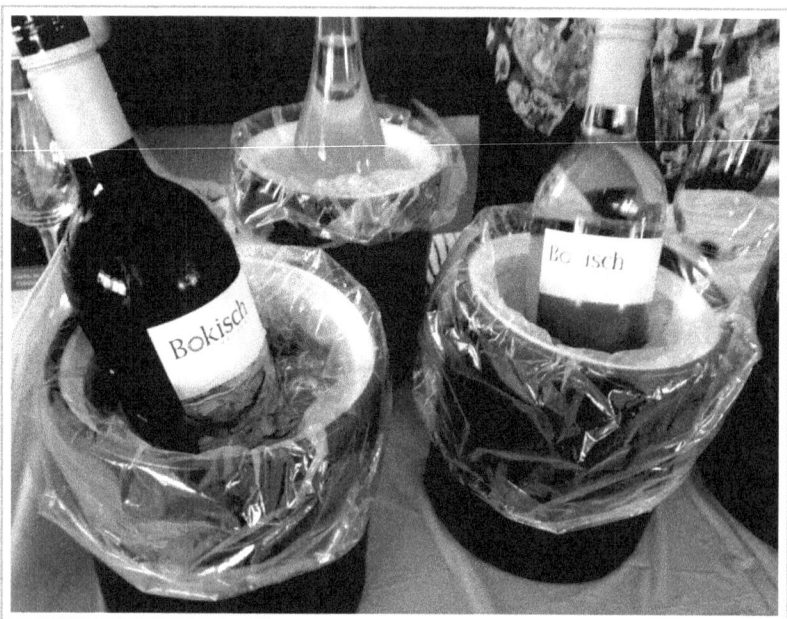

Bokisch wines for Saturday's wine tasting (IS)

Plus de vin?
by Spike

I don't know when I first discovered that Lodi, California -- yes the Lodi John Fogerty of Creedence Clearwater Revival got stuck in -- was the home of good wine. I had a clue that first time I pulled off the highway to get some lunch in Lodi, and encountered the Michael David Winery tasting room inside a cafe and farm store.

My old friend Peter was visiting the Bay Area, and of course we were on a road trip. I wanted to show him a remnant of the old Lincoln Highway, the windmills at Altamont Pass, and the farm roads and levees of the San Joachim River delta. In the good old days we would stop for pie in Lodi, Wisconsin. It seemed important to check out the pie in Lodi, California when the opportunity presented itself.*

I liked what I saw -- a big piece of flatness between Highway 99 and I-5 with a lazy river, the Mokelumne, snaking along one side, and most of the area bisected by a grid of roads, a proper grid, like farm roads where I come from. Meanwhile, fields of corn, wheat and vines were sunning themselves, and the train tracks ran north-south straight through the town. If Lodi was in Iowa or Wisconsin, it would be the county seat, a bustling farm town. But California, with its 58 counties, does things a little differently.

After doing some reading -- Lodi was once known as the "Tokay capital of the World" -- there were more trips to Lodi to try the wine with friends from near and far. Portuguese farmers were early settlers in the Lodi area, and they planted vines from their homeland, like Graciano and Touriga Nacionale. Their grand kids grew up, learned how to farm the grapes to make the best quality wine. Now they are growing the best zinfandel grapes, and they are making wine too. It's not just Robert Mondavi (a Lodi native) putting Lodi on the map.

In 2011, when the annual roving fannish wine-tasting circus called

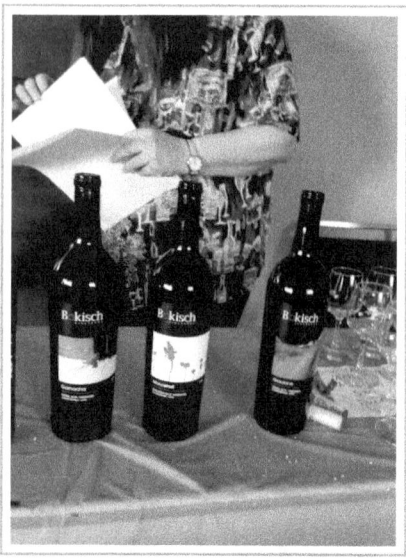

Spike with wine information (IS)

---

* Mr. Google says if you drive nonstop, it's only 30 hours from Lodi to Lodi. Something to think about.

Vintacon announced it's next destination would be Lodi, Tom and I volunteeered to help. We spent a weekend in Lodi exploring dining and wine tasting options, making notes that Tom eventually turned into a zine.

It was on that recon trip that we encountered Bokisch wines. We were checking out the meager restuarants and second hand shops of the old downtown, and stopped at a wine bar/music venue called the Cellar Door. That is where we first sampled Bokisch wine, an albarino or a garnacha blanca that had been recommended at the Wine & Visitor Center. They were building a reputation for producing Iberian (Portuguese and Spanish) varietal wines, but at that time Bokisch did not have their own tasting room.

When they finally opened a tasting room, in 2016, it was outside town at their Terra Alta Vineyard -- a beautiful spot that looks more like Iowa than Napa. I love it.

Lots of great wine is made in Lodi these days. Tom and I especially apprecate the big bodied (but in a balanced way) zinfandels from Jeremy, McCay, Klinker Brick and Fields Family Winery. Although we come for the zins, it's the unusual varietals like those offered by Bokisch that keep me bringing friends to Lodi for exploring the world of wine.

Bokisch Vineyards was named Lodi Winery of the Year for 2019. At Corflu FIAWOL, we tasted two white, one pink, and three red wines from Bokisch one evening in the consuite at Corflu FIAWOL. This is the list:

- **Albariño (Terra Alta Vineyard, 2018)**
- **Gamacha — Tempranillo Rosado (2018)**
- **Garnacha Blancha (2018)**
- **Garnacha (2016)**
- **Graciano (2016)**
- **Monastrell (2016)**

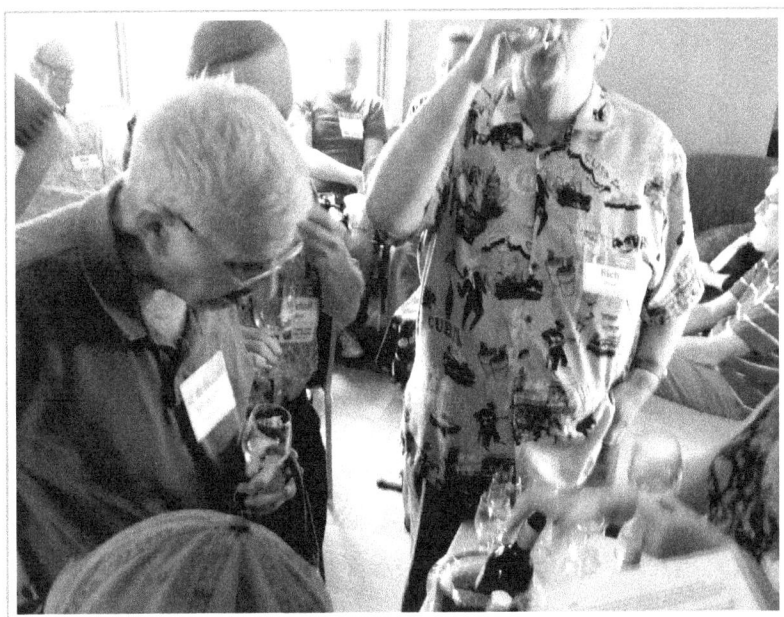

Foreground (l-r) Richard Dengrove, Michael Ward, Rich Coad. Background (l-r) Bob Crain, Jeff Schalles, Steve Stiles (IS)

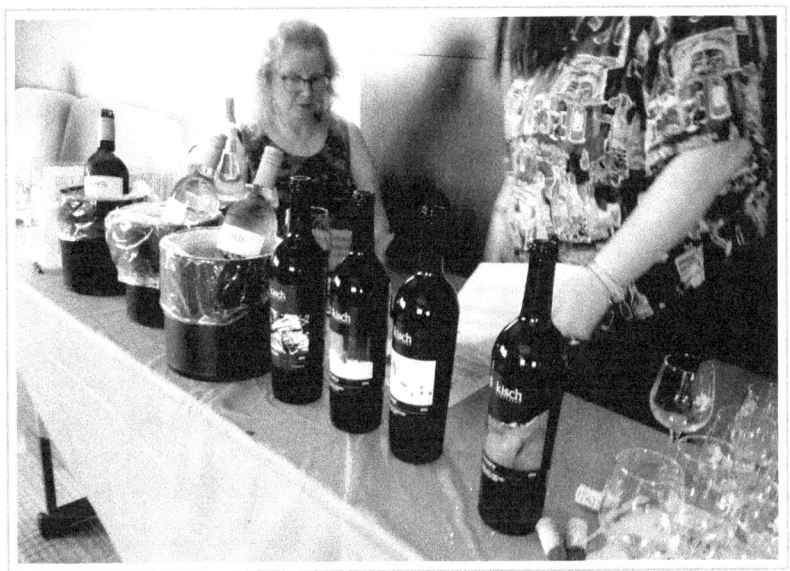

Karen Schaffer, Spike (IS)

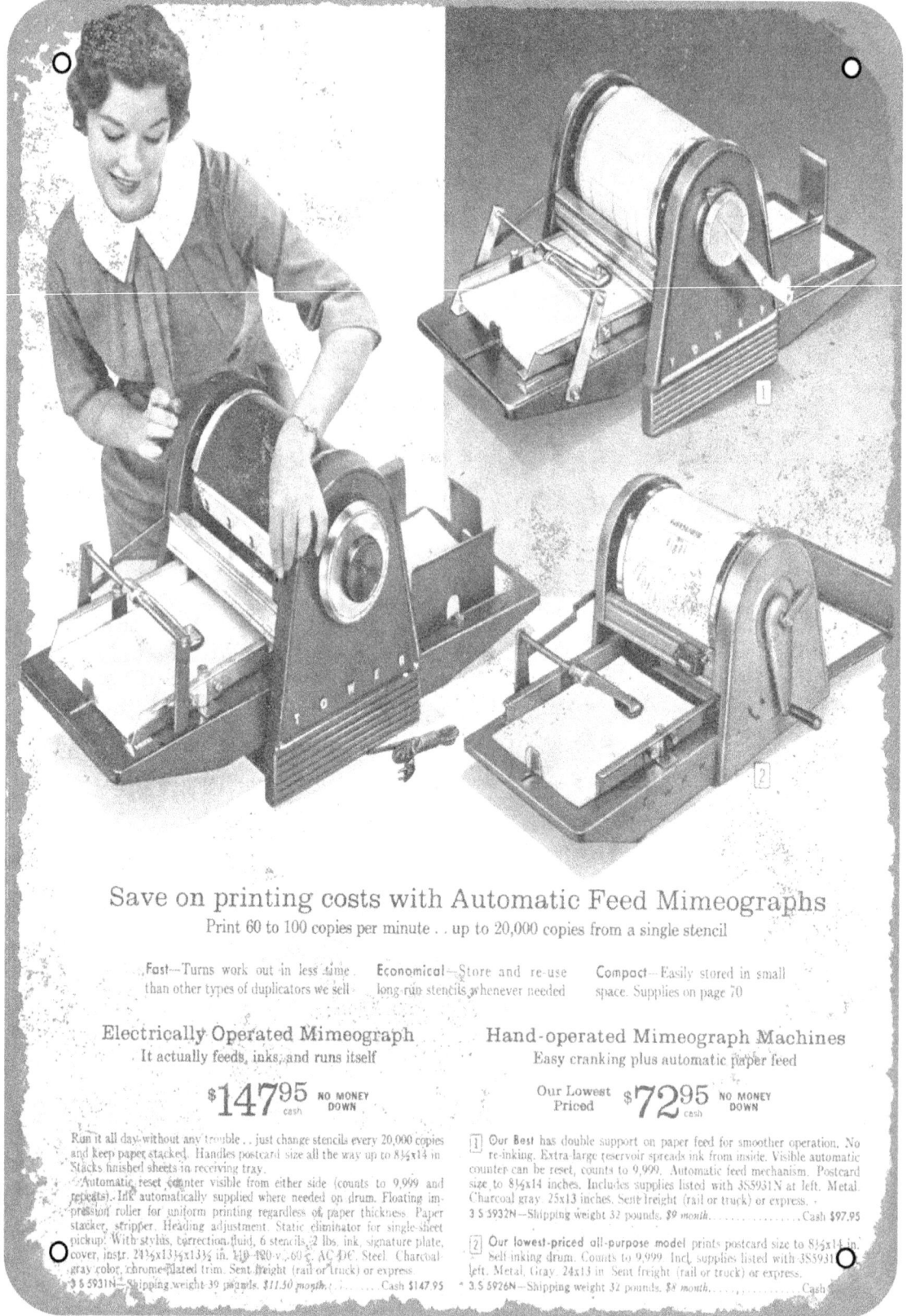

Save on printing costs with Automatic Feed Mimeographs
Print 60 to 100 copies per minute .. up to 20,000 copies from a single stencil

Fast—Turns work out in less time than other types of duplicators we sell

Economical—Store and re-use long-run stencils whenever needed

Compact—Easily stored in small space. Supplies on page 70

Electrically Operated Mimeograph
It actually feeds, inks, and runs itself

$147.95 cash NO MONEY DOWN

Run it all day without any trouble .. just change stencils every 20,000 copies and keep paper stacked. Handles postcard size all the way up to 8½x14 in. Stacks finished sheets in receiving tray.
Automatic reset counter visible from either side (counts to 9,999 and repeats). Ink automatically supplied where needed on drum. Floating impression roller for uniform printing regardless of paper thickness. Paper stacker, stripper. Heading adjustment. Static eliminator for single-sheet pickup. With stylus, correction fluid, 6 stencils, 2 lbs. ink, signature plate, cover, instr. 24½x13½x13½ in. 110-120 v., 60 c. AC-DC. Steel. Charcoal gray color, chrome-plated trim. Sent freight (rail or truck) or express.
3 S 5931N—Shipping weight 39 pounds. $11.50 month........Cash $147.95

Hand-operated Mimeograph Machines
Easy cranking plus automatic paper feed

Our Lowest Priced **$72.95** cash NO MONEY DOWN

[1] **Our Best** has double support on paper feed for smoother operation. No re-inking. Extra-large reservoir spreads ink from inside. Visible automatic counter can be reset, counts to 9,999. Automatic feed mechanism. Postcard size to 8½x14 inches. Includes supplies listed with 3S5931N at left. Metal. Charcoal gray. 25x13 inches. Sent freight (rail or truck) or express.
3 S 5932N—Shipping weight 32 pounds. $9 month.............Cash $97.95

[2] **Our lowest-priced** all-purpose model prints postcard size to 8½x14 in. Self-inking drum. Counts to 9,999. Incl. supplies listed with 3S5931N left. Metal. Gray. 24x13 in. Sent freight (rail or truck) or express.
3 S 5926N—Shipping weight 32 pounds. $8 month.............Cash

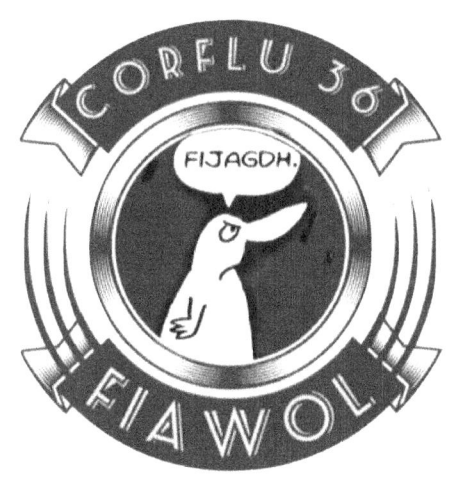

THE BANQUET

Sunday 5 May 2019
12:00 PM

The Corflu FIAWOL Banquet Programme

12 noon — Doors open

12:15p — Banquet Service begins

Menu

Appetizer:

Crottled Greeps en croute

Main course:

Egg + Spam
Egg + Bacon + Spam
Spam + Spam + Spam + Egg + Spam
Lobster Thermidor aux Crevettes with Mornay Sauce Garnished With Truffle Pate Brandy and a Fried Egg on Top + Spam

Dessert: Crottled Greeps a la Mode + Spam

Program

Welcoming remarks: Michael Dobson

Presentation of Corflu Special Awards: Michael Dobson

Presentation of FAAn Awards: Greg Benford and Curt Phillips

Presentation of the Lifetime Achievement Award: Andy Hooper

Selection of the Past President of the Fan Writers of America: Ted White

Guest of Honor Speech: Jim Benford

While the conclusion of the banquet is the official end of Corflu, the dead dogs party long into the night.

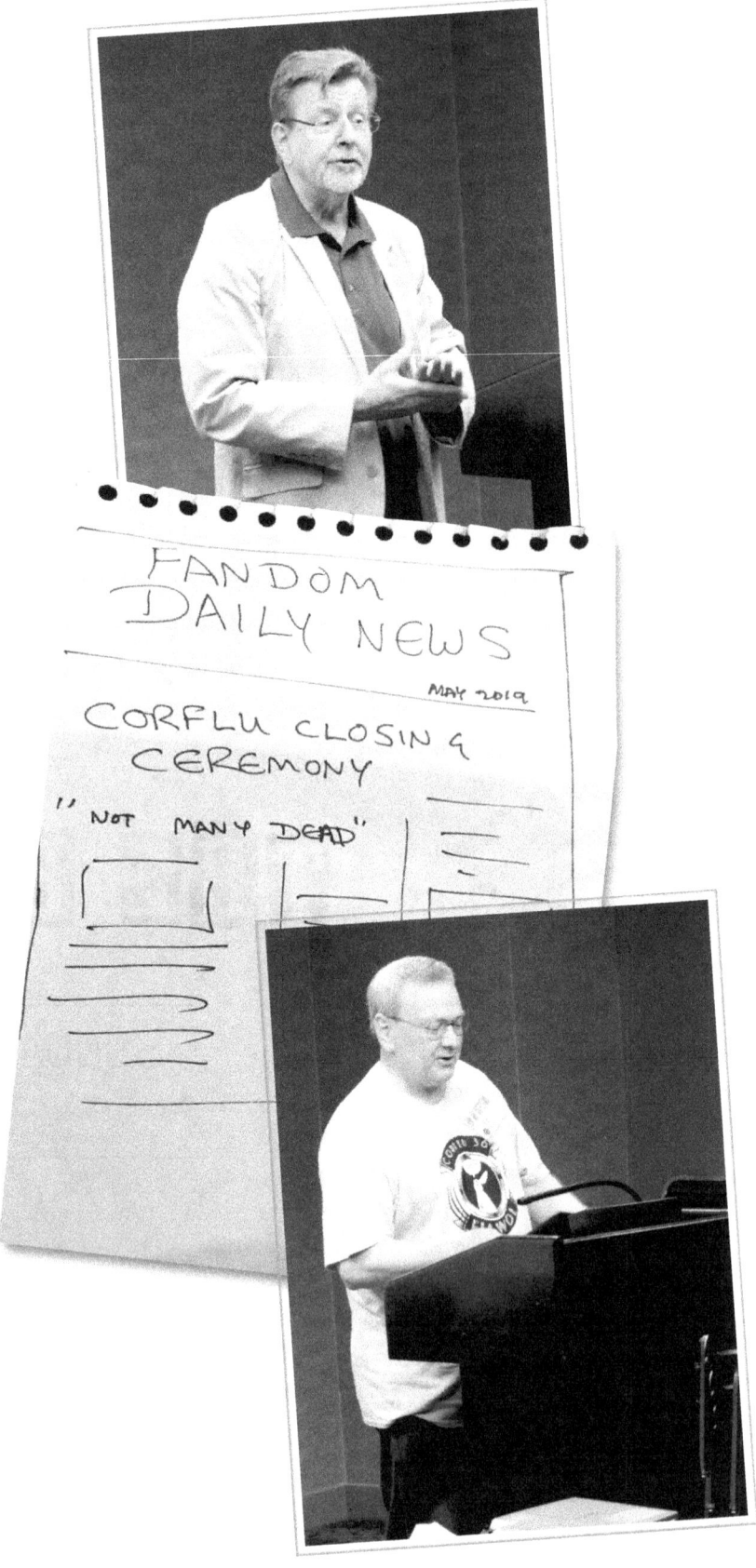

Michael Dobson, Curt Phillips (LS). Cartoon by Steve Jeffery

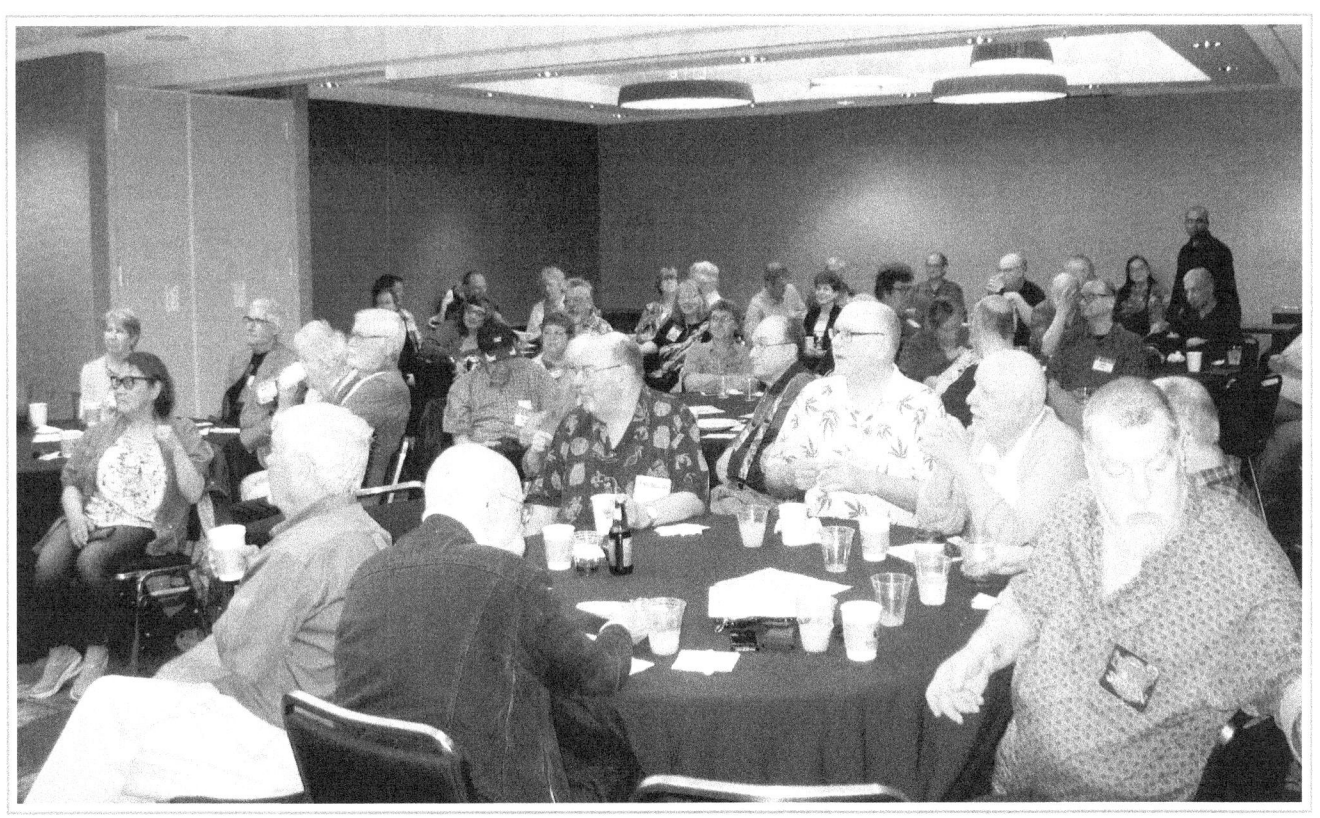
The Banquet (top SJ, bottom CP)

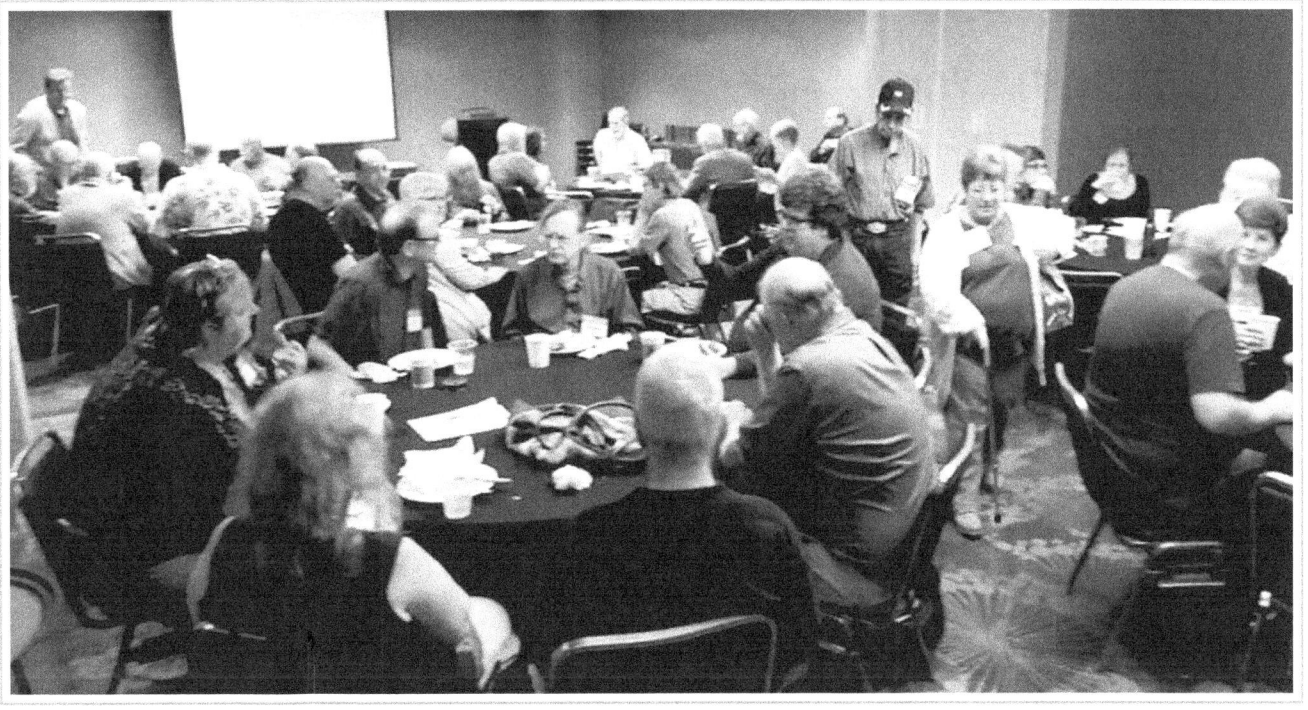

Award Winners

Corflu 50 Recipient

Selected by the Corflu 50 fund to attend that year's Corflu.

Steve Jeffery

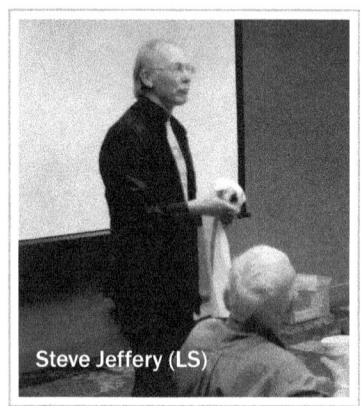

Steve Jeffery (LS)

Corflu 36 FIAWOL MVP Awards

for services to the convention above and beyond the call of fannishness

Curt Phillips

Andy Hooper

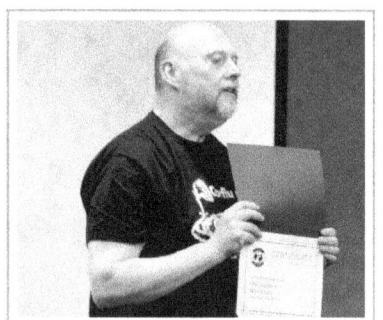

Andy Hooper (LS)

2019 FAAn Awards

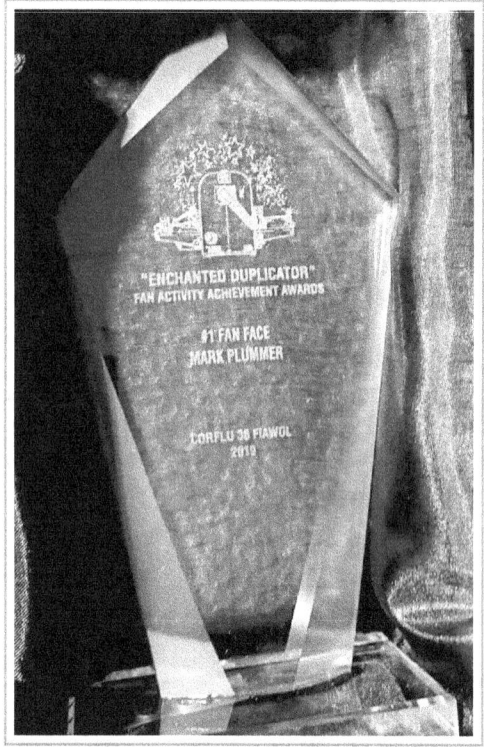

The FAAn Awards "Enchanted Duplicator" Trophy

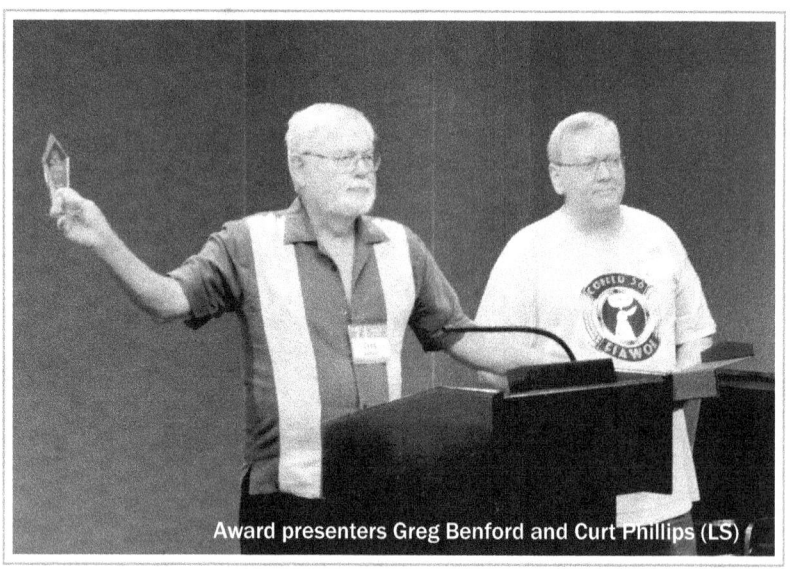

Award presenters Greg Benford and Curt Phillips (LS)

Best Fanzine

Banana Wings
Claire Brialey and Mark Plummer

2nd Place **Trap Door**
Robert Lichtman

3rd Place (tie)
Beam / Nic Farey and Ulrika O'Brien and **Ansible** / Dave Langford

Certificates

Best Genzine
Banana Wings
Claire Brialey and Mark Plummer

Best Perzine (tie)
Vibrator / Flag
Graham Charnock / Andy Hooper

Best Newszine
Ansible
Dave Langford

Best Apazine
Lofgeornost
Fred Lerner for FAPA

Best Special Publication
Lake's Folly
Christina Lake

Best Fan Writer

Mark Plummer

2nd Place **Andy Hooper**
3rd Place **Paul Skelton**

Certificates

Best Article (Fannish)
Worldcon Kaleidoscope
John-Henri Holmberg
Trap Door 34

Best Article (Sercon)
Weisinger's Worldcon
Andy Hooper, *Trap Door* 34

Best Series/Column
Roadrunner
Mark Plummer, *Banana Wings*

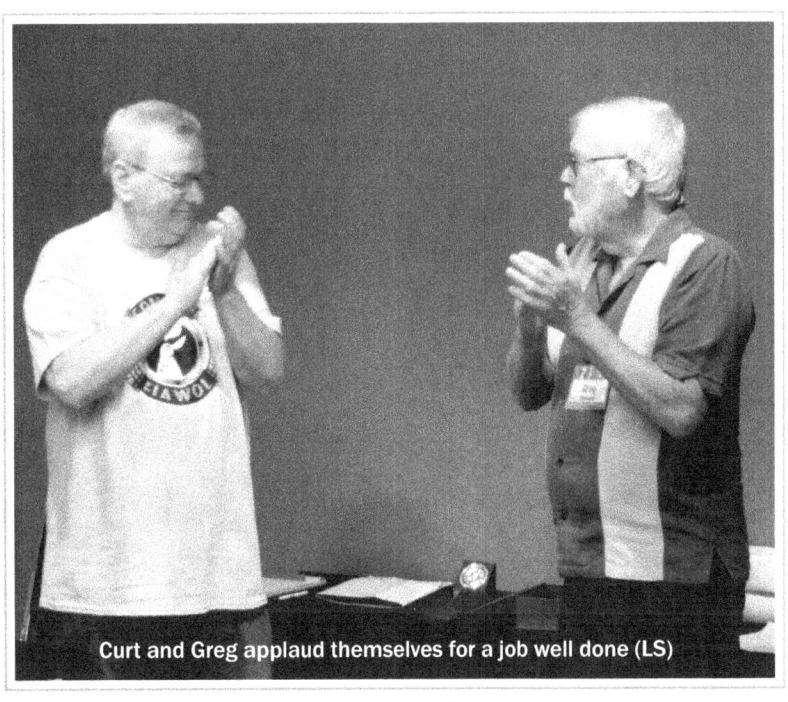
Curt and Greg applaud themselves for a job well done (LS)

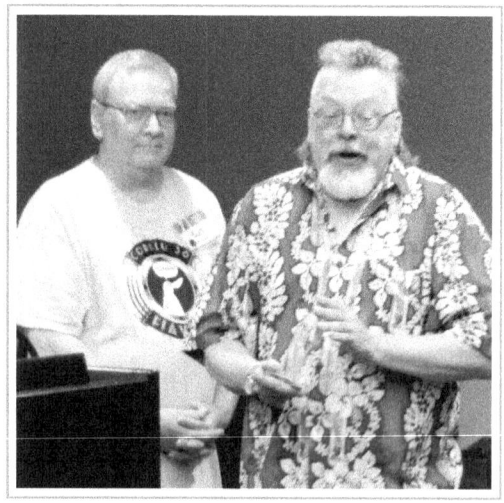
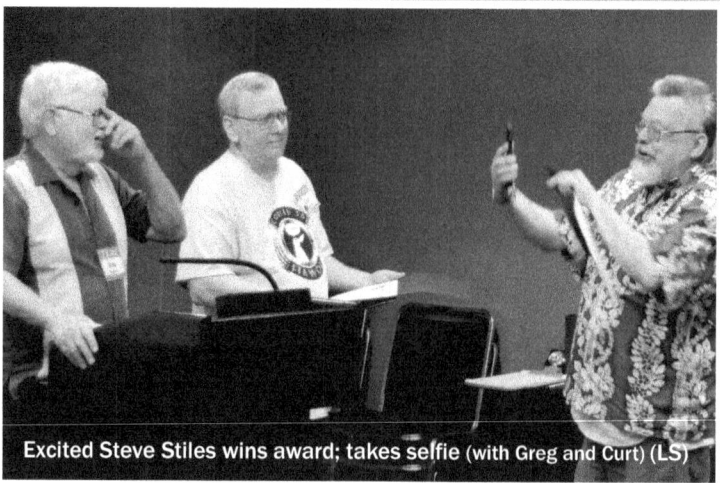

Excited Steve Stiles wins award; takes selfie (with Greg and Curt) (LS)

Harry Warner Jr. Letterhack Award

Paul Skelton

Artistic Achievement

Best Fan Artist

Alan White

2nd Place **Ditmar**

3rd Place (tie) **Brad Foster** and **Brian Parker**

Special Award for Artistic Achievement

Steve Stiles

Certificates

Best Cover (Illo)

Brian Parker

Beam 13

Best Cover (Digital/ Photography)

Geri Sullivan

The Corflu 35 Bheer Tasting Guide

Best Illustrator (Fannish)

Steve Stiles

Best Photographer

Ditmar

Best Graphic Design

Pete Young

The White Notebooks

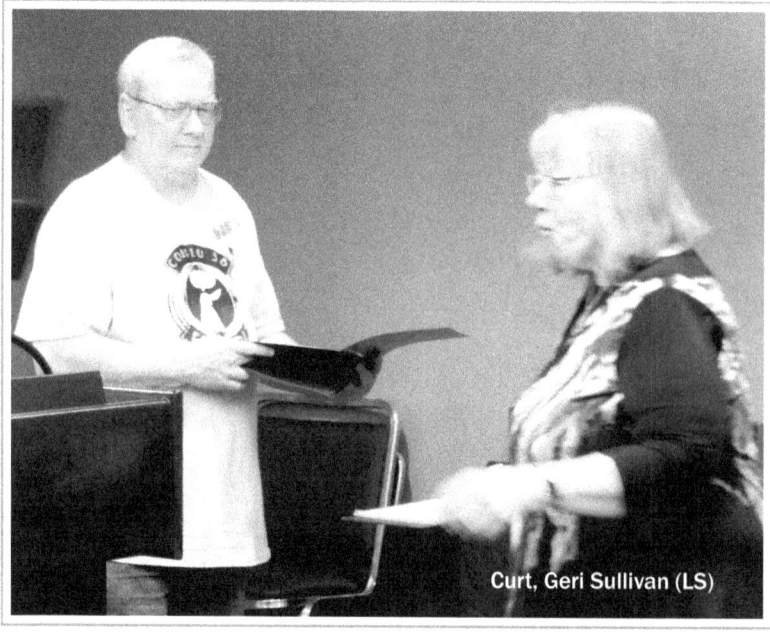

Curt, Geri Sullivan (LS)

Online Achievement

Trophy for Online Achievement

Fanac.org

2nd Place **InTheBar**
3rd Place (tie) <u>file770.com</u> and news.ansible.uk

Special Award for Online Achievement

Bill Burns for <u>efanzines.com</u>

Certificates

Best Online Archive or Resource

Fanac.org

Best News/Information Resource

news.ansible.uk

Best Group or List

InTheBar

General Fanac

#1 Fan Face

Mark Plummer

2nd Place **Dave Langford**

3rd Place **Claire Brialey**

Certificates

Services to the Hobby

Andy Hooper

Smoooth Operator (Bob Tucker Memorial Award)

Spike

Award for Unrecognized Fan Achievement

Taral Wayne

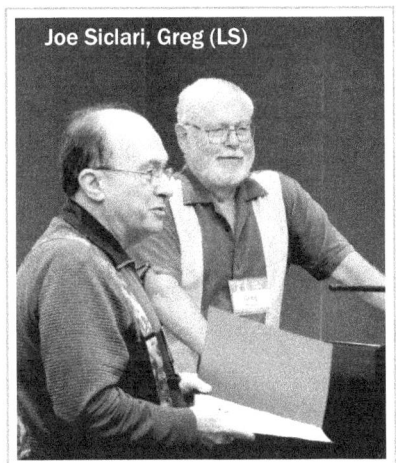
Joe Siclari, Greg (LS)

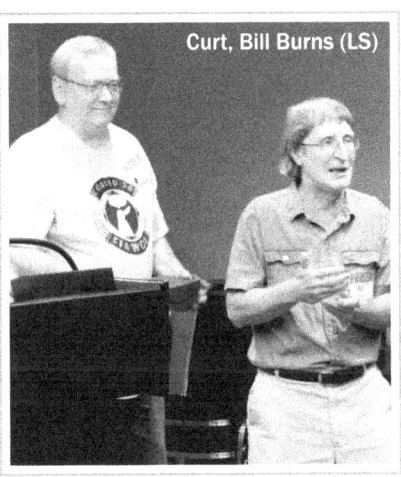
Curt, Bill Burns (LS)

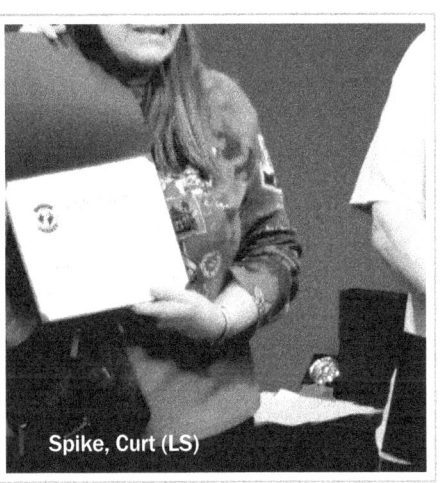
Spike, Curt (LS)

Lifetime Achievement Award

Paul Skelton

Presented by Andy Hooper

Past President, Fan Writers of America

Victor Gonzales

Presented by Ted White

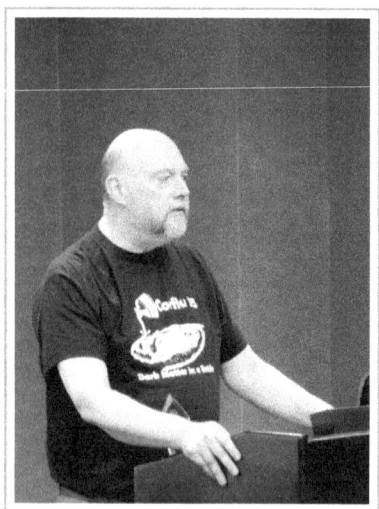

Andy Hooper presents the Lifetime Achievement Award (LS)

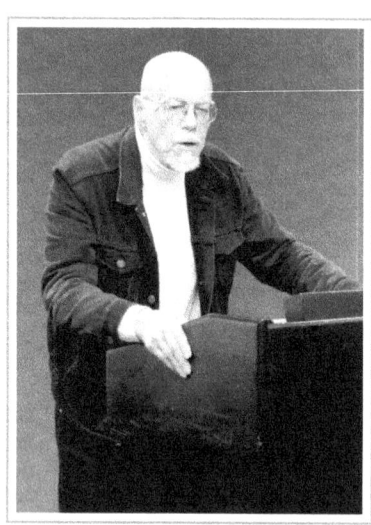

Ted White oversees selection of the Past President of fwa (LS)

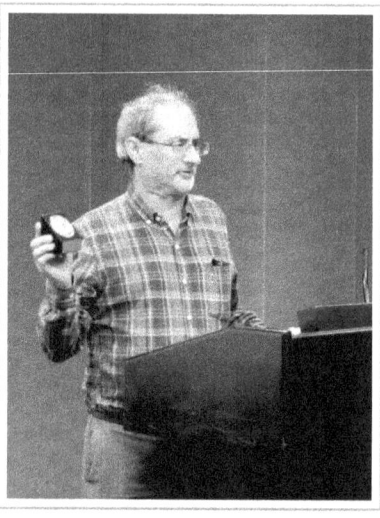

Victor Gonzales accepts his new roles and responsibilities (LS)

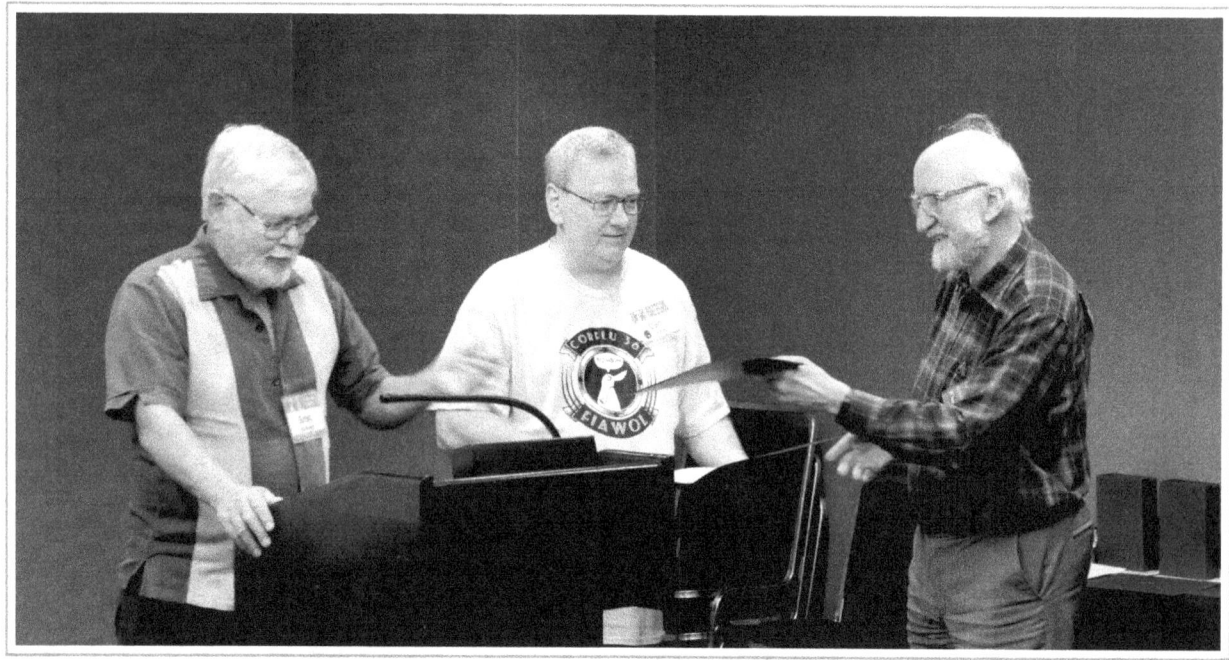

Noted fanzine sherpa Rob Jackson accepts yet another award for a British fan not in attendance (Greg, Curt, Rob) (LS)

Ad Astra via Fandom — Our First Starships
Corflu 36 FIAWOL Guest of Honor Speech
by Jim Benford

After the 13th issue of *Void*, I decided to put all my efforts into my education as a scientist. So, although I kept reading *Void* and have participated in fandom socially ever since, occasionally writing for fanzines. I did nothing to produce fanzines until five years ago when I joined FAPA. Hence I contributed my fanzine *Motley* to that steadily declining organization.

After graduate school, Greg and I undertook our separate careers. I worked in R&D and Greg went on to become a professor (he wrote some novels too). In recent years, we've begun to work together again. We're now working on all sorts of fascinating things: a new form of aero/spacecraft, figuring out what sort of beacons advanced civilizations could make, doing flight experiments using beam-driven sails, planning to use beams from Earth hitting spacecraft in orbit to propel them.

After Void

What was my life was like after my Void Boy days? Briefly, I met a wonderful woman named Hilary Foister in 1964, married her, had two children and am still happily married 53 years later. My major hobby is gardening and I still read science fiction.

After I got my PhD in 1969, I worked for 26 years for Physics International (PI). What attracted me to the company was that they had invented a new technology that could produce incredibly intense beams of both electrons and protons. That enabled an entirely new research area, and my instinct was to explore new things rather than work on details of established topics.

This turned out to be a great decision. Over the years I was able to do fascinating experiments that revealed many properties of the beams and contributed to their applications, such as particle beams for the nuclear fusion research, particle beams for producing intense effects in materials, and most prominently in the generation of intense pulses of microwaves.

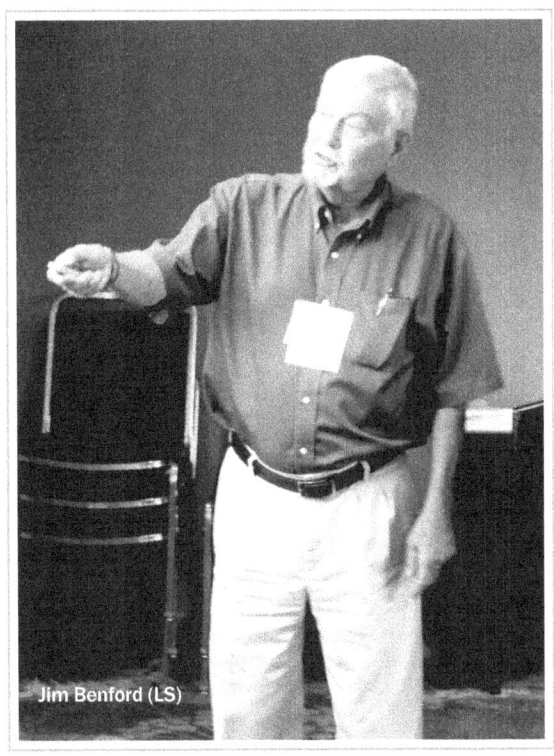
Jim Benford (LS)

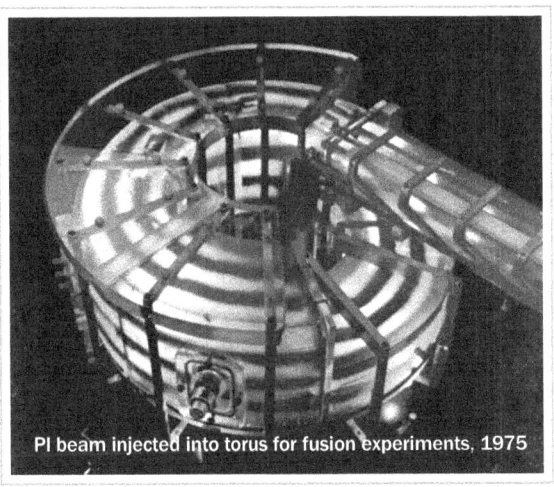
PI beam injected into torus for fusion experiments, 1975

The early *Void* was essential to my development as well as being a lot of fun. I learned many skills in producing ishes on schedule. Later, I used those skills to produce proposals and reports at PI. Compared to fanzines, that was easy. In fact, it had a real impact on my career. Being able to integrate a collection of documents into a coherent whole was one cause of my rapid advancement in research.

To make a long story short, in 1983 I established a high-power microwave division of PI and invented quite a few new devices. After this I realized I had all the skills I needed to go out of my own and pursue my own interests and therefore I retired from PI at 55, the first of my several retirements.

My new company, Microwave Sciences, has been a great success, enabling me to do a large variety of activities which you can see my website, jamesbenford.com. There are also quite a lot of photos and technical papers available there for those of you who want to pursue such aspects.

Researching Starships

The major thing I did in Microwave Sciences was to demonstrate Bob Forward's concept for starships: beam-driven sails. With NASA funding, using equipment at JPL, my team was able to for the first time to fly sails driven by a microwave beam in a vacuum chamber. At JPL in 2000 we achieved accelerations of 13 gees. To date, no one's been able to do better than that.

It was that achievement and subsequent theoretical papers I wrote about beam-driven sails that made the billionaire Yuri Milner hire me in 2016 at the start of his Starshot project. My role there is to be a technical advisor at a fixed stipend. The program is moving Forward, pun intended, and has achieved milestones. Beam-driven sails remains the only practical way of sending probes to the nearby stars.

The Starshot program is ambitious on an astronomical scale: a sail of about 5-m diameter and weighing only a few grams would be accelerated that 30,000 gees by lasers of 10's of billions of watts power to a speed of 20% of the speed of light. The technical challenges constitute a long list: how to build billion watt lasers, how to keep the sail riding on the

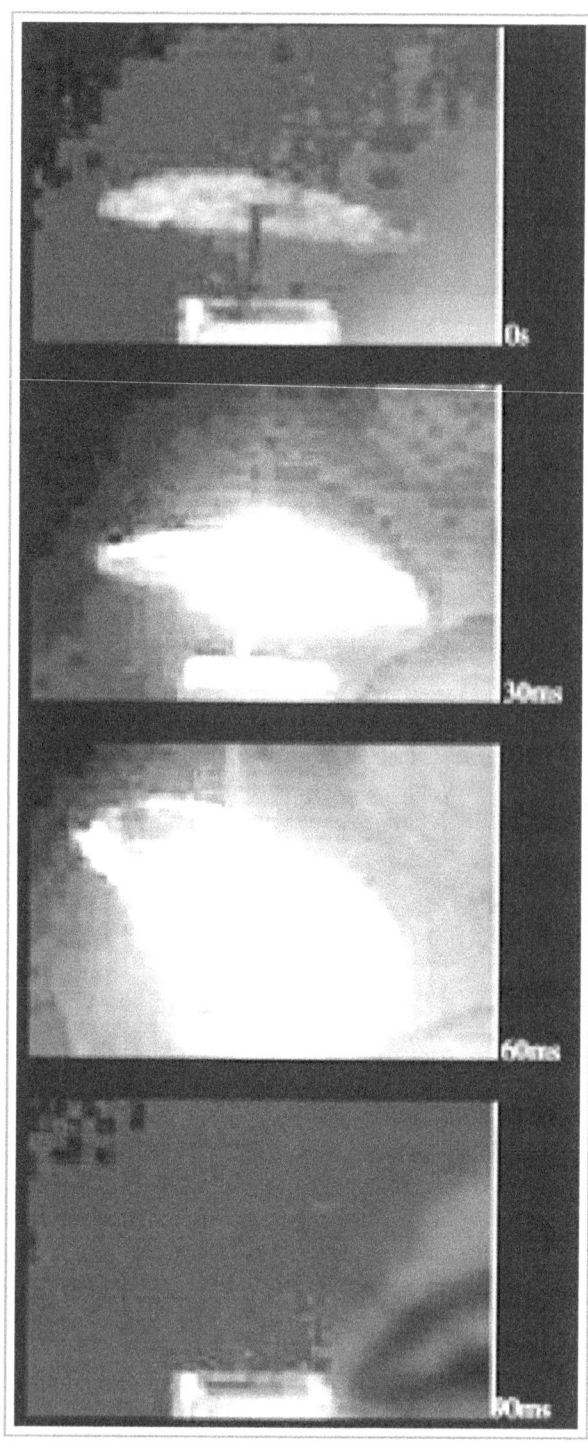

Carbon sail lifting off of rectangular waveguide under 10 kW microwave power (four frames, first at top). Sail before beam onset, at onset, begins liftoff, gone. Frame interval is 30 msec.

beam stably, how to have a sail of materials that absorb so little that it does not overheat, how to maintain operation of the sail over interstellar distances where it will be impacted by dust grains (probable answer: turn the sail sideways), how to take data in a fast flyby of alien planets. And finally: how to return that data to Earth with very little power on the sailcraft.

In my talk, I included a lot of technical information. If you want to hear that part of my talk go listen to it at this site, where it starts at 1hour, 56 minutes:

https://www.youtube.com/watch?v=l0yHFIh6sFg

Although it's early days in this Starshot program, we are increasingly optimistic that we can solve these problems and keep the price of building the system below $10 billion, which is the upper bound that Yuri has set on the capital cost.

So, if the R&D program is successful, in 20 years we will have the prototype Beamer and be launching sails across the solar system. In 30 years we will launch to the stars themselves. In fifty years the first probes begin to sail into alien star systems.

Conclusion

Thinking back over 60 years, when I stopped being a *Void* editor and decided to concentrate on physics, I have this feeling: I wonder what my earlier self would have thought of this now-

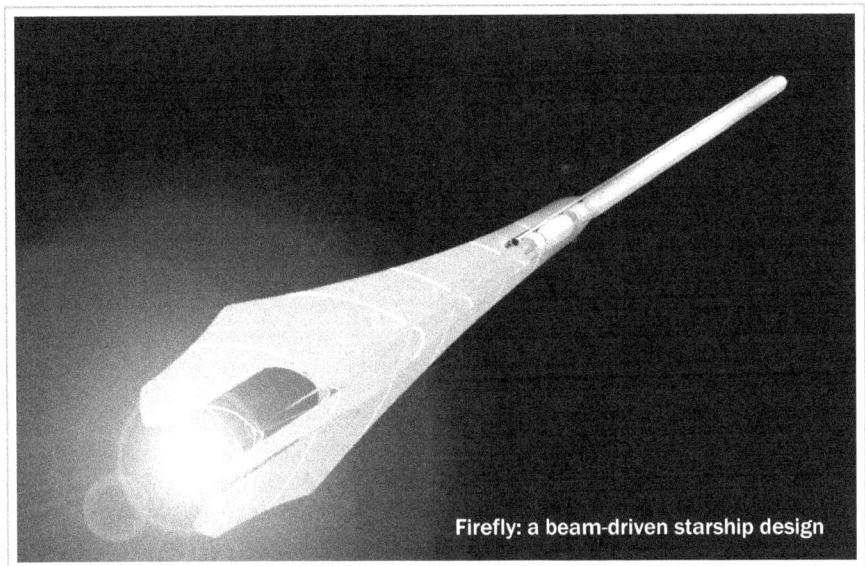

Firefly: a beam-driven starship design

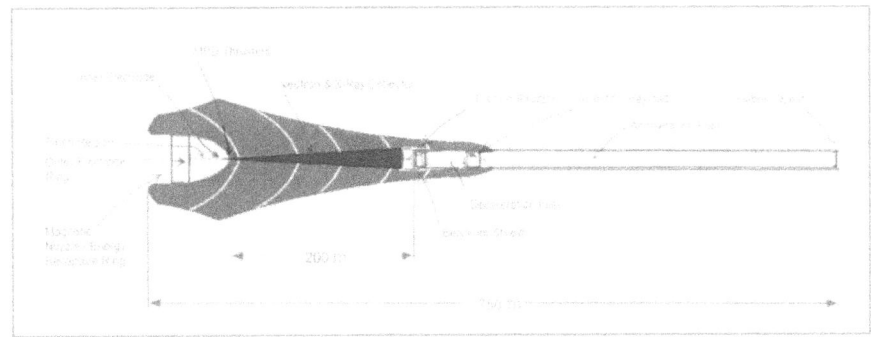

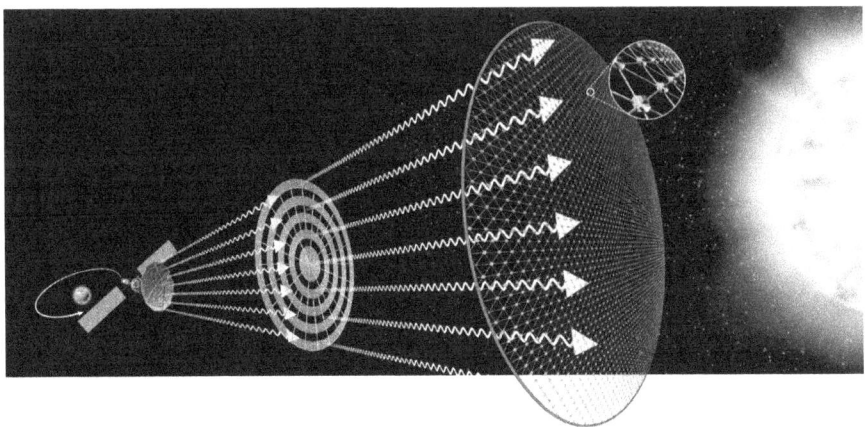

real future? If my self at that time had known that 60 years later he'd be working on the first starships, I think he would be very pleased. I expect it would've seemed quite fantastic, and I think that earlier self would be quite pleased with what I have become.

And today I'm very pleased to be doing something truly science fictional.

— Jim Benford

Sunday Corflu Comments by Various

Rob Jackson

This morning, Curt, Pat V and I had a brief worry about the honesty box which the night before had had plenty of $$$ in and was now empty, but thankfully Michael D had removed it late the previous night for safe keeping.

As the Banquet this time was starting at 12 midday rather than 11, which made it definitely an early lunch rather than a brunch, I had a bit more time to write up stuff about yesterday before the memories faded.

Although it was later than usual, it was still the same sort of brunch banquet fare as at most US Corflus. The food was competent but not outstanding. The Banquet and Awards Ceremony are safely online, and the multiplicity of new awards mingling with the traditional major ones were both efficiently announced (by Greg Benford with assistance from Michael D and Curt Phillips) and well received by the audience.

Elaine Stiles

Most of the banquet food was cold.

Bill Burns

Almost all of the extra awards were greeted with enthusiasm by the attendees. And Spike was very close to tears on receiving the "Smooooth Operator" award, whose description is "In memory of Bob Tucker. Someone you particularly enjoy hanging out with at cons, known for good conversation and a cheerful disposition, or known for excellent gossip ("If you can't find something nice to say about someone, come sit by me.")

Pat Charnock

And, in fact, a lot of the awards went to members of ItB. So well done, all of you!

And a few of them were Brits. Rob J is going to be lugging a lot of stuff home with him.

Rob Jackson

Half of them were for Fishlifters, so S&ra will be taking their stuff. She works within a mile of Fishlifterland.

And as the Skeltons are in Toronto or soon will be, with Susan Manchester, Murray will take Skel's stuff.

Graham Charnock

My favourite comment by Greg Benford on asking who was running the next Corflu and being told it was John Purcell, was "Oh, I thought he had more sense."

Steve Jeffery

Despite being reassured by various people that the only obligation of the Corflu 50 delegate was to show up and have a good time, Curt had other ideas. Every time we passed in a doorway or corridor he would up the ante. From "Have you written your Corflu 50 speech yet?" it became a presentation slideshow ("Our Mission Statement is to drink interesting beers and wines until I start talking incomprehensibly and

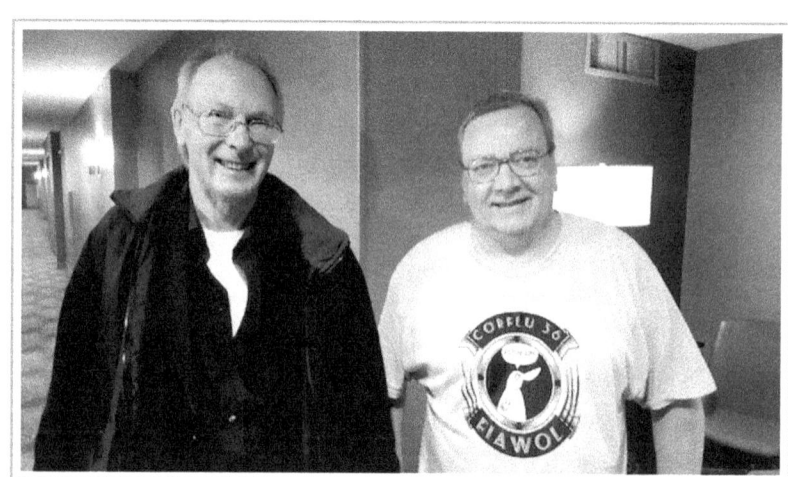

Curt Phillips (right) pesters Steve Jeffery (left) about his Corflu 50 presentation (RJ)

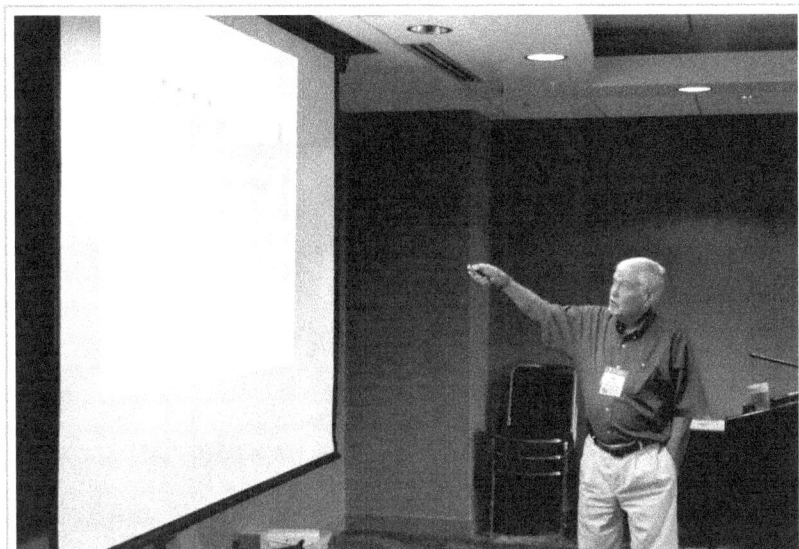
Jim Benford's GoH Speech (LS)

fall over, but not necessarily in that order") to a performance piece in the medium of interpretive dance.

By Sunday morning I fully expected to be composing and conducting a grand opera, complete with sets and working stage machinery. I have actually done the latter before, though with rather more than a day's preparation (where do you buy stage flats in Rockville – a town that seems to consist almost entirely of restaurants?) As for singing, all I can say is that it would probably serve to clear a room as quickly as a fire alarm and with about as much musical range.

In the end, after having hastily scribbled a couple of pages of notes in the half hour before the banquet, I just got up and mumbled my way through a briefly truncated handful of 'thank you's to everyone before sitting down, which seemed to go down as well as anything, although I'm sure Curt was wondering when the Busby Berkeley chorus line and performing seals were going to come on before being enveloped in a sea of dry ice and fireworks.

Sandra Bond

Jim Benford's speech was more learned than Gregg Trend's, but about as long, and the absence of a microphone plus my lack of physics knowledge (I flunked my 'ignoramus' test) made me glad to finally escape upstairs for the group photo. The lounge where this was meant to occur contained two hotel guests one of whom was holding a pair of carved wooden tongs, shaped like... yeah. A fish.

"I know someone who'd really like those," said Carrie Root pointedly, but they shrank away from her blandishments; so Mark and Claire will have to content themselves with the usual shelf full of awards, instead.

Claire Brialey

We will try to console ourselves with those. Well, mostly Mark can console himself and I'll bask in the reflected glory.

And thanks very much for bringing them back, S&ra; it gives us yet another excuse to meet up with you for dinner/drinks etc.

Just watched *Just A Minac* on Rob's YouTube channel. I laughed aloud quite often. Kudos to all involved!

Rob Jackson

Thanks, Claire. I suppose I'd better get into practice at not umming and ahh'ing, as S&ra says she wants me to reprise my Derek Nimmo act sometime. However I suspect that will remain my Achilles heel.

Sadly Sunday's weather was expected to be dreary with rain till about 6 pm, which means the local arts festival this weekend – on-street stalls mainly featuring paintings, photo prints, jewellery and other craftwork – would be a washout for today. That would have been a nice thing to do after the Banquet.

The festival was still there, and it had some attendees while there was a brief gap in the rain, but I went out just as the rain restarted. I did buy a rather lovely photographic print of the Milky Way superimposed on an American rural dusk scene from a guy who runs a website called Dark Sky Art, featuring some lovely astronomy photos, but that was the one bright spot in a very bedraggled set of stalls whose owners were doing their best to pack up without getting their unsold wares too wet.

❖❖❖

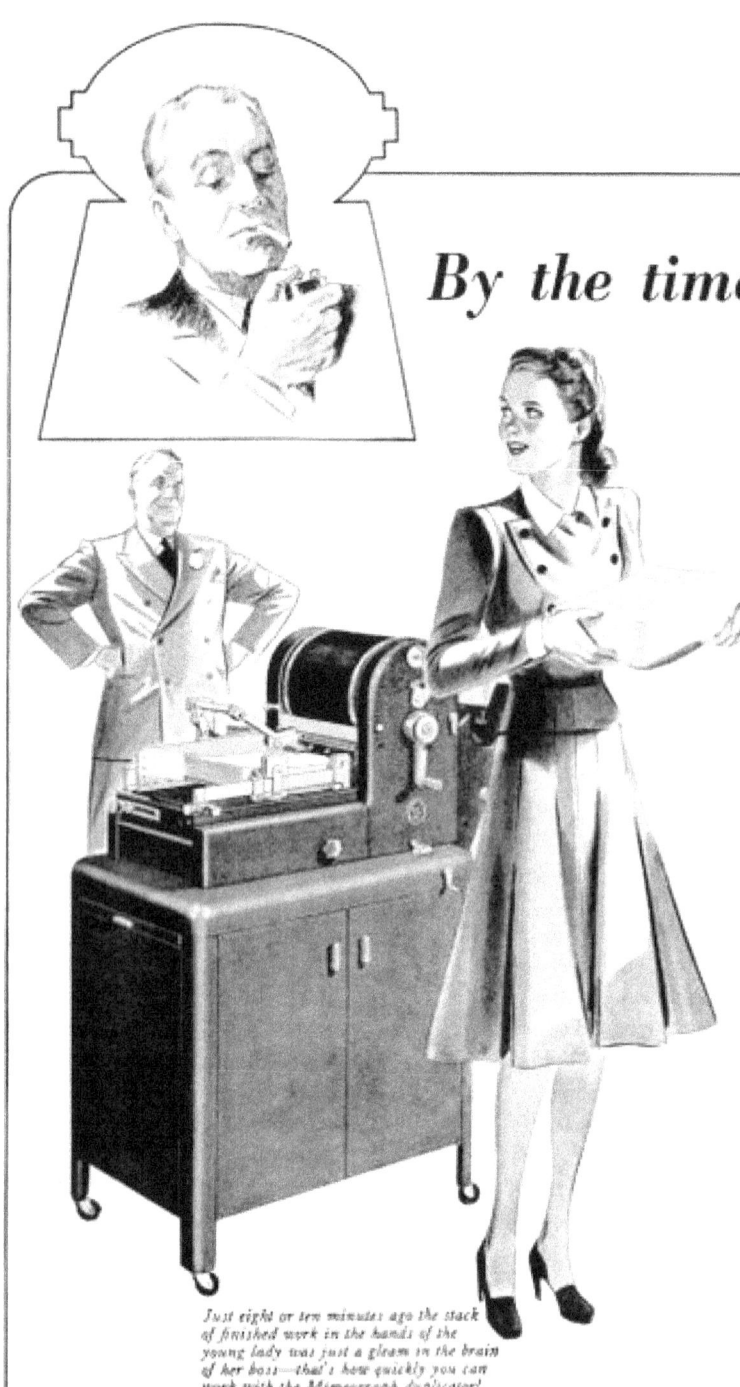

By the time you've smoked a cigarette.......

the Mimeograph duplicator could get out 500 copies of something to make and/or save you money

Those copies might be product announcements that would launch 500 sales... or simplified accounting forms that would save 500 pennies every day. You get out such things with the Mimeograph duplicator without detours, and with pride in their looks.

A simple survey would bring to light a lot more problems it could serve too.

There's now a complete family of Mimeograph duplicators in four price brackets... They are the culmination of a four-year program of modernization, which more than ever makes them the world's standard of office duplication.

They are streamlined in looks, streamlined in engineering, streamlined to make and/or save money for your business. Get the full story from the local Mimeograph distributor listed in your 'phone book. A. B. Dick Company, Chicago.

Just eight or ten minutes ago the stack of finished work in the hands of the young lady was just a gleam in the brain of her boss—that's how quickly you can work with the Mimeograph duplicator!

Mimeograph

MIMEOGRAPH is the trade-mark of A. B. Dick Company, Chicago, registered in the U. S. Patent Office

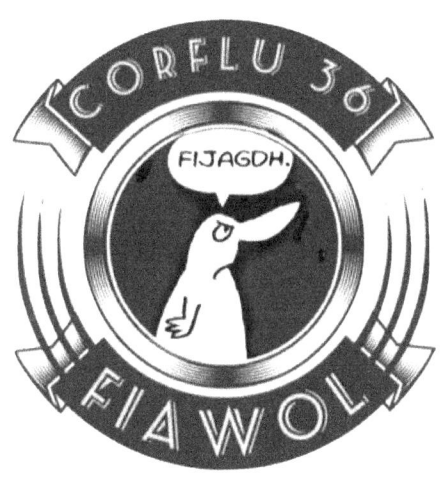

AFTERMATH

Monday 6 May 2019

A PERFECT DAY IN THE BLOODY LANE
PAYING OUR RESPECTS IN HAGERSTOWN AND THE FIELD OF THE ANTIETAM

by Andy Hooper

Originally published in Captain Flashback 7*, June 2019; reprinted with permission. It has been edited for length.*

For the last several years, Carrie and I have enjoyed a special excursion on the Monday following the end of Corflu, the annual convention for fanzine fans. This year, we had a unique opportunity, as the convention's site at Rockville Maryland was less than 50 miles away from several of the most important battle sites of the War of Independence, the War of 1812 and the American Civil War. The Civil War sites included two of the biggest monuments, at Gettysburg and Antietam Creek, which is just outside Sharpsburg, Maryland.

The Antietam National Battlefield is also very close to the town of Hagerstown, Maryland, famous in science fiction fandom as the home of the late Harry Warner Jr. (1922-2003), who was a fanzine publisher, a fan historian and one of fandom's most faithful and prolific correspondents. Harry was a lifetime resident of Hagerstown, a longtime employee of the Hagerstown *Sun* newspaper, and was known for his steadfast refusal to travel to meet the rest of science fiction fandom face to face, always preferring to know us through the mail. The chance to pay a visit to Harry's former home at 423 Summit Avenue made it easy to choose Antietam over Gettysburg this time, and the select group of convention members interested in a post-convention excursion readily agreed.

The Traveling Jiants

I enjoy writing about the day after Corflu, because it is so much easier to keep track of what happens than during the actual con. Corflu is somewhat like a bar fight for me; while it's happening, I am far too busy to make notes or otherwise prepare to write an accurate con report. I spent the first 36 hours preparing for and conducting the fanzine auction this year, and had conversations with several dozen people, all of them recalled in a dim glitter of fragments.

After this glorious 72-hour scrum, I was glad that the cast of characters had been brought down to a

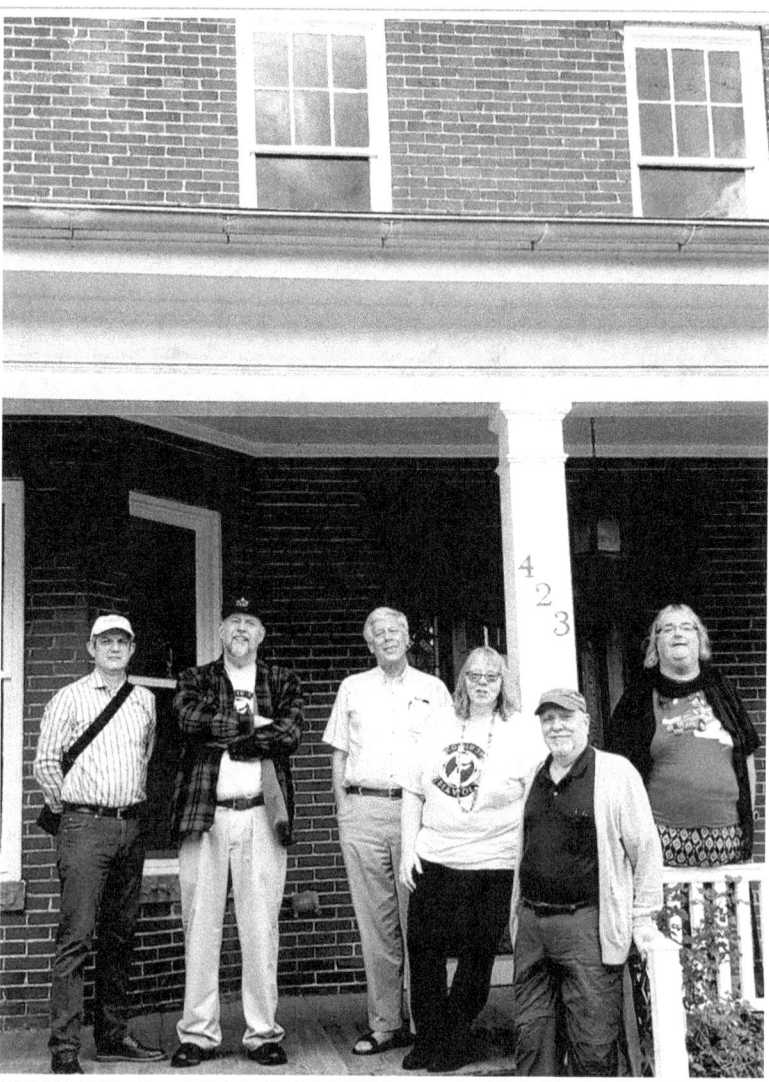

Harry Warner Jr.'s home at 423 Summit Avenue, Hagerstown. Left to right: Nigel Rowe, Andy Hooper, Mark Olson, Geri Sullivan, Grant Canfield, Sandra Bond (CR)

sensible seven: Carrie and I had Grant Canfield in our car, while Sandra Bond had Nigel Rowe as her passenger. Geri Sullivan, who planned to drive to some distant location – Minneapolis? Buffalo? Ohio? – immediately after our tour — was in her own car. And Mark and Priscilla Olson faithfully followed us, despite the understandable inclination to make their drive home while daylight persisted.

I was frankly quite stunned by how close we came to actually meeting in the hotel lobby at 9:30 am, and were indeed on the road to Hagerstown within five or ten minutes of 10:00 am. I think some of those present – Geri and Nigel for certain, and likely Sandra and Carrie too, were feeling some effects of the previous evening's beverages. But the incredible sunny weather made it difficult to feel too low, after the very soggy conditions which had prevailed for most of the weekend. I had fears that the rain might persist, making all unpaved surfaces a bog; but the sun and light breezes made the day perfect for the exertion of walking, and dried the ground out as we made our way to Hagerstown.

The big early-20th Century house at 423 Summit Avenue is currently for sale, and signs posted on the front door suggest that it may have been occupied by some unauthorized residents in the years since Harry's death. Harry left his property to his church, and I believe someone rented the home in the years soon after he died. It looked like it might want some work, particularly electrical, before anyone would want to live in it now.

We tried to be discreet, but the fact that the place was empty was emboldening, and we trooped over the front and back porches and around the back yard. I believe Geri had been there before, and commented on how much larger the spaces were without Harry's stuff crammed into them. We could not see the famous attic where Harry did all of his fan activity, but I was struck by the proliferation of porches, upon which fans visiting Harry in the 1940s had slept. I could ask Curt Phillips to ask Bob Madle where he and Art Widner and Milton Rothman and Julius Unger slept during their early stopover on the way to the Denver World SF Convention in the twilight Indian summer of 1941; but I doubt he would recall if it was the wraparound first floor porch at the front and side of the house, or the smaller balconies outside the bedrooms on the back of the house where they grabbed what sleep they could before setting off west in the morning.

The Best Crab Quesadilla in Hagerstown

After no doubt prompting many of the neighbors to wonder what we were up to, we repaired to the Hagerstown Family Diner to fortify ourselves before departing for the Antietam Battlefield. The conversation wove between Harry Warner and his times, and the events of 1862, which led the Union and Confederate armies to collide in an obscure location in Western Maryland. The food was mostly quite adequate, although what moved three of us to order crab quesadillas is still mysterious to me. The soup was the best part.

I talked a bit about General George McClellan and his effort to make raw Union troops into an actual army, and his frustration in trying to actually use that army on the battlefield in 1862. A new Confederate commander, the dashing Robert E. Lee, was determined to bring the war onto Northern territory, and possibly wrestle the pro-slavery state of Maryland into joining the Confederacy. In September, he marched his army into the quiet farm fields across the Potomac River from Virginia. But appallingly, a dropped copy of his orders for the campaign was discovered

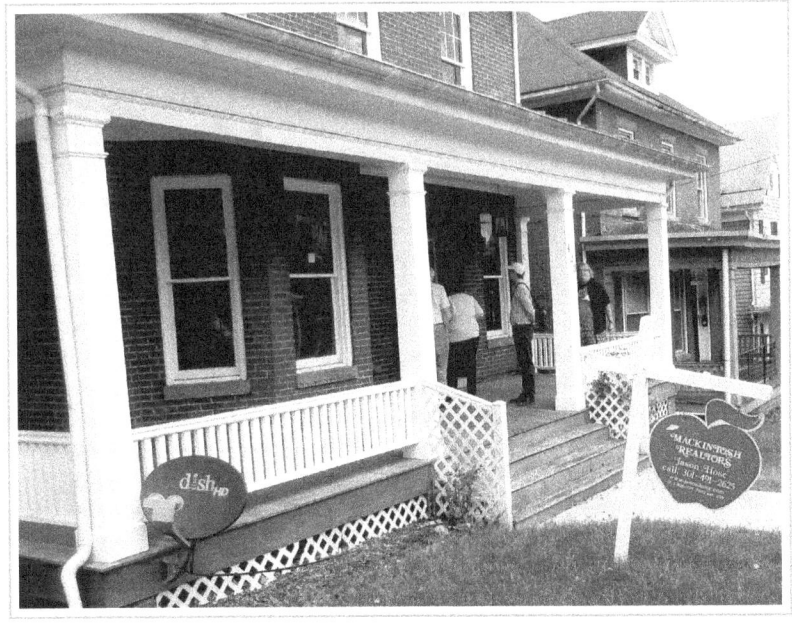

Another view of 423 Summit Avenue

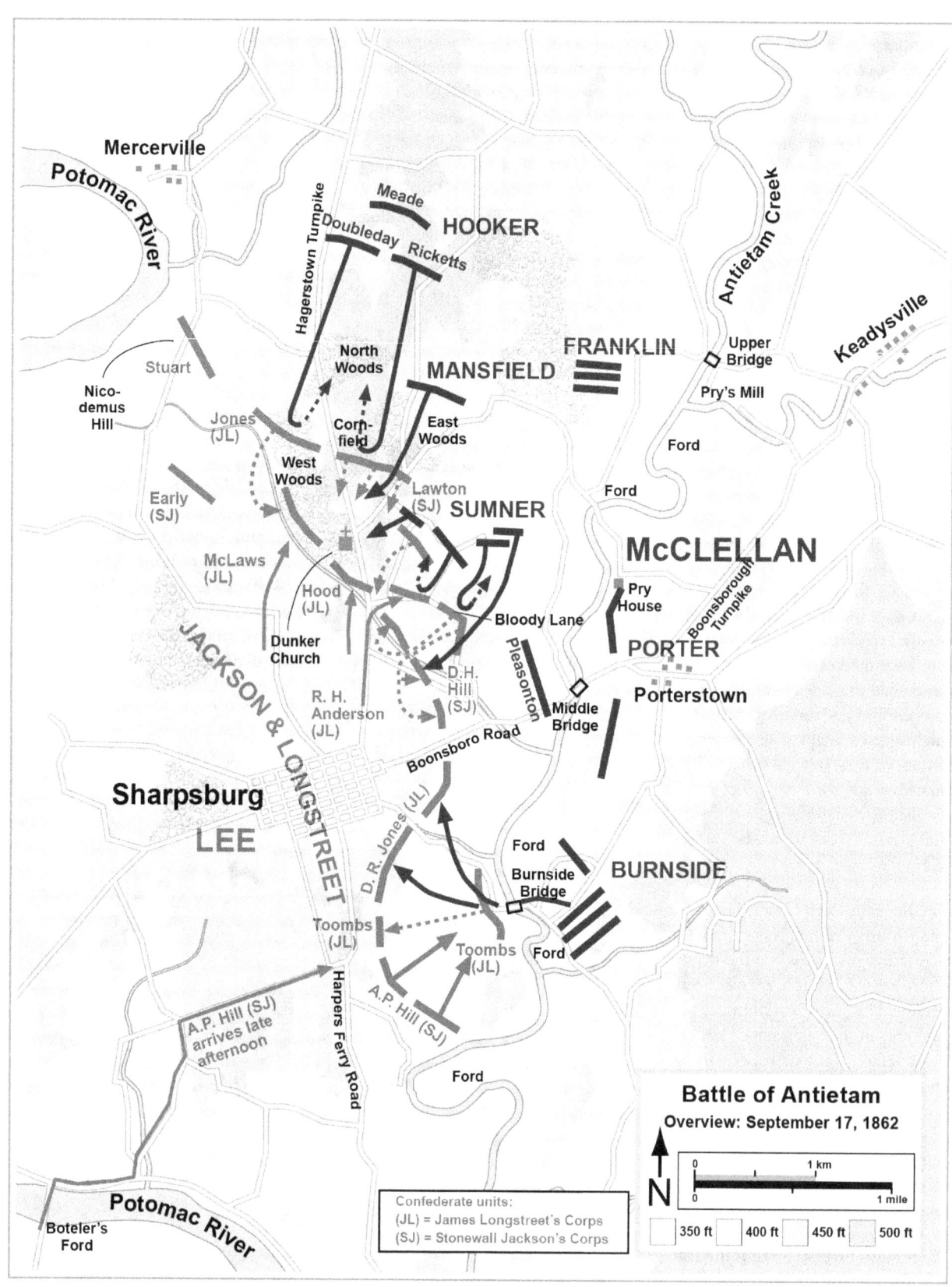

Map of the Battle of Antietam (Credit: Hal Jespersen, www.posix.com/CW, CC BY-SA 3.0; courtesy Wikimedia Commons)

wrapped around a pair of cigars by a Union sentry, and conveyed to McClellan. At last, the General who was never certain of anything knew exactly where his enemy was, and exactly what he was trying to do. Within hours, troops were moving west to meet them. McClellan hoped to catch up with Lee before he finished destroying the Federal armory at Harper's Ferry, Virginia, and could concentrate his army in Maryland.

I was worried that my amateur schematic of the campaign was less than coherent, but it turned out that

defense by the Confederates resulted in the largest loss of American lives in a single day. It is the scale of death that haunts us at the Antietam. 22,717 Americans died, were severely wounded or simply disappeared in a single day: September 17th, 1862.

After the film, we found ourselves listening to another account delivered by a young woman who grew up within sight of the battlefield, and is the third generation of her family to volunteer at the park. She provided a perspective on how the great

to return to the region, and some majority of the burials had been discovered and transferred to the nearby national cemetery, the US Government recognized the unique nature of the ground and acted to preserve it as a battlefield park.

This combination of reverence for history and the toxic aftermath of the battle prevented anyone from building much of anything on the field, and with the exception of a few dozen pieces of heroic sculpture, things look a lot like they did in 1862. This is not an accident; while most of the trees present in 1862 have long since lived their natural lifespans and died, the park service has replanted several stretches of woods and acted to keep them more or less as they appeared in the 19th Century.

The Haunted Corn

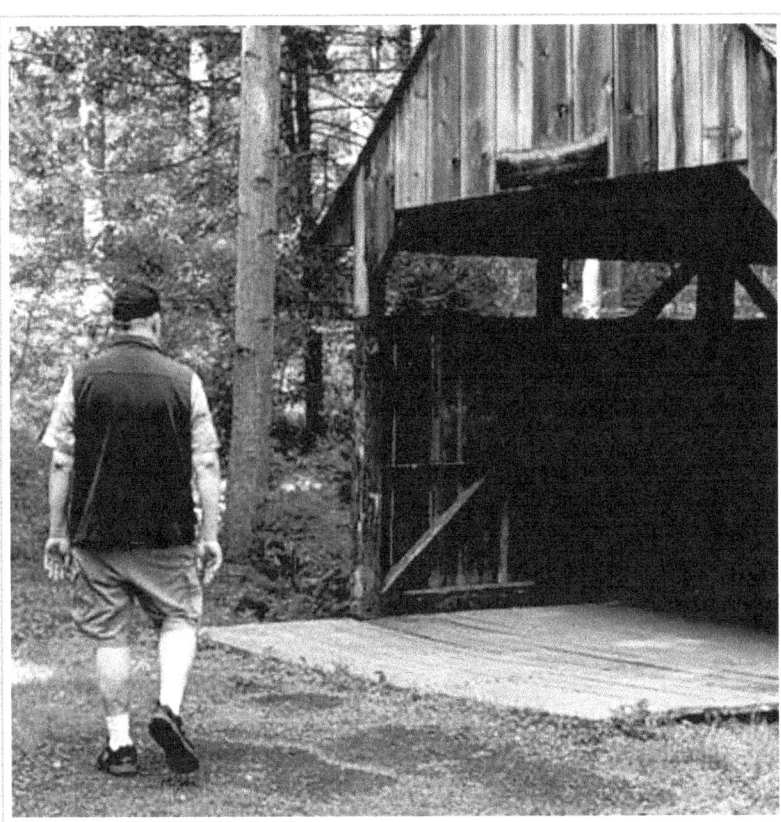

Andy Hooper on the Antietam battlefield (CR)

We decided to tour the field in the order in which the phases of the fight took place: The dawn battle in the cornfield, the morning assault on the Confederate center line, and the afternoon fight at what became known as "Burnside's Bridge," on the far right of the Confederate position, just outside Sharpsburg.

this was just the first of three times we would hear the story of the campaign. When we first arrived at the visitor center, we watched a 30-minute movie narrated by James Earl Jones, which both set up the campaign and explained how aggressive Union tactics and expert

proliferation of shallow graves literally changed the landscape and threatened the lives of the people who lived there. For decades after the battle, bacteria from rotting bodies poisoned the water table; birds and animals avoided the battle site. By the time normal life began

The battle began with a pre-dawn assault on Stonewall Jackson's troops, through a head-high field of corn. It is eerie to imagine so many men shooting at one another in the relatively narrow field, but it is clear what a perfect killing ground it was, just as flat as a concrete floor. Once the Wisconsin and Indiana troops of the "Iron Brigade" made their advance, Jackson sent the Texans of John Bell Hood's Division to stop them. After the battle, Jackson asked Hood where his troops were, and the latter replied "They are lying on the field where you sent them. My Division has been almost wiped out."

We rolled around the cornfield and the "West Woods" which border it, and then toward the slightly elevated ground to the south, where most of the rest of the Confederate army was lined up on the morning of the 17th. Running along the East edge of the hilltop, a deeply-rutted farm lane looks straight down at the long, gentle slope that the Union XIIth Corps marched up, just a little after 9 am. From the slope below, the road is completely invisible; it formed a natural trench from which the rebels were able to fire as a horde of new Union troops tried to walk straight at them. The toll taken by the Confederates in the sunken lane was ferocious; but when Union troops got to ground above and behind them, their perfect position suddenly became a death trap. After the fight, observers said the ground was soaked red with their blood; and ever since this has been known as the "Bloody Lane."

We simply sauntered up in the effort to look over the lip of the lane on the slope that the Union recruits had to climb, but suddenly encountered another example of volunteer interpretation in the park, A former college instructor was giving a battlefield tour to a remarkably varied group of young and old listeners. He was reminding anyone listening that a great many of the troops who were killed trying to reach that road were Irish-Americans, first or second generation immigrants who had joined to do their part to preserve the Union. The great slaughter of the Irish troops turned Irish voters against the war. And when President Lincoln followed the Union's pyrrhic victory at Antietam with the Emancipation Proclamation, they became convinced he planned to give their jobs to freed slaves, and they turned on him as well, voting for his opponent in the 1864 election – who just happened to be George McClellan, the man who had led their brothers into death along the Antietam.

This bit of irony aside, the professor tried to make the point that tactical events and decisions on the battlefield, had great cultural and social ramifications in Ireland as well as America, since so many disillusioned veterans returned to Ireland to fight for independence there.

Whiskey Bridge

So things looked bleak as we set off for the site of the last act of the battle, the afternoon struggle at the far right of the Confederate position. We didn't intend to follow the professor's group, but when we arrived at the parking lot above the bridge, there he was again, talking about the "two 51sts," the 51st Pennsylvania and 51st New York volunteer regiments, who are given credit for the dash across the bridge that would finally force the troops defending it to withdraw.

The volunteer lecturer took great relish in this part of the story: The 51st New York was a salty outfit, sometimes less than completely obedient or disciplined. Not long before the campaign, their whiskey ration had been suspended for some kind of mischief. Their Colonel was man named Edward Ferrero. Born in Granada, Spain of Italian parents, he was a pre-war celebrity, one of the world's foremost choreographers and experts on ballroom dance. When a wiseacre sergeant asked if the Colonel would restore the men's whiskey ration if they took the bridge, he replied "Yes, by God, if I

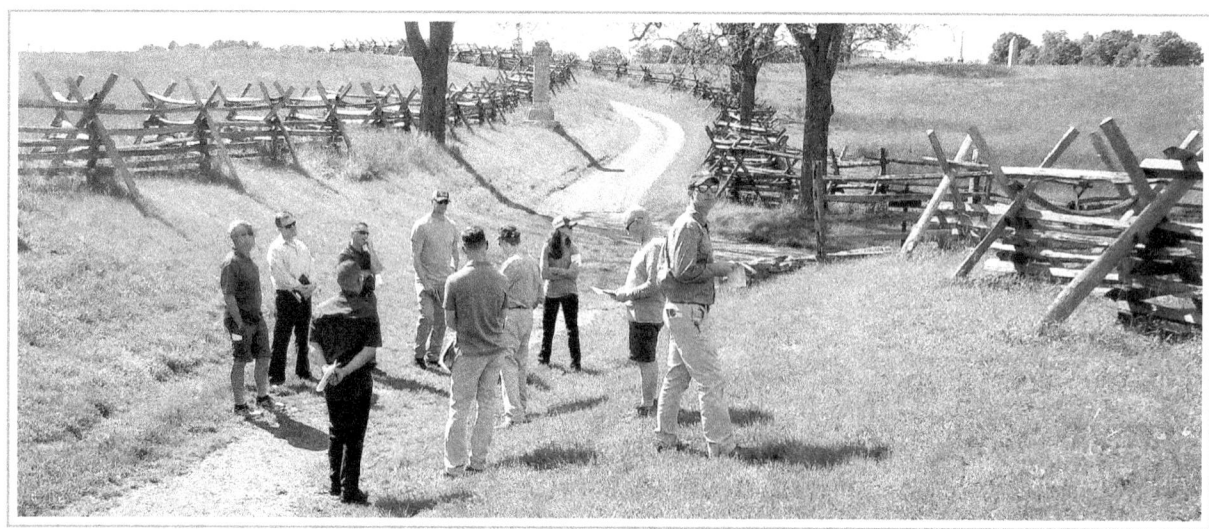

The Bloody Lane (with non-fannish tour group) (AH)

have to go to New York City and fetch it myself." The men cheered and set off to take their place in the line. When some of the troops in the 51st NY noticed that sections of the rebel line had stopped firing – because they had run out of cartridges, although no one in the regiment knew that -- they shouted and surged across the bridge and into the protection of the brush at the bottom of the hill.

Unfortunately, by the time they managed to get up to the top of the hill, and prepared to fall on the Confederate supply wagons and

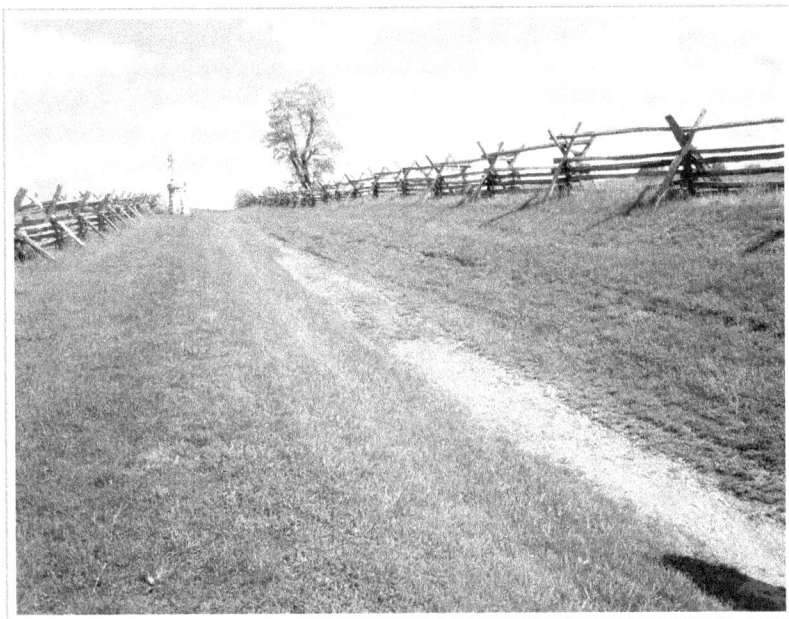

Another view of the Bloody Lane (AH)

ambulances in Sharpsburg, Confederate General A.P. Hill literally wandered onto the battlefield with his entire division. Marching north from Harper's Ferry, he had taken a wrong turn and accidentally reached the point where Burnside's troops were about to attack. Now low on ammunition as well, the Union troops withdrew to the edge of the hill as dusk began to come on.

The Confederate invasion of Maryland had been stopped, but Lee was able to get his surviving troops back to Virginia without any effort at pursuit by McClellan, who felt that his army had been just as close to annihilation as Lee's. Within a matter of weeks, McClellan would be relieved of command again.

The search for a commander with the right temperament to win the war would go on for another year, until Ulysses Grant arrived from the west. The one substantial result of the Maryland campaign was that Lincoln used it as a rationale for the Emancipation Proclamation – not because the Battle of the Antietam was a great victory, but because it was so terrible that he could not imagine asking the survivors to accept that their sacrifice had not been enough to end slavery.

The volunteer lecturer had even more details to share, but we eventually walked away, and the surviving elements of our expedition – Geri Sullivan and the Olsons had left us after the Bloody Lane – walked quietly across the newly-restored bridge, quite enjoying the fact that absolutely no one was shooting at us. As the sun shone through its spring-green leaves, w admired the so-called "Burnside Sycamore," a huge tree growing very close to the Union side of the bridge. A very young tree in 1862, it survived the battle, and has watched over visitors – the mournful and the merely curious -- for more than 150 years. Standing in its shade we agreed we were grateful that it had been allowed to thrive in a place where so many had died and lost everything, even their names. But the process of finding them goes on today. Just a few years ago, a visitor found bones disturbed by a woodchuck, and the lost soldier's buttons marked him as belonging to a New York regiment. There were plans to bury him again in the Antietam cemetery, but the State of New York asked if they could bring him home, and he has a new place of honor at the Greenwood National Cemetery.

We parted with a kind of subdued satisfaction – Nigel and Sandra set off for a rendezvous with Ted White in Falls Church, while we headed for a hotel that would put us close to the airport in the morning.

And I wish I could say that was the end of story, but nothing is ever that neat. Edward Ferrero, the colonel of the heroic 51st New York, would continue to gain promotions and greater responsibility. But during the siege of Petersburg, Virginia in 1864, he was accused of dishonorable and cowardly conduct, remaining in a bomb-proof shelter during the notorious Battle of the Crater, while over half of his command was being killed. He was said to have spent the battle trading pulls at

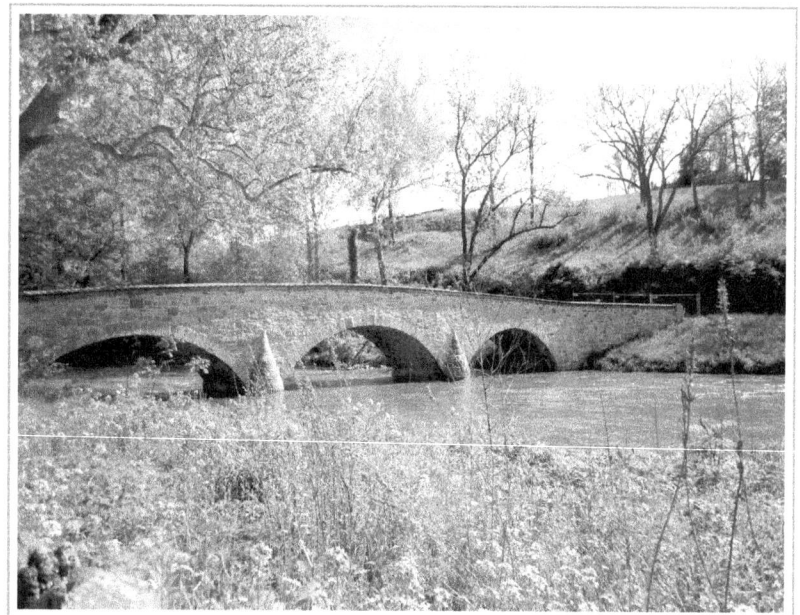
Antietam Creek Bridge (AH)

Monday 6 May 2019

Rob Jackson

I am writing from the Hilton in Crabtree, Raleigh, after a problem-free if rather boring drive down to Raleigh, and a very pleasant evening with my son Hugo and daughter-in-law Madison. They took me to the Metro Diner, which is #9 in the top 20 diners in the US. The Salisbury beef was ridiculously good. Then they drove a long way out of town to a specialist popsicle place, where I chose a mango and chilli popsicle. Imagine an ice lolly composed 50% of small chunks of mango, the rest being frozen chilli-flavoured mango juice. I-i-interesting.

The bottle of wine left over from the wine tasting that Spike let me take home hasn't made it that far. It is just as well I wrapped the top end with paper and 3 plastic bags, as the screw top had started to leak quite a bit.

I have had to open it. What a pity.

What I don't drink tonight or tomorrow can be an extra tip for the housekeeping staff when I leave on Wednesday morning.

a bottle of rum with another officer.

Although put on trial by Gen. Winfield Scott Hancock, and accused of similarly timid conduct during battles in Tennessee, Ferrero seems to have survived with his rank intact, and would eventually repair his reputation. He became active in Democratic politics, and although he never held office himself, he was a frequent visitor to Tammany Hall. In fact, he often rented its ballroom for his dances, as he had not resumed his former haunts after returning from the war.

Wanting to set up in a new building, he chose to lease a recently-completed structure uptown, which would soon become world-famous under the name "Apollo Hall." When he let the lease go in the 1870s, the building was renamed as New York's first "Apollo Theater." Fifty years later, when theater owner Sydney Cohen completely reversed the whites-only policy at what had formerly been known as "Hurtig & Seamon's New Burlesque Theater" on West 125th Street, he selected a name with real history, and rechristened it as "The Apollo Theater." Although the location is completely different, the name remains attached to Edward Ferrero and his whiskey ration, Burnside's bridge, the map, the cigars, amateur night and emancipation. Ferrero died at age 68 in December of 1899. His book, *The History of Dancing,* is still in print today.

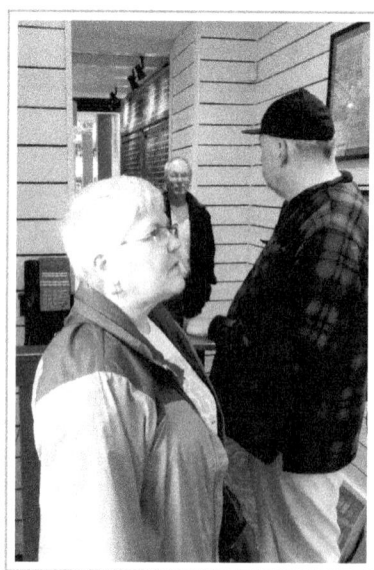
Carrie Root, Steve Jeffery, Andy Hooper (SS)

The End of FIAWOL

Corflu Will Return in

Heatwave

March 12-15
2020

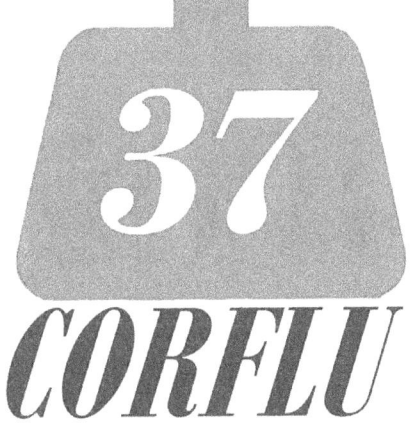

College Station
Texas

37 CORFLU

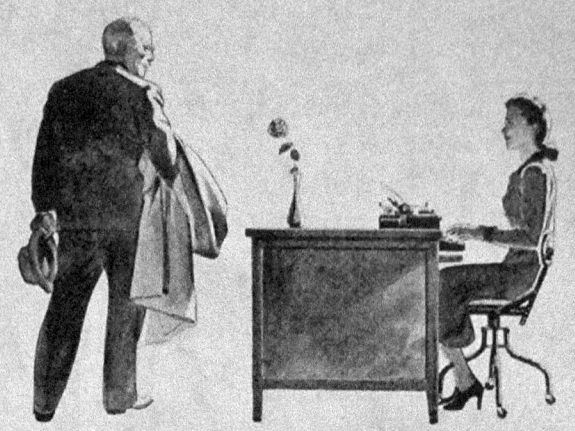

A brain, a girl and a typewriter and you're all set to

Make and/or Save Money

with a Mimeograph duplicator

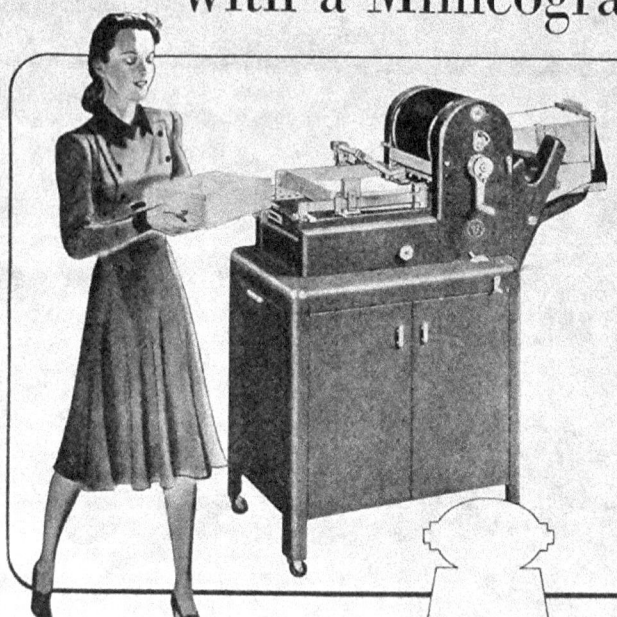

SAID THE BOSS TO THE SECRETARY—
"We've had these problems for years."

SAID THE SECRETARY TO THE BOSS—
"Why haven't we had the Mimeograph duplicator before?"

The Mimeograph duplicator is a great problem-answerer. That goes for problems of production, red-tape cutting and problems of telling customers, employees and friends what you want them to know. It answers those problems fast and economically.

The visibility of fine Mimeograph copies when properly made with Mimeograph brand stencil sheets and inks is equal to the standards set for schools. When you save eyes you save time; and when you save time you save money.

There are four new streamlined models at four prices, and there is probably a Mimeograph distributor in your city to tell you what they can do for you. He is listed in your Classified Telephone Directory.

Mimeograph

MIMEOGRAPH is the trade-mark of A. B. Dick Company, Chicago, registered in the U. S. Patent Office

www.ingramcontent.com/pod-product-compliance
Lightning Source LLC
Chambersburg PA
CBHW080501220526
45465CB00006B/2338